Digital Art Photography
FOR DUMMIES

P9-DOB-373

Cheat Sheet

Auto Modes

Mode	Icon	Look For	Function
Auto	AUTO	A green square or camera	Use for well-lit, non-action daytime shots.
Portrait		A woman's silhouette	Use to photograph people.
Landscape		Mountains	Use when shooting into the distance.
Macro		A flower	Use for extreme close-ups.
Action		A running man	Use to capture sports or other action events.
Night		A person and a star	Use for shooting at night with no flash.
Program	P		The camera sets both the aperture and shutter speed.
Shutter priority	Tv		You set the shutter speed; the camera sets the aperture.
Aperture priority	Av		You set the aperture; the camera sets the shutter speed.
Manual	M		You set both the shutter speed and the aperture.
Automatic depth of field	A-DEP		Use to enable multiple focus points.

Photoshop Tools Palette

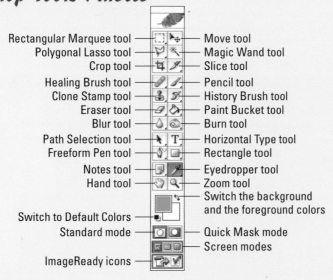

Rectangular Marquee tool — — Move tool
Polygonal Lasso tool — — Magic Wand tool
Crop tool — — Slice tool
Healing Brush tool — — Pencil tool
Clone Stamp tool — — History Brush tool
Eraser tool — — Paint Bucket tool
Blur tool — — Burn tool
Path Selection tool — — Horizontal Type tool
Freeform Pen tool — — Rectangle tool
Notes tool — — Eyedropper tool
Hand tool — — Zoom tool
— Switch the background and the foreground colors
Switch to Default Colors —
Standard mode — — Quick Mask mode
— Screen modes
ImageReady icons —

For Dummies: Bestselling Book Series for Beginners

Digital Art Photography
FOR
DUMMIES

Cheat Sheet

Color Temperature Changes with Respect to Light Source

Knowing a little bit about color temperature can help you get optimum color results. Different light sources emit light at different color temperatures, causing your picture to lean either to a red or blue hue. As shown in this table, a high color temperature shifts light toward blue, and a low color temperature shifts light toward red hues. See Chapter 8 for more about color temperature and getting great color shots.

Source	Color Temperature, Kelvin	Source	Color Temperature, Kelvin
Candle flame	1850° (red hues)	Sunrise or sunset	2000°
40W incandescent light	2650°	One hour after sunrise	3500°
75W incandescent light	2820°	Early morning or late afternoon	4300°
100W incandescent light	2865°	Summer sunlight at noon	5400°
500W incandescent light	2960°	Overcast sky	6000°
Professional photo lamp	3200°	Light summer shade	7100°
Photoflood lamp	3400°	Average summer shade	8000° (blue hues)
Daylight blue photoflood	4800°		

Putting the "Art" in Digital Art Photography

✔ Don't be afraid to take photos on cloudy and/or rainy days (Chapter 5).

✔ Always carry your camera with you so when you see something unusual, you can snap a picture of it (Chapter 4).

✔ Use layers to merge several images to create an entirely new and different image (Chapter 14).

✔ Use a filter when shooting during the day to offset the sun's glare and to make a better picture (Chapter 11).

✔ Study and emulate the work of famous photographers to train your eye but then develop your own style (Chapter 9).

✔ For action shots, set your camera beforehand, get as close as you can to your subject, and keep your f-stop low (Chapter 7).

✔ Study the rules of photography and then break them to attain certain effects (Chapters 6 and 8).

✔ Snap several pictures of a landscape or something tall, like the Tiki shown here, and then merge the pieces to re-create the whole (Chapter 13).

✔ Experiment, experiment, experiment — whether you're out taking pictures or sitting at home fiddling in Photoshop, don't be afraid to try something new.

For Dummies: Bestselling Book Series for Beginners

Digital Art Photography

FOR

DUMMIES®

by Matthew Bamberg, MA

WILEY

Wiley Publishing, Inc.

Digital Art Photography For Dummies®
Published by
Wiley Publishing, Inc.
111 River Street
Hoboken, NJ 07030-5774
www.wiley.com

Copyright © 2006 by Wiley Publishing, Inc., Indianapolis, Indiana

Published by Wiley Publishing, Inc., Indianapolis, Indiana

Published simultaneously in Canada

For general information on our other products and services, please contact our Customer Care Department within the U.S. at 800-762-2974, outside the U.S. at 317-572-3993, or fax 317-572-4002.

For technical support, please visit www.wiley.com/techsupport.

Wiley also publishes its books in a variety of electronic formats. Some content that appears in print may not be available in electronic books.

Library of Congress Control Number: 2005924614

ISBN-13: 978-0-7645-9801-2

ISBN-10: 0-7645-9801-5

Manufactured in the United States of America

10 9 8 7 6 5 4 3 2 1

1K/QR/RS/QV/IN

WILEY

About the Author

Several years ago, **Matthew Bamberg** began to photograph for the articles he was writing while working for the alternative paper, the *Desert Post Weekly*. His writing focuses on popular culture: essays about topics from the Santa Cruz, California surf culture to the mid-century modern architecture revival around the world. Curious by light striking his lens (direct and bold or soft and willowy) and the sounds (especially of the shutter opening and closing), he struck a relationship first with film and then, like so many, with the digital camera's sensor.

Aside from writing about f-stops, shutter speeds, and the fabulous job the digital camera manufacturers have done that permit photographers to take almost noiseless pictures in the dark at high ISO speeds, Matt has written content and provided photographs for articles on Homestore.com, America Online, and The Weather Channel.

Dedication

I dedicate this book to my parents Harold and Estelle Bamberg, who as photographers themselves collected and stored hundreds of negatives, positives, and prints that I took as a kid and that they took themselves. They also supplied me with every trendy camera that came onto the market, which provided me with a foundation to have an additional set of eyes to capture the world.

Author's Acknowledgments

First, cheers to Nicole Sholly and Teresa Artman, who guided the progress of this book and offered dozens of solutions and ideas in its development. To them, a heartfelt thanks. Thanks also to: Robert Stone for his patience teaching me the ins and outs of landscape photography in Paris and Vietnam; Robert Jones of Insightful Solutions for guidance for Internet and Web site photography; Roger Vail for his wonderful nighttime carnival photography (`http://we.got.net/~rvail/recent/recent.html`); the expertise of sports photographer Drew Brashler; and Rich Glass and infrared photographer, Robert Contreras (`www.robertcontreras.com`) who helped widen the book's focus. Also of assistance were the Borgan, Taylor, and Bodon families whose ideas, photos, and patience modeling for dozens of shots made the process not work but fun. I can't forget the valuable assistance in shooting provided by Dr. Suellen Evavold, Trixie Mauleon, and Kelly Lewis and son, Chase. And keeping me on track, offering aesthetic advice on hundreds of photos as they progressed through Photoshop and moved onto the printed page, was Todd Larson. My experiences with all the staff of City Art (Van Nuys, California) helped to make this book a completed cycle by giving insight to one of the most important stages of the art photography process: framing an image. Selling the image, too, needs to be recognized. To that end, I thank James Claude and Miguel Linares of Palm Springs Consignment, a mid-century modern gallery in Palm Springs, who took me in as a street photographer by selling my mid-century modern signage series, a series that took me to some dicey neighborhoods all over the world to capture a piece of the past. Thanks also to John Bernard and Beverly Walker of the modern furnishing gallery, Room Service, who brought and sold my work to the big city (Los Angeles) and Jay Nailor of M Modern Gallery (Palm Springs) who took my work to the gallery level and who was never more than a phone call away.

Publisher's Acknowledgments

We're proud of this book; please send us your comments through our online registration form located at www.dummies.com/register/.

Some of the people who helped bring this book to market include the following:

Acquisitions, Editorial, and Media Development

Project Editor: Nicole Sholly

Senior Acquisitions Editor: Steve Hayes

Senior Copy Editor: Teresa Artman

Technical Editors: Jonathan M. Wentworth, Wentworth Images; Maureen M. McCarty

Editorial Manager: Kevin Kirschner

Media Development Coordinator: Laura Atkinson

Media Development Manager: Laura VanWinkle

Media Development Supervisor: Richard Graves

Editorial Assistant: Amanda Foxworth

Cartoons: Rich Tennant (www.the5thwave.com)

Composition Services

Project Coordinator: Adrienne Martinez

Layout and Graphics: Mary J. Gillot, Lauren Goddard, Barbara Moore, Heather Ryan

Proofreaders: Laura Albert, Laura L. Bowman, Leeann Harney

Indexer: Lynnzee Elze

Special Help: Emily Bain

Publishing and Editorial for Technology Dummies

Richard Swadley, Vice President and Executive Group Publisher

Andy Cummings, Vice President and Publisher

Mary Bednarek, Executive Acquisitions Director

Mary C. Corder, Editorial Director

Publishing for Consumer Dummies

Diane Graves Steele, Vice President and Publisher

Joyce Pepple, Acquisitions Director

Composition Services

Gerry Fahey, Vice President of Production Services

Debbie Stailey, Director of Composition Services

Table of Contents

Introduction *1*

About This Book...1
Foolish Assumptions 1
Conventions Used in This Book 1
What You Don't Have to Read 2
How This Book Is Organized..2
    Part I: The Art of a Digital Picture 2
    Part II: The Photo Shoot 2
    Part III: Photoshop Art: Using Software
       to Enhance or Create Art Photos......................3
    Part IV: The Final Output: Gallery-Worthy Prints.....3
    Part V: The Part of Tens..3
    On the Web site...3
Icons Used in This Book 4
Where to Go from Here...4

Part 1: The Art of a Digital Picture *5*

Chapter 1: Digital Art Photography 101 . . . .**7**

Defining Digital Art Photography 7
Mastering Five Steps to Creating a Gallery-ready Art Print.....................10
    1) Define yourself, your subject matter, and your audience...........11
    2) Master your craft and hone your photographic skills 11
    3) The trek from camera to computer 11
    4) Printing images 12
    5) Framing your masterpiece.................................12
Composing an Art Photograph.....................................12
    Simplicity..13
    Balance 14
    Rule of Thirds...15
    All about light, shadows, and shades 16
    Recognizing lines, shapes, and forms 18
    Subject placement 21
    Deciphering color 23
    Understanding positive and negative space.........24
    Foreground, background, and depth of field 26
    Perspective..28
    In-camera cropping and framing 29

Chapter 2: Making the Digital Leap 31

The Digital Path 31
Film versus Digital..32
Digital Camera 101 36
    Digital camera types 36
    How digital cameras work..38
    The whole megapixel (MP) thing 39
    Lenses 40
    Settings 43
    Flash and flash attachments 44
    Batteries 45
    Supports 46
    Memory and removable storage media................................46
Getting a Digital Image from Camera to Computer....................49
Resolving Resolution Issues 51
Understanding File Types 52
    JPEG 52
    TIFF...53
    Raw 53

Chapter 3: Your Digital Technology 55

Exploring Your Computer 56
    Storage space..56
    Monitors 59
    Calibration...61
    Go-getter graphics add-ons 62
    Choosing a platform...63
Choosing a Printer and Paper for the Results You Want...........66
    Finding a printer that's right for your work 66
    Paper and friends: Selecting the best medium for your prints 70
    Finding the right image size for your print 72
Exploring the Ins and Outs of Scanners 73
    Choosing a scanner..73
    Configuring your scanner..74

Chapter 4: Defining Yourself and Your Photographs 75

Defining Yourself as a Photographer 76
    Shoot what you like...77
    Study the masters 77
    Right-brain, left-brain...78
    All a matter of perspective..80
    Finding the unusual..83
Defining Your Audience: Creating Art That Sells........................84
    Choosing subject matter 85
    Presentation..88

Part II: The Photo Shoot *95*

Chapter 5: Composing a Shot Outdoors ....**.97**

Shooting with Natural Light...97
    Proper exposure 98
    Using auto settings when shooting outdoors............................100
    Using manual settings for creative control 102
    Foreground and background...102
Common Outdoor Lighting Situations...107
    Creating a vivid shot with your back to the sun 107
    Facing the sun..109
    Avoiding and exploiting shadows 111
    Shooting at noon, dusk, and dawn..113
    Glare and flare...114
    Shooting glare on water, ice, and snow 115
    Weather and atmosphere 117
Augmenting Natural Light...119
    Using flash fill..120
    Shooting bright lights in daytime..120

Chapter 6: Composing a Shot Indoors **121**

Setting Up to Shoot Indoors...122
    ISO speed...122
    Manual versus auto settings 124
    White balance 124
Taking Indoor Pictures without Flash...124
    Using available light only 125
    Intentional blur 126
    Taming available bright light 128
    Taking advantage of color imbalance 129
Augmenting Indoor Light 130
    Comparing shooting with and without flash..............................131
    Combining indoor and outdoor light 132
    Using whiteboards...133
    Adding extra light sources; studio set up 133
Shooting Indoors with Flash 136

Chapter 7: Photographing People and Animals **137**

Photographing People...138
    Traditional posed portraits...139
    Candid portraits 147
    Capturing portraits of inanimate objects...................................149
Wildlife Portraiture 150
Pet Portraiture...151

Chapter 8: Shooting for Color in Art Photography 153

Discovering How Light Makes Color...154
  Positioning yourself and your camera.................................156
  Using complementary and contrasting colors 157
How Your Camera Interprets Light and Color.................................160
  Setting ISO speed for maximum color 162
  Setting white balance..163
Using an f-stop to Enhance Color..167
Advanced Color Techniques..168
  Underexposing your photo to enhance color.......................168
  Shooting colors in the shade 171
  Color and the atmosphere 172

Chapter 9: Crafting a Quality Black-and-White Art Photo 173

Why Shoot in Black-and-White? 174
  A brief B&W perspective 176
  Shooting architecture 176
  Shooting portraits 181
  Shooting for journalism 183
Capturing Black and White 185
  Creating a B&W image 186
  Manipulating a color image to become B&W 187
  Getting the best quality image...189
  Understanding the 256 shades of gray 190
  Defining highlights, midtones, and shadows 193
  Printing for best quality...197

Chapter 10: Night Art Photography 199

Taking a Shot in the Dark 199
  Creating a blur-free, flashless night photo 204
  Using fast film and high ISO settings...................................210
  Shooting with a flash..211
Other Nighttime Art Opportunities 212
  Light your subject from beneath...212
  Shoot the moon 212
  Seek nighttime landscapes..215
  Use reflections 216
  Seek out shadows and weather 216

Chapter 11: Achieving Creative Results When Shooting 217

Tweaking Automatic Modes and Settings
  to Achieve Creative Results 218
Playing with Light...222

Come Get 'Yer Effects Here! 223
  Double exposures...223
  Panoramic shots..224
  Reflections..225
  Zooming while shooting 225
  Intentional lack of focus 226
  Intentional underexposure/overexposure 227
  Making flowing water turn to silk...228
  Using filters 230

Part III: Photoshop Art: Using Software to Enhance or Create Art Photos 235

Chapter 12: Adding New Life to Old Photos 237

Using Automatic Adjustments to Refresh Older Prints.........................237
Using Manual Adjustments for Fine-Tuning...240
  Dodge...240
  Burn tool...242
  Smart Sharpen/Unsharp Mask commands...........................243
  Sponge tool 243
  Dust & Scratches filter..244
  Blur tool..244
  Color Balance..245
  Removing a horrible shadow 246
Healing Damaged Photos 247
Making the Corrections 249
Tweaking Color in the Digital World 252
Enhancing Sepia and Other Tones 253
Enhancing Shadow, Highlights, Hue, and Saturation...........................255

Chapter 13: Combining and Manipulating Images 259

Preserving Detail...260
Making an Image Whole Again with Photomerge...................................261
Seamlessly Introducing Backgrounds in Photographs...........................266
Creating Art Photos through Symmetry 268

Chapter 14: Using Layers to Create a Theme 271

Using Layers in Photoshop..271
  Feathering..272
  Creating a simple two-layer project 273
Creating a More Complex Layer Project 277

Chapter 15: Using Photoshop for Special Effects **283**

Photoshop Filter Effects...284
Gaussian Blur filter..285
Unsharp Mask filter..286
Plastic Wrap filter..288
Glowing Edges filter...288
Watercolor filter...288
Sketch filters 289
Emboss filter 291
Constructing a Composite à la Warhol Using Photoshop Filters 292
Making a Background for Your Images..296

Part IV: The Final Output: Gallery-Worthy Prints.........299

Chapter 16: Managing and Preparing Files **301**

Transferring an Image from Your Camera to Your Computer 302
From film/scanning...302
From a JPEG file 302
From a Raw file...303
Are Raw Files a Raw Deal?...305
Understanding the Relationship between File Type and File Size 306
Defining and constructing a TIFF file in Photoshop.....................306
Creating a Web Gallery in Photoshop..307
Resolving Resolution Issues 309
Interpolation 309
Resampling an image 310
Changing resolution without resampling 312

Chapter 17: Printing Prep and Printing **313**

Discovering Proofs and Printing the Final Product 313
Preparing for Output 316
Making a Contact Sheet...317
Previewing Your Print...319

Chapter 18: Framing and Matting **321**

Takin' It to the Mats 322
Comparing mat options 324
Cutting your own mats 324
Creating a mat in Photoshop 325
The Great Frame-Up...329
Buying retail 332
Buying online; finding Internet deals 332
Buying for the bargain 333
Putting Together the Frame..338

Part V: The Part of Tens *341*

Chapter 19: Ten Photo Digital Art Rules 343
Create with Classic Lines and Colors 343
Start with a Good Camera 345
Exploit the Right Light for Your Photo 345
Keep It Small and Spectacular 346
Balance Items Onscreen and on Paper.............................346
Organize Your Photos into Sets by Themes 347
Know the Art Techniques of Thine Masters 347
Create a Story or Message 348
Capture the Unexpected or Unreal 348
Always Have Your Camera with You................................349

Chapter 20: Ten Digital Art Tricks 351
Overexpose and Underexpose 351
Emulate the Masters...352
Shoot on a Cloudy Day 353
Create a Matching Background 354
Meld Layers to Create Motion 355
Build Your Archive of Backgrounds................................355
Don't Overdo Effect(s)..356
Use the Edit⇨Fade Command 357
Keep Your Image in High Res on All Platforms................357

On the Web

Bonus Chapter 1: Telling (And Selling) a Story Using Photo Sets ....On the Web
Crafting a Photo Set from a Storyboard...........................B2
Classifying Your Shots...B5
    Related subjects...B6
    Black and white...B6
    Color...B6
    Composition B8
    Timelines..B8
    Patterns B8
    Media B9
    Theme/emotion...B9
    Historical perspective B10
Archiving and Storing Your Shots...................................B10

Preparing a Set of Prints for Sale B10
    Size..B11
    Printing/polishing in an image editing program B11
    Text B12
    Framing/matting...B12
    Pricing B12

Bonus Chapter 2: Enhancing Art Photos with Text ....**On the Web**

Fonts 101...B14
    Serif and sans serif..B16
    Font styles...B17
    Font size B18
    Font color..B18
    Mixing fonts B19
    Using fonts effectively B19
Creating and Tweaking Text B21
    Text in Word..B22
    Text in Photoshop...B22
    Tweaking text to make it readable...B24
Marrying Text and Photos..B25
Creating an Ad with Text and a Photo B26
Making Art out of Text B30

Index...*359*

Introduction

*I*n this book, I cover the art form of digital art photography. I start by giving you an introduction to the world of film-based photography and how it relates to digital photography. From there, I go on to cover the whole gambit of digital art photography, from shooting great photos to tweaking them in Photoshop to producing final output fit for a gallery wall. If that sounds intriguing, this book is for you whether you're film-based or digital-only or both.

About This Book

Here are some of the things this book will help you do:

- Get a fabulous, well-exposed photograph, no matter what your shooting conditions
- Tweak, edit, and enhance your images to create something entirely new — or just simply better than what you started with
- Produce gallery-worthy art prints
- Find out when it's time to upgrade your computer to handle graphics work

Foolish Assumptions

I don't like to be foolish, but to use this book, I assume that you know the basics of photography, whether digital or film. (I do sprinkle loads of photography tidbits throughout, so no one is stranded.) I also assume that you know how to use a computer and have maybe played around with Photoshop or some photo editor application. Most important of all, I assume that you have a burning desire down deep inside to unleash your creative side by producing — and even selling — truly artistic, awe-inspiring photographic prints.

Conventions Used in This Book

By *conventions,* I simply mean a set of rules that I employ in this book to present information to you consistently. When you see a term *italicized,* look for its definition, which I include so you know what that term means in the context of digital art photography. Sometimes, I give you information to enter onscreen; in those cases, I format what you need to type **bold**. Web site addresses and e-mail addresses appear in `monofont` so that they stand out from regular text.

What You Don't Have to Read

Because I structure this book *modularly* — that is, so you can easily find only the specific information you need — you don't have to read whatever doesn't pertain to your task at hand. You also don't have to read the Technical Stuff icons, which parse out uber-techy tidbits (which you might or might not be interested in).

How This Book Is Organized

Digital Art Photography For Dummies is split into five parts. You don't have to read parts sequentially; you don't have to read each chapter in each part; and you don't even have to read all the sections in any particular chapter. (But I think that you'll want to look at every picture. . . .) You can use the Table of Contents and the index to find the information you need and quickly get your answers. In this section, I briefly describe what you'll find in each part.

Part I: The Art of a Digital Picture

This part serves as an introduction to the world of art photography and how it relates to digital photography. In Chapter 1, I detail the five essential steps to creating a digitized masterpiece and provide a few essentials of composition. Chapters 2 and 3 cover the digital side of digital art photography; I have to admit, this information can get a little dry and techy. (Don't say I didn't warn you.) When it comes time to purchase a new digital camera or to upgrade your computer to handle all the heavy-duty graphics work you'll be doing, however, you'll be glad you have these two chapters by your side. In Chapter 4, things get fun again while I brainstorm with you to decide just what kind of digital art photographer you want to be.

Part II: The Photo Shoot

Part II is all about getting great shots, and so I dive right into ISOs, f-stops, exposure settings, and when to use a flash. This part runs the gamut, from shooting great photos outdoors or indoors (Chapters 5 and 6) to photographing people and animals (Chapter 7) to shooting for great color or outstanding black and white (Chapters 8 and 9) to capturing stunning nighttime images (Chapter 10) to achieving wonderful effects before you ever get to Photoshop (Chapter 11) — whew! That's a lot of photography!

Part III: Photoshop Art: Using Software to Enhance or Create Art Photos

If you're anxious to repair or jazz up some old photos, use Chapter 12 as your guide. In that chapter, I discuss various Photoshop tools and techniques that can bring back vivid color to images 50 years old or eliminate annoying scratches and dust. Chapter 13 is where you can find out how to merge images into one giant photograph, and Chapter 14 gives you the lowdown on using Photoshop layers (a great tool for creating digital art photography). I couldn't not discuss Photoshop's filters, so I include a whole chapter on them (Chapter 15).

Part IV: The Final Output: Gallery-Worthy Prints

Drum roll, please . . . the moment you've all been waiting for. Just itching to click that Print button so you can hold your masterpiece in hand and admire it lovingly? This is the part for you. In Chapter 16, I discuss all things that have to do with managing electronic files (a tedious albeit necessary part of digital art photography), and Chapter 17 covers printing prep and printing. Then comes the really fun part: matting and framing. Chapter 18 has all the information you need to make your art presentable to the world (and paying customers).

Part V: The Part of Tens

I would be remiss in my duties if I didn't include a Part of Tens. So here you'll find ten rules — or if you prefer, guidelines — of digital art photography (Chapter 19) and ten snappy digital art tricks (Chapter 20).

On the Web site

I had so much to tell you about this exciting topic that I couldn't fit it all into the book, so you'll find two bonus chapters at www.dummies.com/go/digital artphotos. Bonus Chapter 1 discusses *photo sets,* which are a great way to present, package, and reuse your saleable art. For example, if you have a slew of dog images — say, several huskies — frame them as a set to create a collection that husky-lovers will sit up and beg for. Bonus Chapter 2 covers using text to enhance your art photography. Here I discuss manipulating text in both Word and Photoshop and adding text to your image to create an entirely new piece of art, like a poster, invitation, greeting card, business card . . . you get the idea.

Icons Used in This Book

What's a *For Dummies* book without icons pointing you toward really useful information that's sure to help you along your way? In this section, I briefly describe each icon I use in this book.

The Tip icon points out helpful information that can make your job — as a *digital art photographer extraordinaire* — easier and hopefully more fun, too.

This icon marks a general interesting and useful fact — something that you probably want to remember for later use.

The Warning icon highlights lurking danger. When you see this icon, pay attention and proceed with caution, or you could end up with disappointing shots or prints.

When you see this icon, you know that there's techie stuff nearby. If you're not feeling very techie, you can skip this info and get to something more fun, like playing with Photoshop filters.

This icon points out interesting or unusual techniques that can lead to intriguing or artful results. Try them! You might like them!

Where to Go from Here

If you're interested in playing with Photoshop, Part III should be your destination. If you want to find out more about digital art photography and photography in general, head straight to Chapter 1. Or you might want to peruse the chapters in Part II to find out some great tips for shooting in a variety of situations. Then again, you could just flip through the book and stop when a particular photograph catches your eye. Whatever you choose, the world is your oyster — now go take a picture of it.

Part I
The Art of a Digital Picture

The 5th Wave By Rich Tennant

"That's a lovely scanned image of your sister's portrait. Now take it off the body of that pit viper before she comes in the room."

In this part . . .

*W*elcome to the world of art photography and how it relates to digital photography! Start your journey in Chapter 1 with the five essential steps to creating a digitized masterpiece as well as an overview of composition essentials. For all those nuts-and-bolts kinds of digital photography issues, Chapters 2 and 3 have you covered. Chapter 4 returns to the artsy side, where I start you thinking about the digital art photographer you want to be.

1

Digital Art Photography 101

In This Chapter

▶ Starting from square one: Digital photography

▶ Creating art photography in five steps

▶ Mastering basic composition elements

*A*rt is the product of human creativity: a medium to create pleasure as well as express the conditions of life and feelings. Art also records history: who we are; what's around us; and how we interpret life, feelings, and interpersonal interactions. This concrete expression has come in many forms: prints, drawings, paintings, and sculpture. With today's digital technology, however, the art form of photography reaches new creative levels, taking on new forms as people flock to this new digital medium.

In this book, I cover the art form of photography. Whether you're a film-based photo purist or firmly entrenched in the digital-only camp, you're covered. This chapter serves as an introduction to the world of photography and how it relates to digital photography. I begin with a brief discussion of digital art photography before moving on to the five essential steps to creating a digitized masterpiece. Finally, I end the chapter with a crash course in composition.

Defining Digital Art Photography

Digital images — whether from a digital camera, scanned from film or print, stills from a camcorder, or something from the Web — can be defined as any artwork stored electronically. After you have a digital image tucked into the hard drive of a computer, the chip of a cellphone, or the memory inside a digital camera, you can

✔ **Manipulate it with a mouse click.** You can change your image's color or size, take away blur (a new tool in Photoshop CS2), make it look like a painting with filters, and emulate many photography techniques without having to go to the trouble of shooting with lots of extra lenses and filters.

- ✒ **Keep it indefinitely without deterioration.** Digital images don't crease, bend, or crumble like traditional hard copies. They don't pick up stains from fingerprints or (yikes) coffee, either.

What few people think of and what makes this book special is how the digital image is conceived. In this book, digital images encompass those born again (or for the first time) into the digital world, including

- ✒ **Scanned original art:** You can scan an illustration or a painting as easily as you can scan a photograph. Then, if the art is yours to manipulate, you can open it in Photoshop and create a digital work of art.

- ✒ **Scanned photo negatives and positives:** Figure 1-1 is a scanned positive (a *slide*). I scanned it into my computer by using a Hewlett-Packard (HP) Scanjet 5470C. I had the original slide tucked away in some old family photos. It dates from the 1960s, but now it's digital.

- ✒ **Scanned print photos:** Scan prints just like you would scan negatives and positives. This is a great way to make repairs to old photographs (see Chapter 12) or to combine images to create a digital masterpiece (see Chapter 13).

- ✒ **Electronically tweaked creations:** After you scan something or download images from your digital camera, you can tweak that digital file in an image editor, electronically enhancing its beauty for sale as a gallery-quality digital print. (For more about printing and preparing your work for gallery exhibition, see Part IV.) Figure 1-2 is an image of a sunset that was tweaked in Photoshop to enhance its color and contrast. Would anyone ever know it was tweaked in Photoshop? That's a question that you should be thinking about when reading this book.

Figure 1-1: A scanned slide becomes part of the digital realm.

Figure 1-2: Tweak photos in Photoshop to enhance color and contrast.

Most of the time, you want to keep your image as natural as possible. Your goal is to clean up dust specks and scratches from print photos or to enhance color and contrast without overdoing it — that is, without producing annoying *noise,* those specs of color that make your images look unnatural. A little tweaking can go a long way.

Long discussions have ensued among many photographers, amateur and professional alike, as to what format is better: digital or film. There's really no answer, but some people are adamant about one or the other. Take a look at Table 1-1 and judge for yourself which is better. Whatever the case and whatever medium you use, don't be shy about trying out both from time to time. Each has its advantages, and it's a fun ride to see what you get when the light shines on your film or on your digital sensor. (A *digital sensor* is a small device inside a digital camera that captures picture info and sends it to the storage inside the camera.)

Table 1-1	Digital versus Film	
Characteristic	*Digital*	*Film*
Cost	No film costs, but high-end equipment is expensive.	Film and developing costs. For cheaper costs, develop as negatives only and scan at home.
Ease of use	More controls in LCD panel in addition to filmlike creative and manual modes controlled by knob at top of camera on most models. Frequent change of batteries or battery removal and recharging required for camera to work.	Fewer controls and no LCD make camera less confusing.
Image quality	Clear and vivid. Some folks notice a "plastic" quality that digital images can have. Edges are crisp (too crisp, according to some).	More natural-looking images when light hits film, which creates observable chemical change that's recorded on the film and that can be kept as a hard copy for decades.
Output tools	Gallery-quality prints can be made at home with new multiple ink cartridge printers.	Gallery-quality prints have to be sent out for processing unless you have complicated developing materials at home along with a darkroom.

Mastering Five Steps to Creating a Gallery-ready Art Print

A gallery-ready art print is one that is defined continually throughout this book — through many examples and for many types of photographs, from old reproductions to the newest, swiftest digital art around. From taking a traditional portrait to making text-based art from a photograph, you'll travel through a land of light, space, time, and patience (remember, anything digital can get quirky) to create some of the most original and high-quality work around. Photographers who take the time to capture and print superior quality images by adhering to these five steps, each a creative process in itself, produce gallery-ready art prints that turn viewers into buyers who will enjoy the work for a lifetime.

1) Define yourself, your subject matter, and your audience

When making choices about what to photograph, think about what interests you. If it's sports, you've got it made with an abundance of uniformed players, cheerleaders, and wild fans in the bleachers. If it's rare and exotic orchids in Guatemala that you long for, your trek is likely a bit more arduous but doable. And if you really don't know what you want to photograph — or whom to create photographs for — go directly to Chapter 4 where I discuss defining yourself as a photographer as well as your audience and subject matter.

2) Master your craft and hone your photographic skills

Photography, like any art form, is based on some basic rules of composition, such as the Rule of Thirds and using a vanishing point. After you master those composition techniques, you can put your own artistic interpretation of a scene into your art photo. After all, it's your art and your photo, and you can do with it what you want. Read through the remainder of this chapter for more specifics on all things composition, including use of geometry, color, and cropping. The more you can create and manipulate in-camera, the less you have to do in your image editor and when printing. Also, see Chapters 8 and 11, where I cover shooting for great color and achieving special in-camera effects, respectively.

3) The trek from camera to computer

Snapping a photograph is only the beginning. Digital art photography requires following certain paths before you can print and frame your *output* (final image), including

1. **Getting the image into your computer:** You do this either by transferring the files from your digital camera to your computer or by digitizing a film photo, in which case you want to scan either the photograph itself or (even better) its negative. (Remember, after transferring a film print, positive, or negative into the computer, it becomes digital.) Chapter 3 covers scanners; see Chapter 16 for more about transferring images.

2. **Digitally tweaking the image:** With your image open in Photoshop (or your image editor of choice), there's practically no end to the tweaking that you can do. You can crop an image, apply filters to it, resample it, use layers to merge it with other images . . . the list goes on. See the chapters in Part III for more about image editing.

3. **Saving your image in the appropriate file type:** Whether you're shooting with a high-end digital single lens reflex camera (dSLR) or a mid-level point-and-shoot model, the files in which your camera stores your pictures are ultimately saved in a high-resolution format called *TIFF,* which is a file format that I describe in Chapter 2. Your digital image might travel across a number of devices and platforms before it's ultimately printed.

4) Print images

After you complete Step 3 — that is, you've tweaked, you've resized, the color is perfect, and the photo is ready for the world — just press Print, and you're good to go. Okay, the printing process is more involved than that. In Chapter 3, I discuss what types of printers are available. And in Chapter 17, I discuss the whole printing process in detail.

5) Frame your masterpiece

When you have your printed image in hand, you're almost to the finish. Following are your three choices for framing your digital photograph:

- **Take your photos to your local framer and have mats and frames made.** This is mostly for those who want a select look for their home or office that matches exactly to their décor. It's not a cost effective route for those who want to sell their prints framed.

- **Cut your own mats and make your own frames.** This is a great way to get your work framed if you're a carpenter. Many people take this route but buy the frames premade from a wholesaler while cutting the mats themselves.

- **Buy your mats precut and your frames from a wholesaler or your local discount frame store.** Hey, for people starting out (and even for people who do the art show circuit), this isn't a bad idea.

For creative framing options, see Chapter 18.

Composing an Art Photograph

The difference between someone who takes pictures and an art photographer is that the latter realizes that the cornerstone of fundamental design is composition. Folks easily take this element for granted, getting swept away by coolness or locale of the subject. Composition is more than what your subject is and how it's posed: It comprises all that plus the background, foreground, color, lighting, and framing. Always remember to compose first and expose second.

All great photographs start with sound composition techniques, which are basic rules of how to put together a pleasing image. When you compare two shots (say, using the same subject and lighting), one of a sloppily composed image with one that's thoughtful and crafted, you can immediately tell the difference. And when you follow these rules, remember that you follow in the footsteps of masters of art and architecture: The ancient Greeks and Romans practiced these same tenets 20 centuries before the advent of photography. It's obvious in their architecture.

Most photographs need a *focus* — anything inherently interesting to your viewer, from a looming tree and its shadow to a church's dome. Figure 1-3 shows a pair of pictures: The left image has too many unnecessary objects in the frame that render the image unfocused; the right image is composed artfully.

Figure 1-3: Provide a focus for the subject(s) of your photos.

And, by the way, call 'em guidelines instead of rules if you want. Know, too, that after you master these guidelines, you can bend them to your artistic desire.

Simplicity

Keeping your shots clean and uncluttered is paramount to presenting a great art photograph. That's not to say that you can't shoot something detailed and ornamented, but make sure your audience sees what you want to show, not a photo cluttered with unnecessary background distractions. Read more about this in the upcoming section, "Foreground, background, and depth of field."

For example, consider the architecture of the Sydney Opera House. People gather around this Australian landmark, snapping pictures left and right. To present this wonderful architecture artfully to your viewer (or to present any subject artfully to your viewer), crop it boldly and closely — either while you shoot (ideally) or later in Photoshop if necessary. By doing so, you can retain your viewer's focus on this monument only and nothing else, as shown in the two images in Figure 1-4.

Figure 1-4: Full frontal photos of massive architectural monuments need to be framed and/or cropped tightly.

 As a general rule for landscape and architectural photos, leave about 1/3 of the top of the photo for the sky.

Balance

Akin to using simplicity is the art of balance. Achieving good balance means paying careful attention to how you arrange shapes, colors, or areas of light/dark to complement one another so that the photograph has interest but isn't lopsided. (Try to avoid centering the subject; read more about this in the section on the Rule of Thirds.)

When using symmetrical balance, the two halves of an object look the same — they are mirror images of each other, if you will. In the Greek islands (and elsewhere), gates and foyers are often built symmetrically, as shown in Figure 1-5.

Figure 1-5: Symmetry is a forced balance.

Shadow dancing

Have you ever been caught playing with your shadow, stretched into a seemingly infinite length at dusk, skipping, jumping, straddling, and stretching to the sky? Well, why not take a picture of it or have someone else photograph those slick moves? Taking a variety of impressions of yourself by photographing your shadow on different backgrounds offers an artful perspective of your life.

You can use asymmetry to give a less formal yet balanced feel to your shots. This image of a bird with its beak sticking out of the cage (Figure 1-6) is unsymmetrical yet balanced. You can use simple geometry to help create balance. For more on that, see the later section, "Identifying lines in photos."

Figure 1-6: Asymmetry offers viewers a less formal perspective.

Rule of Thirds

I show examples of the Rule of Thirds throughout this book. This composition principle is based on the theory that the human eye gravitates naturally to a point about two-thirds of the way up an image. Thus, images with the subject or a dominant dividing line that falls in the upper or lower third of an image is pleasing. *Hint:* By visually dividing the image into thirds (vertically or horizontally), you can asymmetrically balance, as I discuss in the preceding section.

Imaginary lines divide the image into thirds both horizontally and vertically. You place important elements of your composition where these lines intersect. In Figure 1-7, you can visualize those imaginary lines that denote where the one-third and two-third marks fall horizontally and vertically in your photograph.

When you're shooting a wide area of land or water, the third-line will usually be two-thirds up from the bottom, as shown in Figure 1-8.

Figure 1-7: Follow the Rule of Thirds for visual appeal.

Figure 1-8: Even in this thin landscape, the third-line is two-thirds from the bottom.

Conversely, if you want to showcase the sky — like for a remarkable sunrise or sunset — your main line is effective one-third up from the bottom, as shown in Figure 1-9.

All about light, shadows, and shades

Capturing light — how you want to show and exploit it — truly defines photography. After all, photography literally means *light writing*. You can use light to paint, illuminate, mask, shadow, and color your subject almost limitlessly. Use light to your advantage to capture everything from blasting saturated color to ethereal backlit fog and mist to stark silhouettes. For more on reading light when shooting outdoors and indoors, see Chapters 5 and 6, respectively. For great techniques on capturing light when shooting black-and-white, see Chapter 9. And for shooting in virtually no light, see Chapter 10 for the low-down on night photography.

Photographing landscapes and people with strong late afternoon or early morning sun in front of you creates a silhouette, as shown in Figure 1-10.

Figure 1-9: Third-lines that divide sky from sea should fall one-third the way up the frame.

Figure 1-10: Photographing into the late afternoon sun creates a silhouette effect.

You can also use light and shadow at night to add depth to photographs, sometimes making them look similar to paintings. Older buildings that show wear offer your camera's sensor a brush stroke effect in its interpretation of the light's reflection on the worn stone.

Many of the best architecture and landscape photographs are shot at dusk. The long shadows, soft light, and reflections can create dramatic results. For instance, Figure 1-11 shows a quiet street scene made dramatic by the long shadows caught at dusk. (In Chapter 9, I further discuss shooting architecture photos in the context of black-and-white photography.)

Figure 1-11: Shadows cast at dusk add a dramatic dimension to your images.

Don't be afraid to exploit contrast when calculating the proper light for exposure. After you get the hang of your camera's auto settings, master how to set your exposures manually. (More on that in Part II.) For example, in Figure 1-12, you can see how the light paints the outlines of the multicolored leaf.

Figure 1-12: An under-lit leaf is painted with light.

Recognizing lines, shapes, and forms

You probably learned as a kid that two points make a line and that four lines fit together to make a rectangle. Later in life, you also likely learned about intersecting lines, parallel lines, and all the types of triangles. Then 3-D spaces of area and volume were next.

I know, I know: "It's math — ugh, geometry, at that! — and you can't make me like it any more than spinach." However, with a minimum of effort, you can quickly discover how to use lines, triangles, and all things geometric to help compose photographs that are compelling and full of life.

Also, don't overlook capturing texture and form repetition as strong compositional tools.

Identifying lines in photos

Vertical, horizontal, diagonal, curved, zigzag — straight lines come in many forms. And lines don't have to be straight, either: Don't forget ovals, curves, and circles.

In the earlier section on the Rule of Thirds, you can see how a simple horizontal line can effectively divide a shot. Now flip that line on the bias (a 45° angle) to show how using a strong diagonal line can add more interest and a dynamic sense, as shown in Figure 1-13. In this image, the paths of the two women, along with the painted street lines, form diagonal lines.

Figure 1-13: Diagonal lines add interest.

When you're out and about — running errands or just going for a walk — really look at the lines in your world. Try to notice straight lines (fences and sidewalks), parallel lines (railroad tracks), soft and slinky curves (like a cat stretching), or undulating waves (like the overpass shown in Figure 1-14).

Figure 1-14: Undulating lines catch the eye.

Using geometric shapes and forms

After you become better at identifying lines in a potential shot, start looking for geometric forms to mimic. Your viewer likely won't even realize your trick but will be attracted to the composition of an image when you cleverly hide a triangle, like the example shown in Figure 1-15. (Oh, so I did manage to sneak in some spinach, after all.)

Figure 1-15: Natural triangles add interest.

Shapes don't have to be linear, either. You can use a rounded shape to draw attention to your subject, as shown in Figure 1-16. (Image that: Circles and repetition!)

Photo credit: Ausnap! Photography

Figure 1-16: Rotundas provide an excellent study in circles.

Now take the triangle technique one step further, using one to create a vanishing point. When you arrange lines to converge in a distant point — usually at a corner of an image — you create a *vanishing point*. Perhaps the lines don't truly disappear off the edge, but they look as though they could, as shown in Figure 1-17.

More importantly, the lines and geometric shape immediately pull your eye to the place of interest you craft via composition. When lines are repeated — even when they repeat but end in a jumble, like a pile of sticks — you create even more visual interest. In Figure 1-18, notice how the repetition of a line draws your eye up the image.

Figure 1-17: Capture lines to form a vanishing point.

Figure 1-18: Use repeated lines for visual interest.

Repeating a geometric shape can also be quite effective. You can often find this technique in architecture, as shown in Figure 1-19.

Texture

A basic micro-element of art — a mark — can be considered like a mini-line. When that mark is repeated, that creates texture (on a small scale, like the fur of a cat) or repetition (like a woven pattern in cloth), as shown in Figure 1-20.

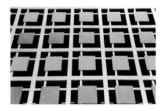

Figure 1-19: Look for patterns built into architecture.

Figure 1-20: Indulge your viewers with texture.

Subject placement

Be cognizant of how you place your subjects. Avoid sun shining right in their eyes (see Chapter 5), having odd things in the background seemingly sprout from their heads (see the upcoming section, "Foreground, background, and depth of field"), and having them in motion to disappear from an image, as shown in Figure 1-21.

Photo credit: Kevin Kirschner

Figure 1-21: Careful how you place your subjects.

The risk of Impressionism

Claude Monet's *Impression, Sunrise* (in the Musée Marmottan Monet, Paris) plays with light and shadow on canvas. About a century and a half ago, Monet took a risk by painting in a different way, re-creating the natural environment that surrounded him. Soon others began painting with dabs of color that come together when you step back from the work and view it as a whole. The Impressionist movement got its name when art critic Louis Leroy commented that Monet's work wasn't finished. Up until that time, works of art were more realistic. A painting of a garden, for example, was expected to approximate reality and not be just an "impression."

Just like Monet took a risk, so can you. The following figure illustrates a risk that a photographer can take when filming and manipulating images to give photographs an Impressionistic feel. Take a picture on a rainy day and you get a picture looking as if it was painted with short brush strokes a century and a half ago.

Take the extra minute and consider these points about your subjects when composing:

- ✔ Frame them in the shot's context.

- ✔ Identify line shapes that you can exploit.

- ✔ Calculate how much (or how little) of the object you want in your picture.

- ✔ Choose what angle to shoot from.

- ✔ Create dimension and, by context, show more than just the face/main portion.

Deciphering color

Looking at color is a matter of observing the world around you. As your kids grow up, their hair changes shades. (Um, yours does, too.) And those bananas you bought at the store the other day morph from yellow-green into deeper shades of yellow (and if you don't eat them, brown). Also, color changes — sometimes extraordinarily — under different light; the shades of the desert re-create themselves from dawn to noon to dusk, from yellow to pink or even green, depending on the weather, light, and season.

And perceptions can play with color. To one person at one moment, red can appear bright and cheery or warlike and aggressive. Color perception also changes on your object/subject when other colors are nearby. A green object can shift to more yellow or blue depending on the colors of the object next to it or the color of the foreground and/or background, as shown in the three fruit images in Figure 1-22.

The colors you see around you can depend on sunlight, atmospheric conditions (clouds, rain, haze), and season. (Light is always softer in

Figure 1-22: Different background colors cause subtle perception changes.

spring and fall.) You can also affect how your camera sees color with some of its settings. For more on color photography, see Chapter 8.

To understand how to effectively capture color, you need to understand a wee bit about the beast. It's all pretty simple, and you likely know more than you think you do. Three primary colors — red, yellow, and blue — inside a triangle are at the center of a color wheel (shown in Figure 1-23). Next come the triangles of secondary colors — orange, green, and violet — that are made from mixing the primary colors. It's this group of triangles that points the way around the rest of the color wheel, to the tertiary colors.

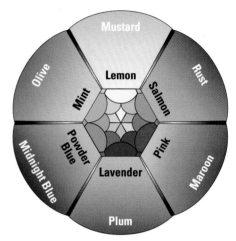

Figure 1-23: Use the color wheel to mix colors and create color schemes.

Use this wheel to find complementary colors that are on opposite sides of the wheel — for example, red and green. You can also use one section or side of the wheel to find colors in the same tonal family — for example, pink, salmon, and orange. (**Note:** These types of color usually go well together but at the expense of contrast.)

To create contrast, choose complementary colors, like the orange and blue in Figure 1-24.

Figure 1-24: Use complements for contrast.

Understanding positive and negative space

In Figure 1-25 are photos of an outdoor sculpture from two different vantage points, which shows how positive and negative space changes. *Negative space* is the space in between and around the object. An object in a picture is the *positive space* of the picture. Sculptors constantly evaluate the negative space as they mold their art, noticing not only the object itself (the positive space) but also the space between it (the negative space). As a photographer, you can exploit both spaces, too.

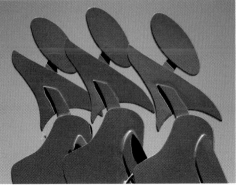

Figure 1-25: Camera position changes positive and negative space.

Positive and negative space tell you the following about your picture:

- **What shape and form the object is:** Forms without jagged edges — smooth and even-rounded — are more pleasing to the eye in an art photo. Smooth round rocks (the positive space) among brilliant sky (the negative space) offer a viewer comfort in nature in Figure 1-26.

- **How much of the object occupies the picture:** If the positive space is small, it should stand out in some other way, such as being a bright color. If it's large, like an extreme close-up of a person, it's more interesting if it shows some sort of emotion: excitement, concern, or disappointment. This emotion can be seen in the eyes or somewhere unexpected, like in puffy cheeks or a toothy smile.

Figure 1-26: Rounded rocks offer a peaceful version of a hard surface.

✔ **How the subject and object interact:** Whether your subject is in motion or static makes a big difference in how the distinction between the spaces is outlined. The way in which the two spaces meet affects how the picture will react to image manipulation. Rapidly changing tones within a small area sometimes gather pixels of disparate colors with tweaks in Photoshop, but more about that in Chapter 15. Also, the more dimension the object has, the more complicated the interaction between the two spaces.

✔ **How busy the space is:** A busy shot is bad for art photos because when too much is going on, the viewer has no focus. That being said, millions of successful art pieces are very busy. It just depends on trends and what's out in the culture and/or community as a whole. Figure 1-27 is a photo that is, well, just too busy with too much going on. Your viewer's eyes will just juggle looking at the picture.

Photo credit: Kevin Kirschner

Figure 1-27: This shot is so busy that the viewer has nowhere to focus.

Foreground, background, and depth of field

Right off the bat, you can't talk about backgrounds and foregrounds in photography without addressing *depth of field*. Basically, the depth of field is how much of your picture is in focus. Some photos have detail throughout the foreground and background with no blur, and others show a subject clearly with blur in the background.

You can use Photoshop to make a blurred background clear and vice versa, but it's done in kind of a roundabout way to get a good result. Turn to Chapter 14 for more about making backgrounds with Photoshop layers.

So why would you want any blur at all in a photograph? Blur creates an illusion of dimension, movement, and, sometimes, even the suggestion of a sixth sense. To make a variety of art with your state-of-the-art digital equipment, keep these points in mind:

✔ **The clarity of the negative and positive space:** If you have a picture with a blurred background and want it clear, you'll probably have to replace it with a clear background from another picture in Photoshop.

✔ **The number and dimension of your subjects:** If your picture is a simple 2-D negative/positive-space photo, tweaking it in an image processing program is fairly easy. You can use almost any option to make a good art photo. For more about cleaning up pictures in Photoshop, see Chapter 12.

The sharper the distinction between foreground and background, the easier you can process, transfer, and manipulate the foreground and background in an image processing program.

Small is relative. Tiny objects cast in massive backgrounds can be missed, so those tiny objects need to have a certain eye-catching something. When you're casting something small in a big background, make that small object colorful and memorable.

Having little or no background can make a photograph dramatic. In a portrait, such a shot is an *extreme close-up,* which is a type of photograph that reveals expression in all the features. In Figure 1-28, the focus is solely on the subject. But note how the subject is shifted to the right, leaving some background — a space that assumes some importance in the picture.

Photo credit: Rebekka Guðleifsdóttir

Figure 1-28: Use background to add intrigue.

Often, pictures with large foregrounds and just a little background can give the viewer a sense of being right in front of the subject.

And don't forget to scrutinize your background when composing and shooting. Who hasn't taken a photo of someone with an errant phone pole or tree growing out of someone's head (as in the top image in Figure 1-29)? Sure, you can probably clean up your image later in Photoshop, but if you're careful to begin with, that's just less manipulation to do later (as in the image on the bottom in Figure 1-29).

Perspective

Showing a different angle or perspective of a subject can lend an artsy feel to a photograph. To experiment with this, walk around your subject, keeping your eye to the viewfinder to see how the light in the foreground or background changes with your different camera positions. Don't forget to move up and down, too. Sometimes shooting from above or below (as in the left image of Figure 1-30) gives you a feeling that's quite different from your normal eye level (as in the image on the right in Figure 1-30).

Photo credit: Kevin Kirschner

Figure 1-29: Be mindful how you place your subjects.

Stay tuned for the weather

All the atmospheric elements (humidity, temperature, wind, and so on) that make up the weather comprise one long color equation. Each item is a variable that on any given day and at any given moment influences the appearance of color in the world around you. Some environmental circumstances have almost no effect on the color you see while others give your eyes a feast of tones and hues.

Figure 1-30: Change perspective to add that artistic edge.

In-camera cropping and framing

Perhaps the most valuable technique at your disposal when shooting is to crop judiciously. Think of this from a pragmatic view: What's the point in all that wasted space that you later have to crop in an image editing application? The more base image you have to work from, the less noise you get when you enlarge your image. See how Figure 1-31 could have benefited from more in-camera careful cropping?

Too, paying attention to in-camera framing lends to the craft of the shot, adding a professional touch. Use framing to visually lead the viewer into the scene or add a softened edge for effect.

Figure 1-31: Close cropping makes a better, more focused photograph.

Making the Digital Leap

In This Chapter

▷ Comparing film and digital cameras and equipment

▷ Exploring digital cameras

▷ Selecting lenses, flashes, and other accessories

▷ Downloading images from your camera to your computer

▷ Understanding resolution

▷ Discovering file types

So you decided to jump into this century and go digital, eh? Bully for you! This chapter (and the next) cover all those nuts-and-bolts kinds of digital photography issues — you know, the *digital side* of digital art photography.

Whether you're a budding photographer whose first foray involves using a digital camera or a film buff who wants to use traditional and digital film technology, this chapter walks you through some of the jargon and nuances between these two formats to help you along your path.

The Digital Path

Any image that ends up in your computer is *digital* — that is, bits of data organized electronically. Even if a photo begins on film, it ends up being digital when you scan it into your computer. Ever look at a photo attachment in an e-mail? Maybe it started out as a hard copy print from film, but you view it in digital format. Your goal when making the digital leap is to manipulate those bits of data with electronic means — your computer, some image editing software, and perhaps a scanner — to create an image that looks simply fantastic and cutting edge, no matter what special effects you do (or don't) apply.

Think of your photographs taken with your digital camera or scanned from film or prints as the beginning of making a product in a factory. The image goes through a process:

1. Snap the picture.

2. Store the image.

   - *Film:* This step has two parts: The first takes place in a processing machine or dark room where the film is developed into negatives and/or positives; during the second part, the image is developed onto photo paper.

   - *Digital:* The image is stored as *pixels,* which are tiny picture elements made of bits of data, inside your camera.

3. Move the image file into your computer.

   - *Film:* Scan a printed photograph or a slide (a *positive*).

   - *Digital:* Transfer the image from your camera to your computer.

4. Leave the image as-is or tweak it within an image processing program.

5. Print the image.

   You can use your own printer or take it to a service bureau.

To get your image through this process, you need a certain amount of equipment: camera, lens, scanner, printer, and so on. Read on for an overview of digital cameras and camera peripherals; this overview is designed to help you acquire the proper tools for your needs. I also discuss resolution issues and file types (two topics that you never need to know to use a film camera!).

See Chapter 3 for an overview of the other parts necessary for digital art photography: computer, scanner, and printer. Then progress to Part III for the lowdown on manipulating images in image editing software. Part IV shows you how to prepare your final output.

Film versus Digital

Because film has been around a lot longer than digital camera sensors, take a minute to compare the new technology with the old. Sure, in some ways, photos taken with a digital camera beat those taken with a film model hands-down, but the digital world isn't a black-and-white world — as with most things in life, there are many shades of gray. For every privilege you get with the technology, you have to be careful because each format has its inherent pluses and minuses, which are described in the upcoming Table 2-1.

For example, compare the viewfinders on a film camera with a digital model. You look through a film camera viewfinder, but most digital cameras use an *LCD display,* akin to a mini TV screen. Viewfinders on digital single lens reflex (dSLR) models, however, are very similar to film SLR models.

✔ **Most cameras that have an attached lens come with an LCD screen viewfinder.** This viewfinder (as in Figure 2-1) is a nice feature to have (no discomfort from the camera against your face), but it does have a slightly different perspective than what you actually get after your picture is taken.

 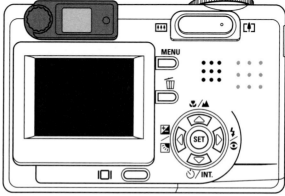

Figure 2-1: Most digital cameras use LCD viewfinders.

✔ **The viewfinder on a high-end dSLR camera uses what a 35mm SLR camera does.** Optical viewfinders on professional digital cameras are the same ones used on professional film cameras. These use a prism to split the view, so the picture you take is pretty much what you see through the lens, as shown in Figure 2-2.

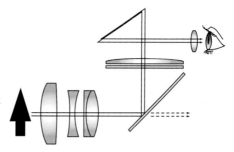

Figure 2-2: SLR and dSLR cameras' viewfinders are similar.

If you've been a film photographer for most of your life, your eye has probably been glued to the viewfinder of your camera. Thank goodness they also put one on digital SLR cameras because that LCD viewfinder takes some getting used to.

Of course, both film and digital cameras each have other advantages and disadvantages. Table 2-1 provides a brief overview. Some factors will undoubtedly matter more to you than to someone else. Similarly, you can also compare digital and film images, as shown in Table 2-2.

Table 2-1	Shooting Digital versus Shooting Film	
Factor	**Pro**	**Con**
Convenience	*Digital:* They're small and portable.	*Digital:* Some models are a bit small for some folks' hands.
	Film: Some folks like the weight and feel.	*Film:* They're more bulky.
Instant gratification	*Digital:* You get to see images right away. Not only is this cool, but you can cull bad shots right away.	*Film:* You have to wait for processing.
Cost-efficient	*Digital:* You don't have to pay for film and processing. (If you do your own image processing, though, you do need a computer, software, printer, and printing supplies.)	*Film:* You have to buy film and prints. (If you make your own prints, you need a darkroom setup, equipment, an enlarger, and printing supplies.)
Durability	*Digital:* They have fewer moving parts to wear out.	*Digital:* They can easily fall from a shirt pocket or get knocked about in a purse.
	Film: They withstand bumps and drops better.	*Film:* They have more moving parts.
Accessories	*Both film and digital:* SLRs can use more lenses, filters, and flash accessories.	*Digital:* Non-dSLRs don't have as many lens options.
Power	*Digital:* They eat batteries.	*Film:* They have much less battery consumption although flash units and motor drives are battery intensive.

Factor	Pro	Con
Memory	*Film:* You're limited only by your film roll size.	*Film:* You're limited by your film roll size.
	Digital: Removable storage media means unlimited shots; you're limited only by the amount you have; memory can be reused.	*Digital:* Because of its size and nature, removable memory can be damaged or lost.

Table 2-2	Digital Images versus Film Images	
Factor	**Pro**	**Con**
Storage	*Digital:* You can store many images in a small amount of space, like on a CD or DVD.	*Film:* Film (negative and positive) and paper archiving takes space and environmental care.
	Film: You don't need a computer.	*Digital:* You need a computer and software to view/edit.
Lifespan	*Digital:* Images don't degrade like film and paper do.	*Digital:* Images can become corrupt or be lost when a computer crashes; also, storage media lifespan is not unlimited.
	Both film and digital: Hard copy images are permanent.	*Film:* Film and prints deteriorate over time.
Flexibility	*Digital:* Images are easily edited and printed; digital images can be transmitted between computers and posted online.	*Digital:* Images can be "faked"; you need a computer and software.
	Film: Digitize film images for archiving and manipulation.	*Film:* Making printing tweaks is limited; moving from color to black-and-white and vice versa is difficult.
Cost	*Digital:* No need to buy film.	*Film:* Processing costs.
Appeal/ art factor	*Digital:* You create amazingly cool images with tweaks, filters, and layering.	*Digital:* Some folks are a tad snobbish in their preference for film over digital; some folks like holding a print for viewing rather than viewing onscreen.
	Film: Some folks (and art pros) like prints from film better; some galleries insist on print images, especially B&W.	*Film:* You're limited in your tweaking options.

Don't ditch your scanner if you decide to use only a digital camera from now on. Just because you have all your images stored digitally on a tiny chip doesn't mean that you don't want to be able to copy some older ones from prints. (You don't want to forget about how you looked way back when.) Sure, old crackly photos can be retouched in Photoshop (see Part III), but they have to be scanned first.

Digital Camera 101

Choices, choices. Just like when choosing a film camera, don't let all the options, bell and whistles, and knobs bamboozle you. Read through the following sections to help make your equipment purchasing decisions. Be prepared to pony up a bit of cash when you go high-end digital, but you can find a lot of features on moderately priced models. And prices come down all the time, so first determine what features you want/need and then shop around.

Digital camera types

You have many types of digital cameras from which to choose. Here's a brief overview of each. Because prices for each drop so quickly, take a look at online and local newspaper ads for accurate pricing. Expect to pay a few hundred bucks for the low-end models (compacts) and work your way up into the thousands for a dSLR with bells and whistles.

- **Ultracompact:** These microcameras are Twiggy-thin.
- **Point-and-shoot:** About the same size as a subcompact, some of these have some manual settings.
- **Subcompact:** These easily fit in your shirt pocket; most have some manual settings.
- **Prosumer:** These are similar in size to a dSLR; some have detachable lenses.
- **dSLR:** These are the best models going, featuring all the manual settings of a film SLR.

Choosing a digital camera that takes good-quality images is easy and relatively inexpensive. You can choose from a variety of megapixel (MP) prosumer digital cameras and dSLR cameras from which you can use a number of controls to create art.

Figure 2-3 shows typical subcompact, prosumer, and dSLR models. (*Note:* dSLRs and film SLRs look very similar when comparing higher-end models.)

✔ **Basic digital cameras:** There are dozens of digital cameras (including the ones that are an option on cellphones) that take your basic digital picture, all great for sending images to friends and/or posting images on the Web. As far as printing a clear 8" x 10" print, however, you're better off spending a little extra on a prosumer model, which I describe in the next bullet.

✔ **Prosumer digital cameras:** Prosumer cameras offer far better quality than those cameras built into cellphones or those cheaper low-end model digital cameras. You could label these as mid-end cameras. If you're getting serious about your digital photography, these are the cameras to buy.

✔ **dSLRs:** These are the gold (or platinum) standard of the digital photography world. Expensive (but coming down in price), these cameras do their best to replicate the best 35mm film cameras. (And an added bonus, you can use the lens from your film camera on the dSLRs.)

If you do have money already invested in lenses, make sure to purchase a digital camera that's compatible with those lenses. You'll also find that sticking with the same brand of camera as you go digital reduces the learning curve — most options and controls will already be familiar to you.

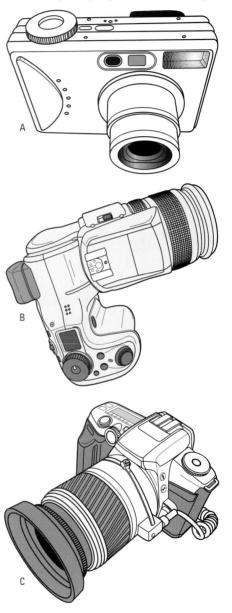

Figure 2-3: Digital camera bodies.

How digital cameras work

Digital cameras use sensors to record the images that you shoot. There are three categories of sensors:

- ✔ **Foveon:** A kind of simulated film sensor, where pixels are processed within the sensor with an added color enhancement similar to film
- ✔ **CCD:** A *charge-coupled device,* where pixels are processed outside the sensor
- ✔ **APS:** *Active Pixel Sensors,* where pixels are processed within the sensor

    You see the acronym CMOS (Complementary Metal Oxide Semiconductor) most commonly for APS devices.

Each uses a technology that forms the image coming through the lens into a digital format. They are easy to use and allow the user to immediately review the photo. You can keep, download, or manipulate the photo electronically in your computer, tweaking and cropping it so it looks like it could be published in a newspaper or magazine, and adjusting the image for best results. A digital camera is basically a computer with a lens that scans an image, stores it digitally on removable storage, has a built-in monitor for viewing, and can download the image to a computer. Digital cameras have most of the features found in film cameras, such as zoom lenses, built-in flashes, lens adjustments, timers, and more. Most high-end digital cameras use optical viewfinders for framing the image.

dSLR cameras look identical to their film counterparts and operate similar to them, too. Both prosumer and dSLR models have different sophistication levels of these features. In a nutshell, consider these factors:

- ✔ **Optics:** The optics of digital cameras comprise the zooms, exposure compensations, white and color balances, and a whole slew of controls that come to your fingertips after you make your selection. The zoom is how the image can be enlarged without losing resolution. For more information about optical and digital zooms, see *Digital Photography For Dummies,* 5th Edition, by Julie Adair King (Wiley).
- ✔ **Metering:** The metering in your camera helps you to use light distributions correctly within the area of the photograph you're taking.
- ✔ **Focusing system:** The focusing systems on most digital and film cameras currently come with an autofocus and also have a manual focus system.
- ✔ **Sensor resolution:** The *sensor resolution* is the number of pixels the image carries at the camera's maximum resolution setting. The more, the merrier — that is, increased clarity.

The whole megapixel (MP) thing

Megapixels determine the quality (clarity) of a digital image that's taken with a sensor in a digital camera. A *pixel* is the composition unit of a digital image. (Just like a *byte* is the smallest unit of memory storage, a pixel is the smallest unit in an image on a display screen.) Images that you take with your digital camera have a lot of pixels — a million or more (hence, *mega*). When you shop for a digital camera in a store, the first thing that the salesman tells you is how many megapixels it has.

The quality of a digital camera's image is measured in millions of pixels (megapixels, MP). The higher the number of megapixels, the greater the resolution. For more about resolution concerns, see the later section, "Resolving Resolution Issues."

Thus, a 5MP camera can capture a shot with more pieces of information than a 2MP camera. Sometimes bigger is indeed better. Again, prices vary and can come down quickly. Assess your needs: For example, are you striving for gallery-quality images, or can you make do with a bit less? You can easily spend over $1,000 for high-end models (>6MP), but you can find a good 2MP model for about $100–$200. Expect to shell out $200–$350 for a model between 4 and 6MP. Of course, pricing for MP capacity also depends on whether the model is a dSLR.

You can compare prices and other options online at sites like

```
www.buyersedge.com/landing/digital_cameras.asp
```

If you're beginning to make art photos, you're best off with a camera that can take a high-quality image that can be enlarged to 8" x 10". After you master that arena, you can move up to giant sizes, and those are determined by the type of printer you have (see Chapter 17). Here's how to tell how much MP muscle you need:

- ✔ **<2MP:** Under-2MP cameras aren't really capable of producing a clear enough image for a high-quality art photograph. To give you an idea of what you could expect, many cellphones have camera capabilities in the 2MP range.

- ✔ **2–4MP:** Cameras with this oomph are great starter cameras and can produce some pretty good 5" x 7" prints that are great, especially if you have a series of them in similar frames.

- ✔ **4–6MP:** These guys can produce some mighty good 8" x 10" images. When shooting these under the right light conditions, you can produce gallery-quality photographs.

- ✔ **>6MP:** These beasts can produce 8" x10" prints — and even larger photographs — of stellar quality.

The physical size of a digital camera's sensor also plays a role in the quality of the image captured. Generally speaking, larger is better. Some digital cameras include a sensor that's the same size as a frame of 35mm film; others use a smaller sensor. When you explore digital cameras, you might also come across the extremely expensive digital backs for medium- and large-format studio cameras, which capture images of 20MB, 30MB, and more.

How is image quality affected if you've got two cameras, both with 8 or more MP but each with a different size sensor? It's the light. The bigger sensor of a dSLR reads light better, creating deeper colors and better contrast. Images from each camera will be clear and can be used for gallery-quality photos, but the size of the sensor does make a difference.

The dSLRs in the near-$1,000 price range are 6- and 8MP models with sensor sizes around 16 x 24mm. In contrast, the two-third-inch (about 17mm) sensor size of some 6-, 7-, and 8MP digital cameras is dramatically smaller, perhaps the size of a man's thumbnail. These models are usually not dSLRs but rather point-and-shoot to prosumer models described in the previous section, "Digital camera types." About a dozen film camera companies offer a wide variety of digital cameras and dSLRs. Canon, Fuji, Hewlett-Packard (HP), Kodak, Leica, Minolta, Nikon, Olympus, and Sony: You name it, and they probably have it — from models that take pictures in JPEG format to models that shoot in Raw format, the latest in digital photography technology. Read about both file types in the later section, "Understanding File Types."

Most of the time, the closer the specifications of the camera are to those of a film camera, the better the digital camera.

Lenses

You can change lenses on your digital SLR camera just like you can with a film SLR camera. And best yet, you can use some of the same lenses from your film camera. This isn't possible with a fixed-lens digital camera. If you're moving to digital for good and don't want to waste your investment in lenses, consider investing in a dSLR model of the same brand as your film camera when switching from film to digital.

The principles of lens attachments and/or digital camera zooms and wide angle lenses are similar to that of film. An all-purpose zoom lens should meet most of your photography needs. Just about every camera has one of these. A *zoom lens* lets you press a button (on digital camera models) to change focal lengths without changing lenses. Many film point-and-shoot cameras work the same way. The variable focal lengths of this kind of lens make it all-purpose. You can shoot at wide angle for one exposure and then use the normal (standard) or telephoto lens for another.

Many cameras and digital cameras come with built-in lenses that have a limited *focal point range* — that is, one where it's a challenge to catch a good bit of horizontal or vertical (if you turn the camera on its side) space.

A good all-purpose lens for art photography should have at least a 28–105mm lens or the equivalent depending upon sensor size. For more about lens size equivalents for sensors smaller than 24mm x 36mm, see the "Focal lengths" sidebar, later in this chapter.

As an art photographer, you need to be quick. Life happens fast — there one minute and not the next — like people on the red carpet of a film opening, a comet in the sky, or a horseless carriage driving on the freeway. You have to think to yourself about what you want to carry with you and how much time you're going to have. If you have to tote a duffle bag with a variety of lenses that have to be changed from shot to shot, you're better off shooting things that are static and/or anchored. A good camera with an all-purpose lens is best to have with you at all times if you need to shoot your art photos fast.

Deciding what lenses to use comes down to the types of objects in your photographs and the amount of time you have to shoot them. On your digital camera's zoom lens push button zoom controller, the T means *telephoto* or *zoom in,* and the W means *wide angle*.

✔ **Telephoto:** Use a telephoto lens (as I did in Figure 2-4 to close in on just one part of a large sculpture) and a dSLR camera if you're going to shoot from far away.

Sports photographers and the infamous paparazzi use telephotos, as do some fashion photographers (who use loudspeakers to communicate with their subjects). The telephoto lens compresses a larger area in front of the subject, which helps to soften human features and blur the background. If you're looking to get close and/or have a picture-perfect portrait, you should, too.

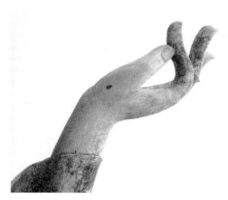

Figure 2-4: Use a telephoto lens to get close.

✔ **Wide angle:** Use a wide angle lens (wide angle zoom lenses have lengths such as 16–35mm and 10–22mm; see Figure 2-5) and a dSLR camera if you're going to shoot architecture and landscapes, or in any situation where you need a panorama. For example, a shot of a swimming pool's length is best presented as a panorama so that the focus of the shot is just the pool (with little or no background), long and ready to jump into.

A panorama doesn't necessarily have to be a picture that's very wide; it can also be a vertical picture showing something extraordinarily tall. Steer your panorama shots with wide angle lenses (or your zoom set to wide angle) in an up-and-down orientation. For instance, take the elaborate doors of European architecture that are ten times the height of the average person. Set a person in the shot and you've got vertical drama, as shown in Figure 2-5.

With this type of photography, you also probably need a tripod to avoid camera shake.

Fish-eye: A fish-eye lens gives you maximum lens distortion so that objects are magnified in the center and diminish in size and clarity in all directions in proportion to the lens's shape. Superwide angles cause this type of distortion. Some would consider it an error,

Figure 2-5: Some architecture is best shot using wide angle vertical shots.

but others would see it as art. Figure 2-6 is a fish-eye view, one that offers offbeat distortion for your art photos.

Focal lengths

Many digital cameras have zoom lenses whose numbers might look funny if you're used to the focal length numbers on film lenses or digital cameras with sensors the size of 35mm film. For example, a 5MP Kodak EasyShare CX 7530 camera has a lens that measures 5.6–16.8mm, which is equivalent to a 35mm film lens that's 34–102mm. The effective length of the lens depends on the physical dimensions of the

camera's sensor — the area on which the light coming through the lens is spread. A camera with a sensor measuring 14.8mm x 22.2mm (rather than 35mm film's 24mm x 36mm) has a conversion factor of about 1:6.

Some companies, including Kodak, have started to put the film equivalent on the lens itself to lessen confusion about the in-fact value.

Figure 2-6: Shoot with a fish-eye lens for remarkable effects.

Settings

Many digital cameras come with different modes: preset settings that you can choose for certain lighting and shooting scenarios. For example, you can choose an auto setting (see Figure 2-7; let the camera choose what it thinks is best), shutter priority, aperture priority, or manual control (you make all the exposure decisions). Some cameras also have drive modes, which allow you to fire off quick shots in succession (great for sports and actions shots). See the Cheat Sheet at the front of this book where I list the modes and their functions.

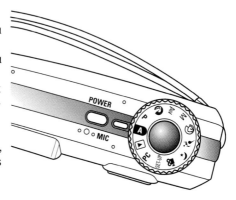

Figure 2-7: Auto settings do all the work.

Settings are influenced by the ISO setting you choose. ISO refers to how sensitive you set the sensor to read light; for more on ISO, see Chapters 5 and 6.

Of course, for total creative control, use all manual settings to control aperture and shutter speeds. For more on these settings, see Chapter 11.

Flash and flash attachments

Ever wonder why people who've been photographed using a flash look scared? The human eye — of the subject, in this case — isn't used to powerful bursts of light, like what a flash omits. Eyes need time to adjust to changes in light. Hence, you often get that deer-in-headlights look. This makes flash photography tricky. Too, you have to know how to achieve adequate and even illumination. To overcome these limitations when using a flash, first begin by understanding the average built-in flash:

- **Range:** Built-in flashes have a range of up to 10 feet. If your subject is farther away than that, the flash will fall short.

- **Quality:** Flash light is harsh unless you soften it by bouncing it off walls, whiteboards, umbrellas, and other diffusing devices.

  The best light is *ambient* light — light that comes from all around you — and that just doesn't happen with a built-in flash.

If you have a dSLR, you can always augment or replace your camera's built-in flash with a flash attachment. (The only type of digital camera that can take an additional flash attachment is a dSLR model.) Of course, any time you add an attachment to your camera, it becomes more cumbersome. Still, here are reasons why you might want to attach a more powerful flash to your camera:

- **Flash technology has become sophisticated.** Some flash units can simulate a good lighting situation from a pretty good distance, some up to 40 feet. There are flash extender units (handy if you're using a lens greater than 300mm) that can shoot light over 40 feet when used as a flash fill. (For more about flash fill, see Chapter 5.)

- **You're shooting outside in low light, and no other light is available.** For example, a flash attachment is very handy if you are filming the red carpet celebs at the Sundance Film Festival in Park City, Utah.

Each camera company makes its own flash attachment. For example, Nikon makes the SB 800 AF Speedlight, which is a flash attachment that is interchangeable on both its film SLR and dSLR cameras.

Work with your built-in and/or flash attachment by taking pictures with it to assess its effectiveness and range.

Your built-in camera flash is triggered when your shutter moves. You can mount different types of flash attachments to your camera. Many in-camera flashes offer uneven light, sometimes blasting all in one place so that your subject looks unevenly lit. Flash attachments work wonders to eliminate these light blasts by providing much more powerful flash over which you have more control:

✔ A *hot shoe* is a space on your camera into which you can secure your external flash. Using a hot shoe enables your camera to control many aspects of the flash from the camera's flash options, such as flash exposure compensation. The flash exposure compensation lets you control the amount of light from your flash that you want cast over your subject/object.

✔ Some flash units, such as the Canon Speedlite 580 EX, can determine your camera's sensor size so that it throws out evenly dispersed light over your entire frame. You can also adjust the way the flash gives off light through options within the flash unit settings. Many of these units swivel and tilt so that the light can be thrown at wide angles and bounced off walls and whiteboards and at varying focal lengths.

✔ Mid- to high-level external flash attachments have motors that move the flash outward in front of the camera. (The closer the bulb is to the camera, the wider the light will be cast.) The zooming motor can be adjusted each time you change your focal length.

✔ Many external flash units use AA batteries. Some can accommodate high voltage battery packs; all operate so that the battery life lasts throughout heavy flash picture taking at long events, such as a wedding.

For more on shooting in low-light situations, see Chapter 6.

Batteries

Digital cameras use a lot of batteries. Many point-and-shoot models use two AA batteries that will usually last through several dozen shots.

Internal battery packs are rechargeable units that you take out of the camera and recharge by securing them into a charging unit that you plug into a wall outlet. Recharging time can vary from several hours to less than one hour depending on the model. If you use your camera's LCD viewfinder and flash a lot, the batteries will be sucked dry quickly. Some dSLR cameras offer optional external battery packs for extended operation.

Buy another rechargeable battery if you do a lot of shooting. When you have an extra, you can charge one while using the other (and you'll always have a charged battery on hand).

Batteries are simple to load. Look for your typical sliding/slot door. If all else fails, read the manual. Check out

        www.imaging-resource.com/ACCS/BATTS/BATTS.HTM

for a comparison of batteries.

Some cameras can use only *proprietary* batteries — that is, made by the same manufacturer as your camera. Thus, you gotta pony up the cash for the ones specially designed for your camera or risk damaging your camera. Not good.

Supports

When shooting at slow ISO/ASA speeds, slow shutter speeds, or in low-light situations, you want to support the camera to prevent unintentional blur. Your best bet is to use a tripod or a monopod (see Figure 2-8). (Read more about film speeds, shutter speeds, and shooting in low light in Chapters 5 and 6.)

A *tripod* is a three-legged (hence the *tri*) stand for your camera. You attach your camera to it with a tiny screw attached to a small platform at the top. Tripods can vary anywhere from high-end ball bearing balanced tools to ultraportable, tabletop models. A monopod works in a similar fashion but (obviously) has one leg. (Just watch out when using a monopod, especially in a public building. Don't be surprised if security personnel want to inspect it. It's the times we live in.)

Just make sure that your camera has a threaded mount hole (look at the bottom plate) to marry to a tripod. Higher-end digital cameras will have this feature. Also, after you attach your camera to a tripod, you can manipulate the tripod's knobs to flip your camera on its side to take pictures vertically.

Memory and removable storage media

All digital cameras store exposures in digital memory of some kind. This "memory" works the way film does in a traditional camera. Lower-end cameras usually have a set amount of onboard memory; when it's full, you're done shooting until you download the stored images. (Think of this as running out of film.) Moderately priced and high-end cameras also use removable media, which is a fantastic timesaver (no more changing film!) and oh-so-convenient (just pop in a new card and keep on shooting!).

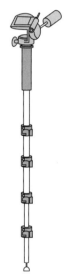

Figure 2-8: Supports come in pretty handy.

TRY THIS

From a different angle . . .

Use a tripod's moveable head (just play with the mounting base handles) to shoot on an angle and get some great canted (oblique) shots, as shown in the figure here. Adjust the tripod's knobs, twisting and turning them so that they are fixed into position. Then practice

✔ **Panning left and right:** Move the tripod left and right slowly and methodically.

✔ **Panning up and down:** Move the tripod up and down slowly, then quickly.

✔ **Moving from place to place:** Move the tripod from one place — say, a flat ground — to another place on uneven ground. Readjust the legs so it sits evenly.

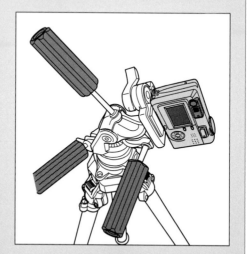

After you get used to moving the tripod head around and panning it in all directions, you can set it up — and adjust it — on the fly and quickly.

Funny thing about memory, though (and no, not just that losing it isn't fun): Different manufacturers like to use their own types, or at least different types, of memory in general. Thus, removable media formats usually aren't exactly interchangeable. Tangentially, if you download images from removable media to your computer (as compared with downloading straight from your camera via a USB cable), your computer must be able to accept these memory devices, too. Some machines come equipped with card readers on their front (usually next to the USB ports), and sometimes you need to use an external card reader (as in Figure 2-9). Sigh.

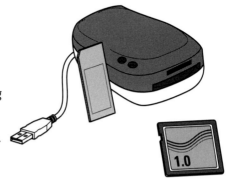

Figure 2-9: Download images on removable media via a card reader.

Here's the scoop, as briefly as I can write it. Check your particular camera model/manufacturer to see what you need. Of course, the greater the memory the card can hold (say 1GB versus 512MB), the more shots you can take on that card and thus not have to swap it out or cease photographing. Likewise, the price will be higher.

Here are the major players. Prices change like crazy, so shop online for the best deals. Too, all these types (with the exception of the mini-CD) come in various amounts of storage — some as high as 8GB (yes, I did say 8 *gigabytes*) — so that factors in to the pricing, too.

- **Floppy disk:** Yes, believe it or not, at least one type of digital camera (a Sony Mavica model) records to a 3½" floppy disk. This storage method is rare.

- **Compact CD:** Some Sony Mavica models use a compact CD-R/RW storage method. These are rare, too.

- **CompactFlash:** This is a common memory card; see Figure 2-10. These are physically a little larger in size than a Memory Stick (see the following bullet), and their capacities range from 8MB to 8GB of storage. The two types of CF cards are

  Figure 2-10: Memory card removable media storage.

  - Type I: These are 3.3mm thick.

  - Type II: These are 5mm thick.

  Cameras with Type I slots cannot use Type II cards. Cameras with Type II slots can use both Type I and Type II cards.

  CompactFlash cards are generally referred to as *CF cards*.

- **Memory Stick:** This is a proprietary format from Sony. These thin and flat removable memory cards are about the length of your thumb. Compared with current SD (Secure Digital) and CF cards, the original MS card is incredibly slow.

  Sony uses a smaller card — Memory Stick DUO — in some of its super-compact Cyber-shot models. A Memory Stick DUO card is half the size of a regular Memory Stick. You need an adapter to bring the Memory Stick DUO card up to the size that a Memory Stick slot or card reader can handle.

- **SmartMedia (SM):** These cards are smaller than a book of matches and not as thick as a credit card. Their design can cause incompatibility issues with cameras made before 2001. Some photog pundits predict the demise of SM cards because Fuji and Olympus — once the biggest users of SmartMedia cards — now both use their new xD-Picture Card. (See the upcoming bullet on that format.) All other camera makers, except Fuji, Olympus, and Sony (which uses its proprietary Memory Stick), have gone with Secure Digital (SD).

- **MultiMediaCard (MMC):** These cards are similar to SD cards (see the following bullet) but are less secure and are physically thinner. A MultiMediaCard can fit into an SD slot, but an SD card can't fit into an MMC slot. MMCs are usually compatible with cameras that can use an SD Card.

- **Secure Digital (SD) Card:** These cards are probably the most popular flash memory format for digital cameras and can also be used in other gadgets like PDAs. SD and MMCs are nearly identical on the outside, but SD cards are much faster than MMC cards. SD cards have become the flash memory card of choice for digital cameras because of their small size and low power consumption. SD Cards hold from 16MB to 2GB.

Because not all cameras that use SD can also use MMC cards, check your camera's user manual.

- **xD-Picture Card:** Man, oh, man! These cards are about the size of a quarter! Olympus and Fuji jointly developed the xD-Picture Card, which boasts an ultracompact design and storage capacity of up to 8GB. These cards are compatible with different digital camera brands.

Getting a Digital Image from Camera to Computer

After you have some good pictures in your digital camera, the next step is to transfer the images to your computer. Images captured with a film camera can be transferred to a computer using a scanner. I discuss scanning in Chapter 3.

When you're ready to download images to your computer for the first time, first install your camera software onto your computer. You then have two basic methods of transfer:

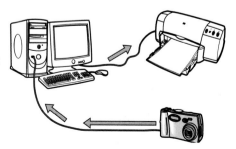

- **From the camera itself:** Connect a USB cable from your camera to your computer, as shown in Figure 2-11. On newer computers, you can find a USB port on the front of your machine. (Some super-jiffy machines have USB ports on their keyboards!)

Figure 2-11: Download images from your camera to your computer.

✓ **From removable memory:** Remove the memory card from your camera and place it in a card reader. These can be external devices that plug into your computer via a USB cable. (Refer to Figure 2-9.) Some computers have card readers built in.

Either way, your images are then on your computer, from which you can edit and tweak away in an image processing program like Photoshop.

Adobe Photoshop is one image editing program that meets the needs of digital artists. It has been around for a while and has many versions. Although the latest version (CS2) has the most features, almost any version from 3.*x* up will do. You can open your downloaded or scanned images into any version of Photoshop.

You can get a reasonable print from processing your image using other third-party image manipulation software. iPhoto (for you Mac users out there) and even your scanner software are enough to print out any image. The key here is to tweak your printer software to get the best print possible. See Chapter 17 for more about printing from programs other than Photoshop.

As a timesaver, you can bypass the whole download-to-your-computer path: Just directly download images from a camera to a printer. You can use

✓ **A docking system** (like from Kodak), in which the camera seats directly onto a printer designed to marry with that camera model.

✓ **PictBridge,** which is a standard that you can use (in tandem with a USB cable) to directly connect camera to printer. (See Figure 2-12.) Many major manufacturers support this technology, including Nikon, Canon, Olympus, Kodak, Pentax, Fuji, HP, Epson, Sony, and a gaggle of others. You can read more about it at

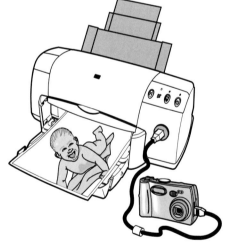

Figure 2-12: Download images from your camera to your printer.

```
www.cipa.jp/pictbridge/index_e.html
```

The downside to taking a direct download-to-print shortcut is that you miss the opportunity to tweak your shots in an image editing program. For more on printing, see Chapter 17.

Resolving Resolution Issues

As I mention earlier in this chapter, *megapixels* determine the quality (clarity) of a digital image that's taken with a sensor in a digital camera. A pixel is the composition unit of a digital image. Remember that a pixel is the smallest unit in an image on a display screen. Images that you take with your digital camera have a lot of pixels. For more information about interpolation, resampling, cropping, and resizing, see Chapter 16.

To view what a pixel looks like within an image

1. **Find and double-click an image file on your computer.**

2. **In Photoshop, enter a magnification level in the Zoom text box at the lower left of the window (see Figure 2-13).**

3. **Input the following magnification levels: 50%, 100%, 400%, and 1600% (the maximum in Photoshop).**

   No need to type the percent sign; just entering the number will do.

4. **Notice how the image changes each time.**

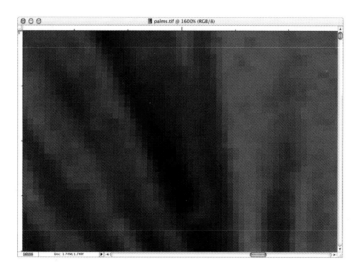

Figure 2-13: You can see the pixel squares in the picture enlarged 1600%.

Notice how an image is clear at low magnification levels. Then the tiny squares that make up the image really take on a life force of their own at high magnification levels (as shown in Figure 2-13). The tiny squares are pixels.

Figure 2-13 probably could be an art photo in and of itself, which is what makes the digital platform a medium that has just begun to see its potential in new art forms.

Whether you take a picture with a digital camera or you take one on film and digitize it, one of your primary concerns in art photography is to maintain image resolution. In order to keep the resolution (that's the number of pixels your image contains) of your printed photo high above 300 pixels per inch, strive for the following:

✔ **When taking photographs with your digital camera, set it to a high resolution photo by navigating within your camera's menu in the LCD screen to the image type/size (varies with camera) you want to shoot.**

✔ **When scanning prints, negatives, or positives, set the scanner to read at least 300 dots per inch (dpi) at your desired final print size.**

✔ **For art photos, input an image size of at least 300 ppi (pixels per inch) in your image processing program before saving.**

Understanding File Types

You need to know a few things about what kind of file formats your digital camera will capture and how they travel from your digital camera to your image editing software to your printer. The main players are JPEG, TIFF, and Raw.

JPEG

You've probably already heard of JPEGs because they're used on the Internet and for e-mailing images. (JPEG stands for the *Joint Photographic Expert Group*.) If you've downloaded digital photos from your camera to your computer and saved them, you've probably seen the file extension .jpg. JPEGs have their pluses and minuses:

✔ **Pros**

• Good for sending images over the Web.

• Easily compressed; can be saved as small files onto your hard drive.

✔ **Cons**

• Degrade (lose image quality) each time they're compressed and transferred. Compression reduces the file size at the expense of discarding information about the image itself. Think of it like reading the Cliff's Notes for Dickens's *David Copperfield.* Yeah, you get the gist, but the nuances fade away.

• Not the best format for printing gallery-quality prints.

The higher-resolution JPEG format is fine for sending images to editors of newspapers for publication as long as the images haven't been compressed (opened and saved in an image processing program) multiple times.

If you must use the JPEG file format and you want to maintain the highest image quality possible, always use the maximum Quality setting on your camera and in your software.

TIFF

The file from which you produce your output is a TIFF file. TIFF means *Tagged Image File Format,* which is a format that can be read on both Macs and PCs.

- ✔ **You produce a TIFF file in a graphics or photo editing program like Photoshop.**
- ✔ **TIFF files cannot be viewed in Web browsers or on the Internet, but the file format does an excellent job of preserving image quality.**

Raw

On many midrange and high-end digital cameras, you can save photos in Raw format instead of the traditional JPEG. If you've noticed that your camera has this capability, use it. Here's why: A Raw image is like a digital negative — the unprocessed image data that your camera sensor captures. Raw isn't an acronym; it just means that the image file itself is unadulterated — that is, it's in a raw state. This untouched (um, raw) state is optimal because you can do your own processing later on your computer.

Different camera manufacturers use different file formats for their own versions of Raw. For example, you might see such file extensions as .nef (Nikon), .crw and .cr2 (Canon), .mrw (Minolta), .raf (Fujifilm), .orf (Olympus), .srf (Sony), and the less-common .x3f (Sigma and Polaroid) and .mos (Leaf).

When you save a Raw file, the camera creates a header file containing all the camera settings, including (depending on the camera) date/time captured, the camera used, exposure, ISO, lens, aperture, flash (if any), sharpening level, contrast and saturation settings, color temperature/white balance, and so on — in total, the *metadata*. When you then tweak a copy of your original Raw file, and process copies, you always leave the original image intact. Very cool. To top that, many camera settings (such as white balance and color adjustments) captured in a Raw file can be undone via special software. Think about that — that's like getting to return to the scene of your shoot and tweak the camera's settings! Time warp!

Okay, okay. Nothing's perfect. The downside to Raw is that Raw formats differ between camera manufacturers and even between cameras from the same manufacturer. Thus, you have to use proprietary software from that company or an image editing program such as Photoshop or Photoshop Elements. And because Raw files inherently contain more data, they take longer to open and process than a JPEG or a TIFF file.

The Adobe Web site (www.adobe.com) has the software plug-ins to open your camera's Raw files in Photoshop or Photoshop Elements for editing and adjustment.

Still, the creative possibilities are very tempting. And, more and more third-party editing and software programs are becoming Raw-compatible with more and more camera models and brands.

- ✔ **Digital cameras generate Raw files.** These files are read by the software from the company that you bought your camera from or by an image editing program.

- ✔ **Each camera processes Raw files differently.** The software to read and convert Raw files to the standard high-resolution TIFF or PSD format is available from the camera manufacturer that produced the format; you need that software to download the files from your camera to your computer. Programs like iPhoto are able to read some models' Raw format. There's also third-party software (such as that available at www.iview-mutimedia.com) that can read most camera's Raw formats.

- ✔ **Raw files are generally the preferred file type for producing an art photograph with a digital camera.** The reason for this is that they can be adjusted for color and tonality more efficiently and with better results than can JPEG or TIFF files.

Only some types of digital cameras have this setting (can capture Raw files) because it is very memory intensive. Look for file formats in the camera's specifications and see whether Raw is listed. You'll pay more for cameras that have this format, but prices are falling rapidly.

That's all you need to know about files for producing art photography. There are only three file formats you have to be familiar with when processing images: JPEG, TIFF, and Raw.

3

Your Digital Technology

In This Chapter

▷ Looking inside your computer
▷ Considering memory and monitors
▷ Macs versus PCs
▷ Selecting a print platform and media for your images
▷ Scanning like a pro

*C*onsider an analogy to illustrate moving a photo file from your scanner or digital camera to your printer. Take your average-size image on the Internet — say, one of those beautiful images that AOL flashes on its welcome page. Those pictures, usually small in size and crystal clear, have been moved from one place to another. For example, they were either scanned from film or taken at low resolution with a digital camera and then moved to a personal computer, a server, or Web space.

Now imagine that you could physically carry the image from one platform to another. No cords or wireless wavelengths to travel through, just moved with your bare hands. Imagine that an image off the Internet would be easy to carry, weighing no more than a cup of coffee.

Comparatively, if you take the average size of a digital rendering or photograph taken with a digital camera or scanned from film and put into a computer or server, you'd have to be Hercules (or Wonder Woman) to transport it from platform to platform because its weight might approach that of an elephant. You'd either have to have supernatural powers or a crane.

The point of this analogy: Big, heavy objects require extra might to handle them. The same reasoning follows for small and large images that go from one place to another. Handling a small image that travels a short distance (say, from a camera to a computer or server) takes care but requires much less power and manipulation than moving a huge image from a camera to a computer and then to a printer — a long way.

The point is that although good images are big, they need lots of power from your computer to be processed. If you're considering purchasing a new PC, make sure that it's powerful. Chapter 2 provides an overview of digital cameras and peripherals. In this chapter, I discuss computers, monitors, printers, and scanners — the other equipment necessary for digital art photography.

Exploring Your Computer

If you're new to digital cameras and digital imaging, take a moment to explore your computer's relationship with your digital camera and your scanner. In this section, you discover the basics of storage, get an overview of monitors, and read about which platform to use (Mac or Windows — the age-old argument), all tied together with a discussion of when to upgrade. Unfortunately, I can give only a smattering of the information regarding these topics within the confines of this book. For further reading, try *Macs For Dummies*, Eighth Edition, by David Pogue, and *PCs All-in-One Desk Reference For Dummies*, Third Edition, by Mark L. Chambers (both by Wiley).

Storage space

Storage space is of paramount importance to anyone manipulating graphics on a computer. In short, you need a *lot* of space and a *lot* of memory to move, edit, and print your photos. Certain components of your computer deal with these issues, and you must be familiar with them. Think of each component of your computer — described in the following bullets — in terms of storage space utilization (and conservation, also).

✓ **Disk drive:** This can be external or internal.

- *Internal disk drives* are *hard drives,* which are part of the total package when you buy a desktop or laptop computer. Look for a computer with at least 80 gigabytes (GB) of hard drive space.

  A clear, gallery-worthy 8" x 10" image uses somewhere around 20 megabytes (MB) of computer storage space. Some pieces of this size, like black-and-white photos, can use as little as 5MB, and others that contain intense color can use more than 100MB.

- *External disk drives* are a great way to add more memory to your computer. At 160GB — considered a smaller size — a drive like that shown in Figure 3-1 can do the trick of keeping thousands of high-resolution photos. And if one external drive doesn't do the trick, you can get more than one; at just a little over $100, the price is right for these workhorses. If you're a professional digital photographer, you need one of these eventually no matter how large a hard drive came with your machine. You can get external hard drives online (I recommend www.seagate.com or www.lacie.com) in a variety of sizes from 80GB to over 400GB.

Figure 3-1: Use an external hard drive for extra storage.

Connect your external hard drive to your computer with a FireWire or USB 2.0 cable (not a USB cable) because these ports transfer data much faster. FireWire and USB are two types of connections that both Macs and PCs use to connect devices. The FireWire and USB 2.0 devices transfer data at over 400 Mbps (*megabytes per second,* a unit of measurement used for describing the speed at which data transfers), almost 30 times faster than a USB cable.

- *CD and/or DVD drives* enable you to store extra images on CDs or DVDs. The different types of CDs and DVDs are mostly distinguished by whether you can reuse them. The capacity of the discs ranges from a CR-R or CD-RW (approximately 650MB) to a dual-sided DVD-RAM (a read/write DVD that holds close to 10GB). The discs are ideal for making hard copies to carry around with you or to send back and forth via snail (ground) mail.

✔ **Random access memory (RAM):** This is the computer's memory that is available for programs to use — to move, edit, save, and print files. Digital photography is a memory-eater: Pictures downloaded onto your computer use up a lot of memory on your machine while being edited or adjusted.

No amount of RAM is too much if you have a choice of models of computers that you're shopping for — go with the higher number. RAM gets used up with each program you open and each time you have your computer process an image with the tools in an image processing program like Photoshop.

Computers sold even a couple years ago didn't come furnished with as much hard drive space as those sold today. The older your computer, the faster you'll run out of space without upgrading the storage space that came with it when you bought it.

Look out for messages that your computer gives you while you're dumping images onto it, such as `Cannot copy X to Y because there is not enough free space`; this message tells you that the disk you're transferring files to is full. While dealing with large images, `Scratch disk is full` or

`Not enough memory` appears onscreen, telling you that you've run out of RAM. You also don't want to hear a grinding hard drive or endure that certain sluggishness that leaves you staring out a window, wondering whether you made your image so big that your computer has the hiccups.

You can help tell the status of your computer by listening to it and watching your monitor:

- **Listen to the fan and the spinning of the hard drive.** A quiet humming sound is best.

- **See how quickly files open.** When you have sufficient RAM and your computer is well maintained, files don't lag when opening.

If you have a new computer that you haven't overloaded with software and files from the Internet, you're off to a great start for image processing. If your system is a bit cluttered, you'll find that moving and manipulating images is a slow process. Clean your system to free some space:

- **Throw stuff away that you've created and don't use.** You can get rid of files that you don't use by right-clicking (Control+clicking on a Mac) and depositing them into the Recycle Bin (Windows)/Trash (Mac). Be careful, though, because you don't want to dump files that your computer needs to run. Stick with dumping old documents and images that you've created or duplicated and that you don't need or use anymore. Or, if you're a packrat, copy them onto your external hard drive or burn them onto a CD/DVD.

- **Empty your trash.** Sounds obvious, but dumping files you don't need is a two-step process. First you put them in the trash; then you empty it. (Files in the trash are still recognized by your hard drive; you have to empty your trash for those files to be really gone.) On the Mac, you click the Trash icon and choose Empty. In Windows, right-click the desktop icon and choose Empty Recycle Bin.

- **Empty temporary Internet files.** Open your browser and navigate to the location where it stores temporary files or to the cache and delete them. In Internet Explorer, choose Tools⇨Internet Options and then click the Delete Files button on the General Tab. In Safari (Mac), choose Safari⇨Empty Cache.

- **Maintain your system by using its maintenance utilities.** In Windows, run the Disk Cleanup and/or Disk Defragmenter, which are both part of System Tools, and just follow the prompts. In Mac OS X, navigate to Applications⇨Utilities and run Disk Utility by selecting your hard drive and clicking Repair Disk Permissions, which corrects files by repairing how they are accessed. (Permissions to reach files can get corrupted over time, causing your computer to slow down.)

Read more about Mac system maintenance in *Mac OS X Tiger All-in-One Desk Reference For Dummies,* Third Edition, by Mark L. Chambers. To give your PC a thorough and deep cleaning, take a look at *Cleaning Windows XP For Dummies,* by Allen Wyatt (both books by Wiley).

Monitors

> *The monitor shut off.*
> *It wouldn't blink and couldn't link.*
> *Then it gleamed like the Big Dipper.*
> *Its light flickered as it started to get chipper.*

> — "Shut Down the Computer, Roxanne" by Matt Bamberg

Your monitor is your window to what you see, in close detail. In order for an image to be successfully *rendered* (that is, for the pixels to be arranged to create a picture), you need to see the details. The only way that you can see the details clearly is with a good, high-resolution LCD flat-panel monitor from a well-known company:

- **Apple:** `apple.com/displays`. Displays start at $799, including a 30-inch display for about $3,000.

- **Sony:** `www.sonystyle.com`. A 17" flat-panel monitor is available for about $700.

Prices change quickly, so visit Web sites when you decide to buy.

Flat-panel monitors (as shown in Figure 3-2) are best. And the bigger, the better. Compared with traditional CRT (cathode ray tube) screens (the ones that look like a TV from the '80s), they don't blink much or flicker. LCD flat-panel monitors also possess a *native resolution.* Unlike CRT screens, whose resolution stays the same no matter what size you set it to (*size* being the number of pixels you see onscreen), LCD resolution has a value in which the screen you're gazing at is clearest. Each monitor size contains a pixel configuration for the native resolution. The configuration for a 15" screen is 1024 x 768 pixels; and 1280 x 1024 or 1400 x 1050 for a 17", 18", or 19" model.

The advantages of a big, flat-panel monitor are

- Images don't get distorted with screen curvatures.

- Bigger monitors give you more room to move around windows.

- When moved or shaken, you don't get any flickering.

Figure 3-2: Flat-panel monitors are perfect for graphics work.

A big, flat-panel monitor is essential for graphics work, but you also need to decide what specifications are best for the type of graphics work you're going to do. What you see isn't necessarily what you get. Brightness is distributed across the *intensity spectrum* (how much contrast you have) of your monitor or the *gamma value* (the value of color perception output from the voltage of the input to the monitor). The differences in gamma between a PC and a Mac can have an effect on the colors you see in your photograph.

The platform that you use — Mac or PC — affects the image you see on your monitor, making it even more important that what you see on your monitor is as clear as you can get. That way, you know what to tweak to make your picture prints the best that they can be. Monitors do act differently on different platforms. You might notice that an image shown on a monitor connected to a PC is darker than one connected to a Mac. You can read more about platform differences in the upcoming section, "Choosing a platform."

Calibration

Thank goodness that the days of blinking monitors are just about over with the advent of the new flat-panel monitors. However, you still might have to *calibrate* your monitor, which involves first assessing your computer's color management system and then making some tweaks so that the colors you see onscreen are as close as possible to what you see in print. Because your monitor is what you see — the king (or queen) of communication in the technology world — you need to make sure that it jibes with where your photo has come from and where it's going. The images shown in Figure 3-3 simulate what I mean.

Figure 3-3: Left: Image on a well-calibrated monitor; right: not an optimal image.

Think *output* — that is, what comes out of your printer — from the very beginning of the digitizing process, when you put your image into a computer. Whether you're calibrating your monitor on a Mac or a PC, this upfront work gives you superior quality prints.

Calibrating your monitor requires that you tweak it to work with your image processing program. The process is *color management,* or matching the color in the image as it's displayed with the color you see in your scanner, on your monitor, and in print.

If you have trouble setting up a color management system for your platform — or if you simply can't determine whether you need to calibrate your monitor — type **"color management"** and the name of your platform into a search engine and look for the latest tutorial. (As with anything on the Internet, however, sometimes information presented there is not accurate or current, so use caution.) The best Web sites for this type of information are the companies that make your product. I recommend the following site for some general information:

www.adobe.com/support/techdocs/329486.html

The Mac's Apple Display Calibrator Assistant can be used to calibrate your monitor in a few easy steps. Note that Mac OS X screens will look a bit different from version to version (10.2, 10.3, and 10.4), but they basically function the same. *Note:* Right out of the box, however, most Apple LCDs work just fine and require no calibration. Open your Mac's System Preferences, click Displays, and choose Adobe RGB as the color space from the Color panel. If you see unusual color reproduction onscreen, you might want to calibrate the monitor.

Go-getter graphics add-ons

Other items to consider when you're souping up your computer for graphics work include the following:

- ✓ **Card readers:** These handy little devices can be connected to your computer with a USB or FireWire cable to directly read the memory cards that you extract from your digital camera. Usually, you have to have your digital camera's software read what's in your camera after it's connected. (For more about these devices, see Chapter 2.)

- ✓ **Graphics card:** All modern computers include a card that processes the video data and sends it to your monitor. A more powerful card can help your computer speed the redraw of the monitor screen, which helps you work faster and more efficiently.

- ✓ **External hard drive:** No amount of hard drive space could be enough when working with a lot of high-resolution photographs. I discuss this in the earlier section, "Storage space."

- ✓ **Mouse:** To make your Mac behave more like a PC, you can replace your one-button mouse with a multibutton mouse. When you do, right-clicking is the same as Control+clicking with a one-button mouse. Scroll wheels also help you navigate the screen.

- ✓ **Graphics tablet:** A graphics tablet is like a drawing pad for your computer (see Figure 3-4). No more crimping up your wrist trying to get a smooth hand-drawn line into your Photoshop document. The tablet comes with a stylus that you draw with. (The tablet is connected to your computer.) In Bonus Chapter 2 (at www.dummies.com), I create text out of a VW Bug image, an activity where using a graphics tablet would be especially helpful.

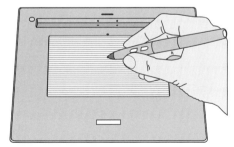

Figure 3-4: Graphics tablets are easier to draw with than a mouse.

Choosing a platform

When you go shopping for a new computer, look for the best platform in terms of ease of use for yourself. If you've been working in a Windows environment for most of your life and know it well — meaning you know how to troubleshoot, combat viruses, and maintain your Windows system — then stick with it. Just because you're going deeper into digital photography doesn't mean that you have to switch platforms, even if most people say that Macs are better suited for graphics work.

If you've never used a computer before, you probably can go with either platform. You'll hear the Mac-is-better-for-graphics argument, but PCs and Windows have come a long way in upgrading their graphics capabilities.

Older computers (Mac systems with OS 9 and Windows 98) and earlier versions of Photoshop that work on less-powerful computers can produce almost the same results as the most recent version of Photoshop and an upgraded computer. However, newer versions and machines are faster and offer more advanced features. You might also find that older computers are incapable of working with the larger file sizes produced by more advanced digital cameras.

Upgrading your platform

Your computer needs some get-up-and-go to run any graphics intensive program — and high-resolution photographs are the most demanding form of 2-D graphics (the most intensive graphics that exist, except for digital video and 3-D graphics). That is, at high resolutions, photographs need a lot of space within your computer and a lot of random access memory (RAM) to manipulate them.

After you do your housekeeping chores, adding more RAM (see the "Storage space" section, earlier in this chapter) to your computer can help it run more smoothly. You can order additional memory, which looks like long wafers, from your favorite neighborhood computer store (or online).

First determine how much memory you have, how much more you can add, and what type of RAM it is.

In Mac OS X:

1. **Click the menu (in the upper-left corner of the Desktop) and choose About This Mac.**

2. **Click More Info to see how many empty slots you have (in the Memory Overview area on the System Profile tab).**

3. **Write down the memory type that you find.**

In Windows, consult the type of memory for the machine you have by looking at the manual or go to your computer manufacturer's Web site.

Adding more memory is just a matter of opening up your box and snapping memory chips into the empty RAM slots. (Think of pushing an ink cartridge into a printer.) If you have an older machine, it's probably not a bad idea to fill up all the empty memory slots.

Always first unplug the machine and ground yourself before touching the chassis of your computer so you don't send an electric shock through the computer and yourself. Ground yourself by touching something metal before handling the memory or the computer, or by wearing an antistatic wrist strap (see Figure 3-5) while snapping the RAM into place.

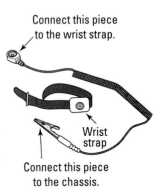

Connect this piece to the wrist strap.

Wrist strap

Connect this piece to the chassis.

Figure 3-5: Always ground yourself first.

Realizing the PC's improved graphics capabilities

Because the computer-connection world (for the most part) works via USB and/or FireWire ports (connections that work on both platforms), you can use the same external hard drives described in the Mac section for your PC.

The two types of USB products are 1.1 and 2.0. The newer, 2.0, is a much faster connection, as fast or faster than a FireWire (both have tested to transmit data at speeds at or over 400 Mbps). When you plug a USB 2.0 device into a USB port, you can expect USB speeds of up to 12 Mbps. Likewise, plugging a USB device into a USB 2.0 port won't speed up the data transfer rate.

Here are other things that make your graphics programs and image processing work go faster and smoother on a PC:

- **Get more RAM.** Get lots — as much as you can afford. On a PC, Photoshop runs slowly when you're working with high-resolution photos if you don't have enough RAM.

- **Consider getting a workstation.** *Workstations* — computers designed to handle high-resolution graphics — have come down in price (some down to around $1,000) and offer all the high-end graphics card and memory capabilities of a souped-up PC. Dell and Hewlett-Packard (HP) offer these systems, once used only by graphic designers and engineers.

Tech styles of today are tomorrow's art photography ops

Think about it: Those stylish iMacs (as shown here) will be collectibles in 30 years! Take an art photo of it today, just as you would of a 1940s Olivetti Chevy typewriter or a psychedelic '60s telephone. *Hint:* Anything made of clear plastic or colored plastic, with style, is great material for an art photo.

PCs are definitely catching up with Macs in terms of exceptional graphics. New systems come with great graphic cards that make their displays comparable with a Mac. If you have an older PC, certainly upgrade your graphics card for better performance and speed from image processing programs. (If you're a video game addict, you know exactly what I mean.) Here are some key points to keep in mind:

- **AGP:** Your computer has to have an Accelerated Graphics Port (AGP) connector. (To look for accelerated graphics devices on a PC, choose Start➪Programs➪Accessories➪System Tools➪System Information; under Components, click Display.)

- **RAM:** Get at least 128MB of memory on the video card for the best shadows, highlights, tones, and colors in your display.

- **Graphics card:** nVIDIA (www.nvidia.com), ATI (www.ati.com), or Matrox (www.matrox.com) graphics cards are the most efficient — that is, they give you speed and stability when you work in Photoshop.

  An 8X graphics card (the data transfer speed) is good. Because Photoshop isn't a 3-D game, though, 4X will do just fine. A 4X card will save you over $100.

Choosing a Printer and Paper for the Results You Want

Ahh, printers. When you finally get to the step where you actually print something out, that's an achievement. Pat yourself on the back.

In order to understand printers, you have to understand the files from which a print originates. You can print out straight from your digital camera, but the prints you get probably won't be gallery-worthy because you haven't had the opportunity to adjust the image's color, composition, and content. Transforming a high-resolution photograph to a gallery-worthy print means that you print from an image processing program, like Photoshop.

If you're wondering what Photoshop (or another image processing program) has to do with buying a printer, try to fill a swimming pool with a hose that's the width of a straw. That's right — you don't want to spare pixels and resolution by buying a printer that sputters out pixels here and there. Just as you would want to use a normal-sized garden hose to fill your swimming pool, you want a printer that uses as much of the data coming from your computer as possible and covers your paper with breathtaking color or well-contrasted shades of gray (for a black-and-white photo).

Software such as Photoshop and Photoshop Elements allows you to make your images any size from tiny, high-resolution prints to huge grainy blow-ups that look like they came from Marilyn Monroe's old family photos. (See Parts III and IV for more about image editing and printing.)

Finding a printer that's right for your work

Gathering information about the different types of printers available is a big help in understanding your choices in the world of printers. Educate yourself by talking with others in your situation and by doing a little research:

- ✓ **Talk with other artists.** Go to art shows and street fairs, look at folks' digital art, and ask what type of printer they use. If you like the look they present, you might have found the perfect printer. Conversely, if you don't like their quality, you can eliminate that printer from your list.

- ✓ **Research.** Read printer reviews at sites like *PC World, Macworld,* and *Infoworld* online magazines.

The following list highlights those issues you should be most concerned with when printer shopping:

✔ **Printer resolution:** A measurement of the detail of the printed photo-graph, this resolution is different from computer screen resolution and is measured in dots per inch (dpi). The lower the dpi your printer prints at, the less clear your prints will be. However, any printer rated at 1440 dpi or higher is sufficient.

✔ **Paper types:** You have literally dozens of papers to choose from — from glossy to matte and fine art. See Table 3-2 (later in this chapter) for a quick comparison of paper types.

✔ **Print speed:** Any art photo that's of gallery quality — that is, has a high resolution — will take at least a few minutes to print out. If you want high quality, you have to be patient.

✔ **Print quality:** Epson products hold up pretty well in terms of the ink that's sprayed on the paper. Mid-level HP glossy prints don't do as well. (I've had some of mine for a few years, and much fading has occurred on those that were printed on HP glossy paper on a Photosmart 1215 printer.) Look for the term *archival* when shopping for a printer so that you know your prints will last for decades.

Most high-end Epson printer models require that you switch between two different shaded black ink cartridges when you print on different papers. You have to change your ink cartridge depending on the paper you use. Matte black ink is used for matte paper, and photo black ink is used for glossy papers.

Different printers use different colors to closely match the colors of your computer screen. Printer software converts whatever colors you use in your photo editing program to CMYK (cyan, magenta, yellow, black) format. CMYK is one of a few color systems used by printers for creating color in your print. An Epson 2200 printer, for example, takes seven cartridges of the following colors that fit within the CMYK mold: matte or photo black, light black, cyan, light cyan, magenta, light magenta, and yellow. Remember, however, that your digital image remains in the RGB (red, green, blue) color mode — let the printer's software convert to CMYK (or CcMmYKk in the case of a seven-ink printer).

Generally speaking, the more ink cartridges your printer has, the better variegation in tone and color your print will have.

For the purposes of printing art photography on a variety of papers, you'll be working mostly in RGB mode. Another common mode in Photoshop is the CMYK mode, which is what printing presses use. In this mode, many colors in Photoshop become *out of gamut,* which means you can't see them in print if you don't change them to colors readable in that mode. You don't use CMYK color mode with inkjet printers.

Several types of printers currently on the market are suitable for art photography:

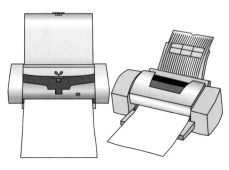

Figure 3-6: Inkjet printers are affordable.

- **Inkjet:** *Inkjet printers* (see Figure 3-6) spray ink onto paper using replaceable cartridges. They are great for economical prints. An 8" x 10" print costs a dollar or two (depending on the type of paper used). Despite their slowness (perhaps several minutes to print a 5" x 7" at a high resolution), inkjet printers have become the number-one choice for the art photographer (like yourself). Produced by a number of different computer and printer companies, they vary in price ($100–$8,000). You can spend a pittance for one that uses a single combo ink cartridge or a lot for one that uses many individual ink cartridges. (The printers with 44"-wide printing capabilities with special inks are the pricey ones.)

Everything you want to know about inkjet printers is at the `http://inkjetart.com` moderated forum page. You can also find some very good prices/deals on ink cartridges here, too.

Figure 3-7: Color laser printers aren't your best option.

- **Color laser:** A laser printer (shown in Figure 3-7) uses static electricity to make an image on a drum covered with *toner* (a solid black/different colored powder), which then prints the image onto paper using heated rollers that melt the toner onto the paper. Color laser printers are good for creating charts and other graphics but not for printing art photography. Perhaps the technology will develop some day to make these printers produce photography that's comparable with that produced in a darkroom. Prices for the printers range from $400 to $2,000, varying mostly with print speed. The cost per-page of less than a quarter makes a color laser printer great for printing out fliers, but the inferior quality compared with an inkjet makes it a no-go for art photos.

✓ **Snapshot:** Snapshot printers are mini models that print fast (prints made in about a minute) at home or on the road. However, you can't make images larger than 4" x 6" with them. Too, your prints end up being more expensive than those you can get at the drug store from the photo guy. Prices range from $100 to $300. These printers, capable of producing high-quality photographs, can be used to make art photos by setting up a kiosk to take and print photos of people, say, sticking their heads on top of the bodies of hula-dancers, and then selling them at a fair. Models (all printing at 4" x 6") include Kodak's EasyShare Printer Dock dye-sublimation (about 62 cents per print), and Epson's PictureMate (about 29 cents per photo). Figure 3-8 shows examples of three models of snapshot printers.

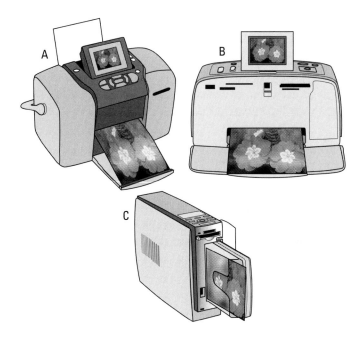

Figure 3-8: Snapshot printers.

✓ **Dye-sublimation:** Also called *thermal dye transfer* printers, *dye-sub* printers (see Figure 3-9) use heated ribbons to imprint an image onto specially coated paper with the resulting print looking just a like a darkroom-produced photograph.

What's the verdict in terms of choosing a printer? Probably some kind of inkjet would be your best bet. Check out Table 3-1 for a handy comparison of some pros and cons of various printers.

Figure 3-9: Dye-sub printers give good results.

Table 3-1		Printer Comparison		
Type	*Pro*	*Con*	*Cost*	*Maximum Size Print*
Inkjets	Low cost; many to choose from; some models print larger than 8" x 10"	Slow	$100–$8,000	Unlimited length with paper rolls: Epson 7800 prints up to 24" wide; Epson 9800 can print 44" wide
Color laser	Faster than inkjet; good for charts and graphics	Cost; not photo-quality	$400–$8,000	HP LaserJet 5500 can print 11" x 17"
Snapshot printers	Convenience	Can't print larger than 4" x 6"	$100–$300	4" x 6"

Many entry-level professional digital photographers print with the Epson Stylus Photo 2200 inkjet printer, which can produce gallery-quality prints. Available online from Epson (www.epson.com), this one will set you back about $700. That's not a bad price for a printer that uses seven ink cartridges and prints at resolutions of 2880 dpi, leaving you with knock-your-socks-off art photos. This model produces prints as big as 13" x 19". If you attach the printer to its roll feed (it comes with the printer) and roll paper (you have to buy that extra), you can print out a maximum print of 13" x 44" inches. The Epson Stylus Photo R1800 model uses eight inks, can print 13" wide, and produces archival prints with a lifespan over 100 years — all for $549!

Good-quality prints will have your printer drinking ink like a runner drinks water after he's just finished a marathon. Make sure to keep extra ink cartridges on hand!

Paper and friends: Selecting the best medium for your prints

Kodak, Fuji, HP, Epson, and even Office Depot make and sell their own photographic print paper. Some printers can handle any kind of paper, producing good-quality prints that you can sell. Others produce superior quality prints that your friends and customers will be in awe of, exclaiming, "How'd you do that?!"

You can choose from a variety of media on which to print your art: all kinds of paper, acetate, and even canvas. (Epson offers its PremierArt Water Resistant Canvas to print your photos with certain printers.)

For printing your art on paper, you have a wealth of options (see Table 3-2 for a quick-and-dirty comparison). Paper comes in a number of varieties: ultra-premium glossy, enhanced matte, velvet fine art, and so on. What you use depends upon the type of art you want to create:

✔ **Any paper is fine as long as it's inexpensive.** Cost is important, especially if you're on a budget and/or want to keep your expenses down. If you want to sell a lot of prints and you plan to do your own framing, you don't need the artsy velvet stuff. Enhanced matte or premium glossy works just fine. Many papers are arranged by thickness. For example, HP glossy papers are categorized by Ultra Premium (the thickest), Premium (next thickness), and so on. 8½" x 11" HP paper runs about a dollar a sheet for the Ultra Premium Glossy, the paper that looks most like a photograph. Epson enhanced matte paper produces a stellar print that among some circles has been considered archival. (At any rate, the print will last at least a couple of decades behind glass.) The paper under glass looks mediocre and much less thrilling than HP glossy paper. Set an Epson matte print inside a glass frame and it looks super, while the HP glossy looks great outside the frame but picks up glare behind glass.

✔ **Your paper choice is your first shot at getting into a gallery.** Epson's enhanced matte is still a fine choice for a show or for a presentation in a gallery. Although the fine glossies look good, they still don't have the ability to take to the ink as a matte paper does when it's applied with an inkjet printer.

Table 3-2	Paper Comparison			
Type	*Use*	*Pro*	*Con*	*Cost (per 8½" x 11" inch sheet)*
Matte	Test copies at low resolution, printer calibration	Cheap	Not much different than regular printing paper	A couple of cents per sheet
Enhanced matte	Art photography prints at low cost, for selling mass quantities at moderate prices	Lasts a long time; looks great behind glass	Looks like a piece of white cardboard	A little more than 50 cents per sheet
Glossy	Art photography prints to emulate darkroom photography prints	Looks great outside frame	Susceptible to glare under glass	About $1 per sheet
Velvet	Fine art prints for high-end galleries	Looks like it belongs in a high-end gallery/ museum	Expensive for mass production/ multiple copies	About $1.25 per sheet

Consider these points regarding your choice between glossy and matte paper prints printed on an inkjet printer:

- **Glossy paper looks great but is inferior to matte paper in print quality.** The highest-quality glossy papers that HP, Kodak, and other companies offer are thick. And some brands do have a tendency to roll. HP machines do well with many brands of paper. Higher-quality glossy paper is about a dollar per sheet.

- **Glossy paper looks better than matte paper — or does it?** That great glossy print is what photography is all about, right? Well, yes, no, and maybe. An inkjet print on glossy paper behind glass can display bothersome glare on an image in direct light.

- **Matte paper fed into wide-format, high-end printers has superior print quality.** I recommend using the paper produced by your printer's manufacturer (rather than paper from other paper makers). Other paper might be cheaper, but you probably won't get as good a print, and you could be spelling disaster in the form of clogged ink cartridges and wasted paper. Enhanced matte runs about 50 cents per sheet for 8½" x 11" to a dollar and more for 13" x 19".

- **The newer inks don't fade on some matte paper.** In fact, the paper degrades over time faster than the ink fades. *Note:* I'm talking decades here, especially with paper and ink behind UV-coated glass.

- **You want to set product pricing to be profitable.** A print on velvet fine art paper commands more money than one on enhanced matte paper. However, both print types will last a very long time and give outstanding digital prints, which is why both papers would be accepted as saleable items at galleries and consignment stores.

Finding the right image size for your print

The size of your image that you should make all depends on how powerful your equipment is. If you want to dabble in producing your own framed prints, start small — say, produce 5" x 7" prints. This is a good starting size because it's a little bigger than the prints produced by a drug store's film processing machine.

The most common size prints are 4" x 6", 5" x 7", 8" x 10", 11" x 14", 11" x 17", and 13" x 19" inches. Of course, you could opt for smaller or larger, the latter dependent on your printer's maximum printout size. These standard sizes work well because

- People are accustomed to these standard print sizes used in film photography.

- You can easily find premade frames for these standard sizes.

- Smaller size images (4" x 6", 5" x 7", and 8" x 10") can be printed on 8½" x 11" paper, which is the size of paper most printer companies make for printing on their printers.

Exploring the Ins and Outs of Scanners

Flatbed scanners — the type that you use to scan prints, negatives, or slides (positives) — are the devices that bring a nondigital image into the digital realm. You're probably familiar with the concept of scanning a hard copy photo print: Just like using your everyday copy machine, you lay the image face-down on a glass plate, close the lid, and press a Copy button. However, instead of getting another hard copy duplicate, that image is stored digitally on your computer. You're not limited to scanning only prints, though. Many scanners can also scan transparencies — negatives and slides (positives) — as well.

Why would you want to use film instead of buying a digital camera? One, scanned images' are still technically digital art because your final product has been digitized. Two, some galleries don't accept digital art: They consider any image printed from a computer to be digital art, even if you started from film.

The main advantage of digitizing film images is that you have a hard copy of your work. This is important because

- **A hard copy can't be corrupted, like a file on a computer.** Hey, life happens. Hard drives hiccup and crash. Sure, you can make CD back-ups of your images' files, but those won't last forever, either (ten years, maybe — depending on how much the CD is used and handled). No one knows how digital media will perform over long periods of time as a storage system.

  Practice safe print and transparency storage to keep your originals pristine. Dust and scratches are the enemy!

- **You can scan these images again and again, each into a new file.** Your creative possibilities are endless, all starting from the same hard copy original.

  Film-processing cost isn't that big of a back-breaker: Developing 35mm film can be really cheap if you order develop-only (no prints). (The price to develop 24 images versus also getting prints drops by more than half: And you still get to know the local photo guy/girl.)

Fortunately, within the realm of digital photography, film still has a role via the scanner. You can scan prints. Better yet, you can scan negatives. And best yet, you can scan slides at really high resolution, making the film-digital divide not a divide at all.

Choosing a scanner

When you go shopping for a scanner, many numbers are thrown at you, with a variety of prices that are associated with them. In their product specifications, computer companies refer to scanner power in dots per inch (dpi). Earlier in this book, you can read about pixels per inch. The difference between ppi and dpi has to do with image resolution and print resolution.

✔ **ppi:** ppi has to do with image resolution: Monitors use pixels.

✔ **dpi:** dpi has to do with print resolution: Printers use dots.

You can set the resolution of the image that you are importing. The number of pixels per inch (ppi) is determined by the number of sensors inside the scanner.

For the sharpest color prints that have been scanned, you need a scanner that creates a print image with more dpi.

✔ The least expensive scanners have a print resolution of 300 x 300 dpi to about 2400 x 2400 dpi. The Visioneer One Touch 9220 USB FlatBed scanner is priced at under $100 and includes a negative reader. Not bad for a machine that scans at 4800 x 2400 dpi. Also, for about $100, you can get an HP Scanjet 3970 with a negative reader, which scans at 2400 x 2400 dpi.

✔ The most expensive scanners have print resolutions around 4800 x 9600 dpi. Coming in at the low end of expensive — at near $300 — is Microtek's ScanMaker 6100 Pro with a negative reader into which you can slip negatives up to 4" x 5". (Don't laugh; I've found more than a couple of these in my old family photos.) Resolution for this workhorse is 6400 x 3200 dpi. A little over $400 will buy the Epson 4990, which scans film and/or transparencies up to 8" x 10" at 4800 x 9600 dpi.

Sharpness depends mainly on the quality of the optics used to make the scanner and the brightness of the light source.

The few pages I have to explore using scanners can't really do the topic justice. For more information, I recommend a book dedicated to the subject, such as *Scanners For Dummies,* Second Edition, by Mark L. Chambers (Wiley).

Configuring your scanner

After you buy your scanner, you need to do two things:

1. **Connect your scanner to your computer using a USB or FireWire device.** (See the earlier section, "Storage space," where I discuss external hard drives because scanners use the same connection ports as do other peripherals.) If your scanner and computer have USB 2.0 or FireWire ports, use them — they're much faster than the regular USB.

2. **Download the software to run the scanner.** Scanner software comes with a companion CD to download into your computer. You can also (and should) access the scanner manufacturer's Web site to download the software (because it will be more current than the CD in hand), just in case you misplace your CD or its files become corrupted or outdated.

Read more about scanning in Chapter 12.

4

Defining Yourself and Your Photographs

In This Chapter

▷ Making age-old creative decisions in your photography

▷ Identifying interesting photography subjects

▷ Creating photos that intrigue viewers

▷ Turning old family photos into art

▷ Transforming your life experiences into digital art

*N*o doubt about it: Photographs are a personal thing. After all, a photograph is a way for you to show the world how you see something — your perspective. In order for you to create *art photos* — you know, images with impact . . . more than the average snapshot — you have three tasks ahead of you:

- ✔ Define yourself as a photographer.
- ✔ Define your audience.
- ✔ Master your tools and hone your craft.

You have dozens of possibilities at your disposal to bridge that gap. First, you have to do a little introspection — investigate who you are. Then you move on to identify your audience. Peruse this chapter to help you identify yourself, choose subjects to express your creativity, and pinpoint those folks who would be interested in your art.

After you have those parts of the puzzle knocked out, you have to choose your subject matter. The world that you can catch on your camera is one very big place. From your immediate surroundings to your neighborhood, your town, your friends, your family, your state, your country, your travels . . . the list is endless. You have tons of choices as subjects for your digital art photography.

Finally, read other chapters of this book to find help with the photography tools, rules, tricks, and tweaks to take your images from average to art.

Defining Yourself as a Photographer

Making art is one of the most rewarding activities that you can pursue because it's something you create yourself with your own personal touch. How personal you want to get is up to you. Some traditional photography artists have work displayed in modern art museums, brushing the edge in controversy. For example, Robert Mapplethorpe, in the 1980s, made headlines when he used the medium to reflect on the pain of his personal life.

The list of photographers who have taken a personal look at their lives is long, and there probably isn't one who didn't evaluate his or her life to come up with the subject matter for his photographs. To name but a few, look at the work of William Eggleston, Annie Leibovitz, David Hockney — and even moon-walker Neil Armstrong.

So if you're going to be an art photographer, should you hang out at cafés and smoke hand-rolled cigarettes? Well, not if you don't want to. (But if you see someone who's smoking a hand-rolled cigarette in a café and who looks amiable to having his picture taken, by all means ask him. That could be an art photo opportunity.)

Perhaps you have no interest in people or their interactions. This certainly doesn't mean that you can't be an art photographer. Take pictures of what appeals to you visually — like in Figure 4-1 — to help define yourself as a photographer. For example, perhaps you're drawn to color (think carnivals, marketplaces filled with rainbows of fruit, or fields exploding with poppies). Or maybe you're attracted to the shapes and forms of nature, such as winding streams, gnarled trees, and majestic peaks. You get the picture.

Figure 4-1: Capture what interests you.

Shoot what you like

To figure out what type of pictures you take the most, look at your pictures you've taken and sort them by categories. If you find that you take a lot of pictures of the same things — say, street scenes — you're on your way to finding a subject that you like (and learning about yourself as a photographer).

Many well-known photographers choose the streets of famous cities as the subjects of their work. If you find that you have a tendency to shoot a particular subject (like street scenes, as in Figure 4-2), then by all means, concentrate on that subject. The more you practice, the better you'll get at capturing and finding different ways to showcase your fave subjects. When you really know your subject, you can better find niche markets for your photos, too.

Study the masters

If you find yourself gravitating toward classical poses and subject matter, study what well-known artists through the ages chose for their subject matter.

Figure 4-2: Street scenes make good subject matter for photographs.

Notice how the subject matter evolves from cave men drawings to religious figures and still lifes (as in Figure 4-3) to nature. The summary of the subject matter of the history of art ends with social commentary about the Great Depression. Art has progressed to modernity through many evolutions. What comes next is up to you. For more detailed information about the subject matter that classical artists have used throughout the ages, you can look at *Art For Dummies,* by Thomas Hoving (Wiley).

After you study the classical masters, take a look at some photographic masters at www.masters-of-photography.com. Works from all the biggies of photography are featured there. Check out

Photo credit: Victoria Archer
Figure 4-3: A simple still life.

Helen Levitt for some cool 1940s grafitti, Ansel Adams for the world's greatest landscapes, Diane Arbus for weird but wonderful people, and E. J. Bellocq for early 20th-century characters. Throughout this book, I reference more artists to help you interpret the masters' photos and refresh their ideas a bit so you refine your own photographic style.

Dadaism

Dadaists (yes, a term that sounds as if a toddler has butchered an art term) stretched the definition of art into new territories: a world of the offbeat and bizarre. In 1917, French artist Marcel Duchamp exhibited a urinal by moving it from a bathroom into a museum and calling it *art*.

He called this art because his viewers saw something that they wouldn't normally expect. The school of art devoted to everyday, ready-made, objects was called Dada. Duchamp was a founding member.

Dadaists see everyday surroundings with new eyes, layers of life that transport new ways of thinking into pieces of art — a roaring of tense colors and a juxtaposition of opposites. Dadaists often use collages to communicate often complicated and/or convoluted ideas.

When you take two disparate images and put them together to spell out a connection, maybe you've got some Dada going. For example, if I decide to go on a diet, I might put something on my refrigerator (like the photo here) to discourage me from eating.

Right-brain, left-brain

Maybe you've heard the phrase, "Oh, he's a left-brained guy," or "She's right-brained." Having one part of your brain dominant over the other shouldn't stop you from taking good digital pictures. This cognitive tendency will, though, probably affect the type of subject matter you choose and the perspective that you choose. It could also affect how you take a picture. Consider right- and left-brained tendencies in terms of an art photographer.

If you're left-brained, you're

- **Logical:** You can figure out patterns. You're good with numbers, problem solving, measuring, and data collecting.
- **Analytical:** Given a set of circumstances, you can provide the answers. You like organization and specific details, preferring to know how things will turn out.

If you're right-brained, you're

- ✐ **Intuitive:** You're ruled by gut feelings. You can delve into subjective thinking and make up stories.

- ✐ **Holistic:** You accept randomness and use what's given to synthesize something. You like the creative process and can tackle more than two things at once.

If you're left-brained, you can assume the following:

- ✐ **Your photography is more ordered and shot more professionally, with more and better equipment.** If you need a tripod, you'll get one. You take more time shooting. You have more posed shots and take the opportunity to use a planned lighting scheme.

- ✐ **Your photographs address technical issues before creative ones.** You probably won't be the kind of photographer who shoots spontaneously. Figure 4-4 shows a posed photo, a nice photo that was planned and not spontaneous.

Photo credit: David Helán

Figure 4-4: Work your left brain to help you plan your portraits.

If you're right-brained, you can infer that your photography will be

- ✐ **Random: You'll "shoot from the hip," so to speak, taking pictures unexpectedly of whatever you want.** Sure, you might plan some, but you realize that the creative moment is fleeting, especially if you don't take the time to compose your photo. Figure 4-5 shows a creative use of the environment — in this case, the ocean, to create a spontaneous and fun shot.

- ✐ **Creative: You'll seek and find the strange and unexpected and capture it quickly with your camera.** Taking a walk with your camera strapped around your shoulder means that it won't stay there long. You seek out new ways to use your camera, taking pictures of nooks and crannies, close up with settings that you're not supposed to use.

Photo credit: David Helán

Figure 4-5: Working your right brain creates spontaneity.

So are you one or the other — or perhaps both? Could be. And more. With the special innate human ability that we have to learn new things, you can do things that you ordinarily wouldn't instinctively do. You can be a left-brained photographer using right-brained techniques if you train yourself, or just take the brain you have and specialize in the type of photography you want to pursue, be it randomly shooting pictures of what you want or planning for large-scale professional photo shoots.

All a matter of perspective

Have you ever gazed at a series of pictures of someone and noticed that the person can look very different in each shot? A person can vary so much from one photograph to another that he might not even look like the same person. In a way, that's *perspective,* whether from the advent of time (cough, aging, as in Figure 4-6), mood, lighting, setting, angle, and so on. Perspective is everything: Changing its focus is the difference between a birthday bash in full swing or showing the remnants when it's over. The more you can personalize the perspective in your photos, the more you define yourself as an art photographer.

Figure 4-6: Perspective includes how people, fashion, and photography styles change.

For more about the popularity of nostalgia photos and how to retouch them, see Chapter 12.

Classic perspectives

Over the centuries, artists from other media and painters have given us standard perspectives, such as the color and texture of natural elements and the joy and pain of humanity. In 1885, Vincent Van Gogh painted a series of portraits, including *Portrait of an Old Man with Beard* and *Head of an Old Man.* Both were close-ups and showed a side (profile) view.

From the religious scenes painted by Leonardo da Vinci (perfect anatomy of subjects expressed in detail and clarity) to the photographs by Dorothea Lange (the realities of the Great Depression), artists use their expert eyes to balance light and composition to capture their situation, feelings, and emotions. These are the perspectives of people that viewers of your photos will probably like best. That doesn't mean that you can't bend a few rules, though, and put your own spin on perspective. You can read more about perspectives regarding portraiture in Chapter 7.

Photo credit: Mario Aguila

To experiment with perspective, photograph something — anything — from close up, far away, from all different angles (as in Figure 4-7), and in different lighting situations.

Figure 4-7: Perspective also includes angle.

After you get the standards under your belt — perhaps by visiting museums and checking out the masters — study the up-and-coming artists to see how they "twist" some of the rules. Then branch out on your own to give your viewers something unexpected.

Finding the unusual

You can take your photography a step further by including the unexpected in a portrait — for example, by including a close-up of a subject that's not human. For instance, instead of a human being, how about using something else — say, a mannequin? Figuring out how to take an art photo of a nontraditional subject is worth your while because viewers stop to look at art photos in which you add a little more than what they expect — as I've done in the portraits in Figure 4-8. (I guess you could call this trio a *photo set;* for more on those, see Bonus Chapter 1. And for more on capturing non-human subjects, see Chapter 7.)

Figure 4-8: Manny and his kin provide interesting non-human portraits.

Statues and inanimate objects present an intriguing opportunity to present the unexpected to the viewer.

Macro or micro: That is the question

Close-up photography is another means of perspective. But is it macro or micro? What's the difference and why should you even pay attention to these lenses/settings? When you think of a *micro* lens, think of looking through a microscope lens to make really small things look bigger. Makes fascinating photography, but not the kind of best-selling art photography you would probably want to make.

A macro lens/setting works on the same principle — to make something small appear larger. However, macro lenses also allow you to get your camera/lens really close to your subject. Compare this with using a telephoto lens. Sure, you make something small appear larger, but a macro lens lets you get right on top of your subject, capturing very fine detail and color.

Hey, wait a minute. Nikon calls its close-up lenses *micro,* but they're really macro. Perhaps Nikon just wanted to be scientific about what it calls its lenses.

At any rate, a *macro* setting comes on a lot of cameras these days. It's a quick turn of the knob (usually found within the Auto modes on your camera; see Chapter 2). You can catch anything up close, like my "flower" here.

To make a macro shot crystal clear, use a tripod when shooting to prevent blur.

TRY THIS

One step further: Consider other take-what-you-already-know-and-add-a-little-more possibilities by throwing potential *Did you know?* questions at the viewers of your art photos. For example, many people think of coconuts as brown, but in their husks, they're green. And most coconuts in Florida are bright golden yellow as they ripen (as in Figure 4-9).

Figure 4-9: Capture the unusual.

Defining Your Audience: Creating Art That Sells

After you initially define yourself as a photographer, it's time to define your audience. Maybe your audience is just yourself; nothing wrong with that.

Perhaps, though, you're looking to turn an avocation into a vocation: that is, sell your photos. There are plenty of markets for art photos, from local stores and restaurants to home decorating outlets to stock photo houses to galleries to online venues to publications to. . . . Get the point? If you want to try to create marketable art photos, the horizon is wide open. However, you do need to figure out who will buy what. After all, folks at a tractor convention likely aren't interested in your photo collection of mannequins. And that focus is what defining your audience is all about.

So how to define your audience? Take these factors into consideration:

- What type of art does your audience like? Portraits, landscapes, action (as in Figure 4-10)?

- What type of art does your audience collect?

- Does your audience have religious or political leanings?

- Where will they purchase your art? Online? Shop?

- What can they afford?

Photo credit: Kevin Kirschner

Figure 4-10: Many folks like action shots.

Keep in mind that a potential audience collects "things." Maybe they yen for pricey items, like vintage cars or delicate *objets d'art,* as in Figure 4-11. You can offer these folks an affordable way to add to their collection.

Choosing subject matter

Your audience (or your taste) will dictate what you photograph and how you photograph it. So what should you shoot? How do you find interesting and compelling subject matter? Do you need to go on safari to exotic lands and hobnob with the jetsetters to find exciting and dramatic subjects? Nah. Start in your own backyard (which you probably

Photo credit: Victoria Archer

Figure 4-11: Capture what your audience wants.

know pretty well) and always keep your eyes open for the art that exists all around you.

In your own backyard

Many people spend a significant part of their life in one area. Any area — rural, suburban, or urban — is a great place to take art photos. To find objects to include in your art photos, just take a look around. As a start, focus on the colors, the landscape, the art, the lifestyle, the sports, the architecture, the wildlife, the flora or where you live.

Through all your waking hours, you pass art, see art, and even make art. With a digital camera in hand, your life is art. Everywhere you look, it's there — colors, shapes, forms, people, places, things — all art, all the time.

Notice, too, that your locality (and those to which you travel) is kind of an independent and unique place on the world map, a place where unique things happen and where pictures of life and art go unnoticed most of the time. Figure 4-12 shows a local carnival. Carnival scenes are extremely popular both among the museum/gallery set and among buyers all over the world. They show both simple, colorful pleasures and sometimes-tawdry scenes with color playing tantamount roles in what amounts to plays of the old Technicolor days of film.

Photo credit: Notley Hawkins

Figure 4-12: Carnivals make for interesting material.

Find the art all around you

Think of your community as a place to find art objects for your photographs. Whether a big city or small town, art abounds — you just have to find it. In the art world is the concept of *found art:* namely, objects you find that you put in an artistic context. Pieces can include almost anything, such as the following:

- Nuts and bolts
- Rusted signs
- The plastic holder from a six-pack of cans
- A stick with perfect symmetry
- A fossil

Figure 4-13, an old sign weathered by time, is a perfect example of an artful found shot. As an artist, check out and shoot different close-ups within the context of your found art — nooks and crannies and even the critters within — just as sculptors do for their works using found art.

Photo credit: Timothy K. Hamilton

Figure 4-13: Shooting this found art up close enhances its artistic edge.

See what sells

Another way to determine your subject matter is to research what sells. This has two advantages:

- You know what subjects are popular.
- You can tell whether you've found a hole — that is, a niche market that no one else is filling. Figure 4-14 shows a motel sign from the middle of the last century, one of a series that I've produced for a niche market of digital art photography. There are many takers for the pop-filled, so-called *Googie images.* Photos of Googie architecture sell. Googie landmarks are everywhere, built in the 1960s, featuring swoops, geometrical figures of steel, and sometimes neon.

Figure 4-14: Mid-century motel signs are extremely popular everywhere around the world.

If you're unsure what to photograph that's saleable, you can do some searching on the Internet to help you. There are many ways to do this and millions of sites to choose from.

Here are two ways to get started:

✔ **In your search engine, type in "stock photo" (include the quotes) as keywords to find what type of images they show.**

Stock photos are the images that editors of magazines and newspapers buy to print in their publications. The images are usually listed by category, so that you can do a search for the type of image you like by typing a word in the search of the stock photo Internet site. Searching a stock house's offerings shows you what images are saleable and what kinds of images you might offer the stock house for sale.

✔ **Go to your Internet search engine and type the name of your community and the word "art" in the image search.** What better way to find images of your community to take a step further than seeing what's out there to begin with?

Presentation

Above all, your presentation must be stellar and unique. After all, you want your photographs to stand out, be memorable, and be enjoyed for years. That's what presentation is all about. This is the culmination of your craft: your subject, your perspective, composition, image finessing, printing, and framing. Here are some ways to make your art stand above the common herd.

Push the envelope

Digital photography is an evolving art form. A ground swell of interest in the subject is brewing, but much more can happen as the medium develops. You can do much to develop the art form of digital photography:

✔ **Move beyond traditional photography techniques applied to the digital realm.** Digital photographers can develop new ways to work with the medium before and while shooting and composing (as in my crazy zoom in Figure 4-15). You can also manipulate your shot in an image processing program like Photoshop as well as during printing. This book covers lots of techniques to help you express yourself through your photographs; the more adventurous of you will want to home in on Chapters 11, 13, 14, and 20.

Figure 4-15: Get a little nuts and be creative!

🖝 **Collaborate with other artists to produce new works of art.** Existing paintings often can be photographed with new results when they are printed digitally. One example is a photograph of a painting on velvet. Photographs of this type of work actually turn out better than the painting itself. (Maybe it has to do with the fact that velvet collects dust easily.) The portrait on velvet in Figure 4-16 is almost 50 years old; picked up at a garage sale and photographed, this image was digitally upgraded with great results.

Figure 4-16: Digitized paintings appear poplike.

You must be careful, however, not to commit copyright infringement. Rather than be sorry, consult with an attorney about this important issue.

✔ **Take a photograph that makes a statement.** Many photographers choose to spotlight social issues, such as homelessness (as in Figure 4-17). These types of compelling photographs make their way into many art museums and high-end galleries. For more information about these types of issues as they're related to photojournalism, see Chapter 9.

Before using anyone's likeness, consult a publications lawyer to make sure you can use the image. Generally speaking, if the person or persons in your image are identifiable, you'll need to get signed model releases. You can read more about these in Chapter 7.

✔ **Use the knowledge and methods to make other art forms.** And you can help your viewers identify other disciplines that might interest them. What better way to get your kids to look at their multiplication tables than to photograph them written by them on a piece of paper or off a black/whiteboard?

Photo credit: S. Gold

Figure 4-17: Social issues are often the subject matter of great photography works.

Offer great quality

Target, Wal-Mart, Ikea, and similar stores all sell framed photos. Most are of an inferior quality compared with what a photographer can print out on his home computer and good-quality printer (say, Epson Stylus 2200 color inkjet). Your personal touch adds a little more to what the big-box stores are selling, making it a competitive, saleable product:

✔ **The road to good photo art has finally been paved for the consumer.** Maybe the big-box outlets will catch on and sell the more artsy pieces, too, but a creative digital artist is likely to outpace the art sold that is mass-produced.

- ✒ **The digital artist can find the niche in subject matter for his community (as in Figure 4-18) that a big-box store probably wouldn't invest in.** Subject matter for a big-box store is limited to that which is derivative: that is, tried and tested to not offend every person in every community in the country. They don't represent risk takers: That's left to the individual photographers and the museums, galleries, and smaller shops that display their work.

- ✒ **The digital artist can create images from photographs that he took, using equipment and processing tools and printers that he chooses.** The big-box stores use the same materials pretty much nationwide.

Figure 4-18: Find niche markets.

Teaching students to create art with each year of their lives

Aside from smoking hand-rolled cigarettes, many artists have been known to wear black. The truth of the matter is that whether an artist wears black or not, he has been trained one way or another. Much of that training involves how to paint (photography is painting with light), how to frame, and, believe it or not, an investigation into his or her life events as well as the history of art and current events.

In the '80s and early '90s, when art came in the form of video installations, and artists were just beginning to play in the digital medium, professor Christine Tamblyn (San Francisco State University) engaged her students in an activity that helped them to recognize where they were coming from. She taught her students how to mine their own life for material for their art. The point of this exercise was to stimulate students' creativity or find out what they already knew, so that perhaps they could add a little more.

The students had to find a space to perform their most memorable public events (a reenactment of a part they had in a play when they were eight years old, for example) for each year of their life. One student made little models with *found materials* (readily available and in a natural state), models, toys, and pictures (hand drawn or photographs) for an event that occurred each year in his life. He then put each model representing the event in lockers in the locker room. For instance, he had taken a trip across the country in an Airstream trailer when he was 15, so he put a picture of one in locker number 15.

Repurpose the past

Going up into the attic and tossing through your great-grandfather's WWII gear, old JFK memorabilia, and perhaps a depression glass collection wrapped in vintage 1940s *The Kansas City Star* newspaper sounds like a challenge . . . maybe something you've been putting off for a long time. Don't miss the opportunity to search through all these wonderful treasures and photograph them before you toss them in a garage sale.

Whether what you find are prints or slides (a *positive* image, in photographic terms) or negatives or anonymous hand-drawn items that are about to fall apart, you have a treasure trove of photographic and restoration opportunities awaiting your creativity. Scan these precious images and work your magic with them, retouching them and reproducing them.

 Again, just be careful about infringing on a copyright inherently or obviously (signed) belonging to another photographer or creator. Consult with an attorney to learn more about copyright and copyright infringement — to make sure you don't infringe upon someone else's work and also to protect your own.

Here's an example of how you can preserve and repurpose an old image, bringing it into this millennium. Figure 4-19 shows an older image before and after sharpening it and then applying the Photoshop Colored Pencil filter. The digital photo on top in the figure was taken with a digital camera from an original slide (a very old one at that, too) set on a light table. Being of an artistic mind, I decided to sharpen it and run it through a Photoshop filter to create my own version of the turn of the last century.

Figure 4-19: Refurbish old art photos into new art pieces.

If you think it's not worth scanning a bunch of old family photos, think again. If you have a scanner — and especially a negative scanner — you can transform the old stuff in that dusty attic into a collection that spells a-r-t.

Here are four reasons to go up in the attic, bring down those photos, and digitize them, either scanning the prints or scanning the negatives and/or positives:

- **Enlargements of these types of photos are being sold in the trendy LA stores for lots of money.** No kidding, prints of women and men in wild '40s, '50s, and '60s outfits are fetching hundreds of dollars.

- **Looking at an old photo's patina onscreen or in print is like taking a time machine back in time.** These treasures need hardly any manipulation in Photoshop because they're amazing aged, just as they are, like the picture shown in Figure 4-20.

- **You discover how your older relatives (and the dead ones) looked when they were young.** Geez, you find out that you look like them! (Check out such a timeline in Figure 4-6.) You're also saving the photos for future generations to see. Remember that photos on photo paper don't last forever.

Figure 4-20: A photo's age can enhance its quality.

- **You can add to your existing photo collection.** Fill your photo folders with old and new and hang them on the wall together. For example, combine the new street scene photos with older ones.

Be wary when repurposing vintage photos. You might need permission, or at least a model release, to reuse an image of someone. Even if that person is deceased, you might have to contact their heirs for permission. See a copyright attorney for the exact rule about this and let him know what type of photo you have as well as what you plan to do with it. Also, see Chapter 7 for more about this issue. Also, practice with your image editing program (like Photoshop) to iron out scuffs and creases in old photos (see Chapter 12). Above all, bring something new to the image: You could create a photo set, tweak the color, use it in a montage — after all, if you're just copying an old photo, that doesn't make you a photographer.

Part II
The Photo Shoot

In this part . . .

You're at the right place to see how to create great shots in any situation. Read all about how to use ISOs, f-stops, exposure settings, and flash to your creative advantage. This part covers the photography spectrum: shooting outdoors and indoors (Chapters 5 and 6), photographing people and animals (Chapter 7), crafting compelling color and dramatic black-and-white images (Chapters 8 and 9), and capturing stunning nighttime images (Chapter 10). If that isn't enough, I finish off this part in Chapter 11 with how to create special effects while you're shooting — even before you tweak your digital images in an editor.

Composing a Shot Outdoors

In This Chapter

▷ Using natural light to your advantage

▷ Mastering common outdoor situations

▷ Boosting natural light

*Y*ou have many ways at your disposal to compose a shot outdoors. Fortunately, natural light is more than adequate, rain or shine, to give you a decent image provided that you compose your shot with care. When composing a shot outdoors, remember to assess where the sun is, what distance you want to be from your subject, and how many objects you are focusing on.

Keep in mind, also, that as a digital art photographer, you have help — in the form of an image processing program that comes later in your digital safari.

Shooting with Natural Light

When you shoot outdoors, light is your natural friend. After all, light is what drives photography. However, the tricks that light can play on your exposures can prove to be gremlins that can haunt — or help — your shots. You can creatively master how your camera reads light via its settings, which help you set the exposure you want, manually. Of course, auto settings are at your fingertips as well, and can come in handy when shooting under less-than-optimal lighting conditions, like an overcast day, as in Figure 5-1.

When you set your camera to automatic, you don't need to know much about f-stops, shutter speeds, and depth of field. Automatic settings let your camera calculate how the f-stop and shutter speed should work together to give you the best picture under the circumstances that you are shooting in. Experiment a little, though, and adjust these numbers, especially when you want to shoot moving objects (like waterfalls, to see them behave dramatically) or to shoot at night (when you want the lights to look like stars). In the next few pages, I describe f-stop settings and shutter speeds so that you can make the adjustments necessary to achieve your desired results. I discuss depth of field in the aptly named "Depth of field" section, later in this chapter.

Figure 5-1: Auto settings can come in handy when shooting on an overcast day.

Proper exposure

Photography is all about light. To get the correct exposure for the art photo you want, you need to know the settings that you can adjust and what they do. The main players are ISO, f-stops, and shutter speed.

ISO

ISO settings determine how sensitive your camera is to light. When you shoot at a lower ISO (less sensitive), you get better image quality with less of the undesirable digital noise. However, when you shoot at a higher ISO (more sensitive), you can capture *stop-action* (fast-moving) shots better, like sports scenes or bounding gazelles on the plains of Africa. As always, there's a trade-off. When shooting at a lower ISO, you must use wider f-stops and slower shutter speeds. That means that you lose depth of field and increase chances of blur. Conversely, when shooting at a higher ISO, you lose some detail and increase the amount of noise in the photo.

For more insight on ISO, skip to Chapter 6. For more on f-stops and shutter speeds and how they interrelate, stay right here.

f-stops

Alert: There's a hole in your camera, but that's okay. Think of the hole in the pinhole camera you probably made in grade school. That hole (the *aperture*) in cameras lets light shine through the lens to expose the film or sensor, depending on your camera type. On some cameras, you can manually adjust the aperture size, which you want to do, depending on your lighting conditions. Most prosumer camera models can change aperture size for you automatically.

For low-light situations (like indoors; see Chapter 6), you typically want a larger aperture to let in more light. For brighter lighting conditions — such as being outdoors on a sunny day — you want to use a smaller aperture to let in less light. Think about how your pupils are wider in the dark and smaller in sunshine, and you get the general idea.

Your camera's f-stop setting controls *depth of field*, which is how much of the image is in focus. With a shallow depth of field (a low f-stop), the subject is in focus, while areas behind (and in front of) the subject are softly blurred. With a higher f-stop, you have a greater depth of field and everything in the image is in focus. (This assumes, of course, that you have actually focused on the subject!)

How wide an aperture opens is measured in *f-stops*. Some common f-stops are f/2.8, f/4, f/5.6, f/8, f/11, f/16, and f/22. The larger the number, the smaller the opening. Low numbers such as f/2.8 (a digital camera shows only the number 2.8 in the LCD display) mean that the aperture in your camera is open wide — perfect for night shots outside, say at night when the snowflakes are wet and big. A setting such as f/22 (22 in the LCD of your digital camera) means that the aperture is small — settings good for landscape shots, say atop a hill overlooking a bluff on a sunny day.

Figure 5-2 shows what happens when you set your aperture to open a little bit (on top — a high f-stop) and a lot (on bottom — a low f-stop). You get more background blur when your f-stop is low (big aperture opening).

Make sure you have a clear focus when using a low f-stop so that at least one object/subject is in focus.

Photo credit: Kevin Kirschner

Figure 5-2: With a larger aperture, you get more blur in the background.

Shutter speed

When cameras could be only manually adjusted (at a time when the Earth's crust was just being formed; hey, it could seem like that for some of you!), you also had to choose a *shutter speed,* which is the amount of time that the shutter lets in light to expose film. (On a digital camera, this is the length of time that the sensor is exposed.) A shutter is like a curtain covering where the film/sensor lies within a camera. Think of playing peek-a-boo: Your hands over your eyes are the shutter, and your eyes are the film/sensor. Figure 5-3 illustrates what happens when the shutter stays open long enough to capture blur.

Photo credit: Kevin Kirschner

Figure 5-3: Longer shutter speeds can cause blur in your photo.

Shutter speeds are commonly marked as follows: 1, 2, 3, 8, 15, 30, 60, 125, 250, 500, 1000, 2000, and 4000. Except for 1, these time measurements are fractions of a second. (The 1 means ⅛ second, or one whole second.) Thus, 2 means one-half second, 3 means one-third second, 4 means one-fourth second, and so on. Note how as the numbers grow larger, the speed actually decreases — less light is allowed in the camera. Your camera also likely permits you to set the shutter speed for longer periods, perhaps as long as 30 seconds. Those same speeds now appear usually on the small LCD screen attached to your camera. For special effects using long shutter speeds, see Chapter 11.

Using auto settings when shooting outdoors

Both digital and film cameras have automatic settings, which are handy for shooting under a wide variety of circumstances, like for art photos captured on the fly (often the best way to go when taking a picture). Here are the settings and what happens to the shutter speed and f-stop when you set them:

- **Auto:** Everything is set for you: flash, focus, and *exposure* (the amount of light reaching the sensor or film). The camera automatically adjusts both the shutter speed and the f-stop for the amount of light on the sensor or film to make a clear picture.

- **Portrait:** Choose this setting when you're taking a photograph of people up-close. This setting blurs your background but makes the profile of the person clear and in focus. This happens when your camera's f-stop is small (the opening of the aperture is large, like f/5.6 or smaller), and the shutter speed is quick (over 250).

- **Motion (Sport):** Opt for this setting when filming subjects in motion or for when you're in motion, like traveling on a train or in a car. Shutter speed is quick. Figure 5-4 shows the action is stopped in mid-air with this setting.

✔ **Night:** With this setting, shutter speed is slow so more light can be let in through the aperture.

Use the night setting during the day to catch action for blurred motion. Of course, you won't have control over how long the shutter stays open (like you have with a dSLR camera or SLR camera).

✔ **Landscape:** Use this setting for far-away objects. The aperture is open only slightly (high f-stop). Use this setting also if you want your background and foreground clear. Figure 5-5 illustrates a clear foreground and background in a landscape (waterscape?) photo due to a small aperture.

✔ **Close-up:** Use this setting for shooting, um, close up, like a flower. You focus on your subject, and the rest of the picture is blurred (similar to using the portrait setting). On many prosumer digital cameras, you can get as close as five inches to the subject.

Photo credit: Kevin Kirschner

Figure 5-4: The sport setting stops action in its tracks.

Photo credit: Joshua Lennon Brown

Figure 5-5: High f-stops are good for landscapes.

When you use a slow shutter speed or an automatic setting with a slow shutter speed, be sure to keep the camera steady or use a tripod. If the camera wobbles, you'll get blur; this happens when the shutter is open long enough to record your hands shaking.

Using manual settings for creative control

Auto settings can certainly come in handy, like when you're grabbing a quick shot. Life doesn't always stand still, you know. However, for the ultimate in creative control for your art shots, here are some techniques that you can control via manual settings to help you compose exactly the shot you want — what message you want to convey in your art photo. To set your camera manually for really cool special effects and more complicated shooting, see Chapter 11.

Foreground and background

Foreground and background identification is sometimes easier said than done. Although many of the examples in Chapter 8 depict images with clear divisions between foreground and background, sometimes you can't distinguish one from the other. For example, maybe the foreground runs right into the background with no lines or distinctions in between. Here are some examples where foreground and background are not clear cut:

Photo credit: Ian Lumb

Figure 5-6: Blending foreground and background to create an artsy effect.

 ✔ **The foreground and background lead to one another.** You know those shots — the ones where the curvy road leads through a prairie where you can see the grass in front lead (and get smaller) as it extends to the back. Or then again, how about a dock that leads to a neighboring mountain, like the one in Figure 5-6.

In this image, a small aperture gets you a clear shot all the way across the water.

✔ **There is no background.** If you want nothing but the object itself, there is no background, as shown in Figure 5-7, which was taken with a mid-sized aperture to let the colors soak in. The face of a map is another example of a photo that technically has no background.

✔ **The background camouflages an object in the foreground.** In some cases, such as in wildlife photos (see Figure 5-8), the backgrounds and foregrounds are similar. The young lion is colored similar to its surroundings.

Figure 5-7: A shot of stained glass has no background.

Eliminating foregrounds, middle grounds, and/or backgrounds can create unique shots. These types of shots are like the sets of a theatrical production and make the viewer feel as if he is within the photo, perhaps a character in it.

Photo credit: Ian Lumb

Figure 5-8: Background as camouflage can be deceptive.

Last, what does a picture look like when there are objects in the foreground, middle ground, and background? It sounds like that would spell c-l-u-t-t-e-r, but not necessarily, especially if the objects are enhanced or diminished with varying amounts of light and/or no light at all.

Figure 5-9 illustrates how one part of a picture, foreground, middle ground, or background, can frame another part.

Figure 5-9: Foreground objects frame a middle ground object with a dark background.

Depth of field

The distance away from your lens in which your image retains its clarity is *depth of field.* Long depths of field are created by using small apertures (or large f-stops). When photographing landscapes, you can set your camera to landscape mode to have it calculate a depth of field so that your image stays clear throughout. In Figure 5-10, the image on top (of a tunnel lined by unusual rock formations) has a long depth of field — taken with a high f-stop; the image on the bottom (of a bird in its nest) has a short depth of field — low f-stop.

Figure 5-10: Top: deep depth of field; bottom: shallow depth of field.

TIP

For the greatest depth of field, shoot on clear days when you can see forever with your back to the sun later in the day, and set your camera so that its aperture is small (f-stop is high).

An intentional shallow depth of field can be quite desirable because it makes the subject of the shot truly the star — it's the only thing in clear focus. For example, see the raindrop on a leaf in Figure 5-11. Because its background is not in true focus, the raindrop's graceful beauty shines even brighter.

Photo credit: Rebekka Guðleifsdóttir

Figure 5-11: Shallow depth of field makes the subject stand out.

Bracketing

You can use your high-end dSLR or film SLR to get a variety of images at different exposures — hedging your bets, as it were. Exposure bracketing is a setting that lets you adjust your exposure to lighten or darken it by measured intervals, capturing a series of individual shots with differing exposure settings. Using this technique is obviously easier with a digital camera because you can see the images right away and toss the ones that you don't want. Figure 5-12 shows how changes in your exposure affect the tones and color of your image.

TIP

Sometimes in less-than-perfect weather situations or when it's overcast, using bracketing can help assure a properly exposed shot.

Keeping white balance when outdoors

Indoor and outdoor light is different; each gives your picture an entirely different hue. Most digital cameras give you a setting to adjust this: white balance. The function of white balance is to find a reference point for what is "white" and then to correct offbeat hues (based on this reference point) in your entire photograph while you shoot. Most film cameras have no white balance setting, so you have to deal with brown tones indoors and blue outdoors. Most digital cameras, however, have a manual setting for white balance that ensures the best results. (For more about white balance, see Chapter 8.)

On most digital cameras, you can set white balance as follows:

⮞ **Auto:** This is the default setting, in which the camera automatically sets itself when you take a picture. It's great for general picture taking.

⮞ **Daylight:** This setting is good for natural lighting — all sun, outdoors, with no artificial light coming into your picture.

⮞ **Indoor:** Some cameras use this as a setting. Other cameras divide the Indoor setting into the types of light you find inside — tungsten or fluorescent. For more about lighting subjects indoors, see Chapter 6.

Figure 5-12: Two pictures, each at a different exposure.

Common Outdoor Lighting Situations

The more you shoot outdoors, the more you'll find that the sun can be your foe or friend. This section covers the most common outdoor lighting situations that you'll encounter — and how to use them to your art photo creative advantage.

Creating a vivid shot with your back to the sun

Color. A lot of people want it. Color can help a photo sell, but bright colors without harsh shadows are what gallery owners like. Simple prosumer cameras require that you set them to a daylight setting. Although this setting does a pretty good job, higher-end dSLR models can be manually set in most of the same ways as a film SLR can. For more about setting your camera for maximum color, see Chapter 8. For more information about prosumer versus high-end dSLR cameras, see Chapter 2.

So how do you get a lot of color in a photo shoot? For starters, by following these basic guidelines:

✔ **Have your back to the sun.** With the sun to your back, your subject is lit from the front and devoid of shadows. You'll probably get a better exposure reading, too, because your aperture won't have to open wide and your shutter can open and close promptly, without blur where you don't want it.

Just try to avoid making your human subjects stare into intense sun to prevent them from squinting.

✔ **Have lots of ambient light.** Ambient light is good anytime during the day in winter when the sun is low in the sky. In summer, it's best to stick to morning and/or afternoon sun, staying away from times when the sun is directly overhead, a time when the sun is so harsh it can overexpose parts of your image. Figure 5-13 shows how the afternoon sun can help to create just the right amount of light to make the picture crystal clear.

Figure 5-13: Photograph outdoors with your back to the sun during late afternoon to get great exposure.

✔ **Have a good camera.** A high-end point-and-shoot or an SLR or a dSLR — where you can manually set the shutter speed and/or f-stop — will help you get better exposures for different kinds of foregrounds and/or backgrounds.

✔ **Have a subject full of bright colors.** Fill your photos with bright colors or unique features, like broad steel vertical beams that are often placed on high-rises to accentuate their strength, or appearance of strength.

✔ **Place objects in clutter-free backgrounds.** Clutter usually gives a bothersome disruption to the flow of a photograph. Making your background clutter-free is dependent on the size of the object:

- **For movable objects:** Place them on a clutter-free surface (the ground will do) and shoot standing up with the sun at your back.

- **For immovable objects:** Position yourself with your back to the sun and find the part of the surface where there are no shadows.

Taking close-ups of people outside requires that you use the portrait mode. However, this mode does not protect your subjects' eyes from squinting when you're sitting comfy with your back to the sun and they're facing the sun. You can, however, move your subjects to the shade or wait and take your photograph during the magical moments of the sunset when the light is less harsh.

To get finer detail in subjects that are washed out because of *overexposure* (too much light around them), get close to the subject, lock the exposure (lightly press the shutter control and hold it there), step back, and then take the picture. *Note:* You get a very bright white background doing this.

Take a look at the picture of part of a church in Figure 5-14. You've got two things working in your favor here, just the state you want when you're shooting with your back to the sun:

- ✔ The surface of the object is nearly free of harsh shadows.

- ✔ The light is bright, so the color is deep. (For more about light and color, see Chapter 8.)

Facing the sun

Shooting into the sun is not always a bad thing. This technique can provide many opportunities for unique art photos, determined by the shapes in the foreground as well as the effects created by light — specifically, the backlighting of the sun. This technique is the opposite of shooting with your back to the sun, as I discuss in the preceding section ("Creating a vivid shot with your back to the sun"). See Figure 5-15 for a comparison of the two photographing techniques, both with very different effects.

Figure 5-14: Shoot with the sun at your back to capture vivid color.

Photo credit: Kevin Kirschner

Figure 5-15: Camera position makes a world of difference in sunlight.

Ansel your landscapes

When you think depth of field, you might think of Ansel Adams, one of the greats in landscape photography. Adams captured the essence of America's coast-to-coast landforms from scenic overlooks in U.S. national parks to the close-ups of flowers there. His imagery illustrated the fine art of texture from smooth rocks to the jutting sticks of tree branches. If one word could be used to describe how Adams photographed landscapes, that word would have to be detail.

Adams worked with film: big format film, film several inches long by several inches wide, film that required a special lens. He waited for the right time to take a picture, and he got to know the places where he photographed. Emulating Adams using your digital camera can be pursued first by knowing a place where there's nothing but nature around, knowing when the weather will be good, knowing a viewpoint from which to photograph, and knowing what time of day to go there for the best light.

You can get pictures from high-end digital cameras with the same clarity that Adams got, provided you find that special natural place that you know well and use a tripod when shooting. Try a variety of shutter speeds and exposures, and then pick out the best of a series. This landscape shot is the best of a series taken by a photographer with a 6.1MP Olympus point-and-shoot camera at Joshua National Park. Aperture openings were small to create a long depth of field in this shot.

The effects you get shooting into the sun are just the opposite of shooting with the sun behind you:

✏ **Subjects lose their color.** The more aligned your subjects are in front of the sun, the darker they are until they become total silhouettes when they block the sun. Notice in Figure 5-16 how the subject and his kiosk are so dark that they appear almost black. You don't always get a lot of detail with this technique, but you get some really cool light rays (and sometimes lens flare).

If the light at sunset or sunrise is blasting into your eyes and you see a subject in a beautiful silhouette, snap a picture of it.

Photo credit: André Sá

Figure 5-16: Shoot directly into the sun for flare.

✔ **Backgrounds lighten.** With a lightened background, colors turn to pastels (not bold primary colors) because of the distance and all the atmospheric particles that your camera picks up from its lens to the edge of the world (the horizon, that is). In Figure 5-17, the background has turned to pastel blue.

Avoiding and exploiting shadows

Obviously, shooting either with your back to the sun or facing the sun can cause unwanted shadows. Think of the shadow cast by a sundial, and you get the idea. Take care when composing your shot that you don't capture a shadow that you don't want — especially one that you, as the photographer, unwittingly cast.

Photo credit: Notley Hawkins

Figure 5-17: Lighten a background when shooting into the sun.

In an informal shot outdoors, harsh shadows can darken features so they communicate practically nothing. Take, for instance, the picture of the young woman in Figure 5-18. The picture on the left was taken with a flash in the sun. And the one on the right was taken without a flash. When you take a picture outside in the sun using your flash, you have used the *flash fill* feature, which lessens the harsh daytime shadows in portrait mode.

Setting flash fill is easy. On the body of most camera models there's a picture of a lightening stroke. That's the flash control. Press the button and look in the LCD. Navigate to where it says flash fill and set your camera to that option. Take your picture.

However, the art photographer in you can master how to exploit and take advantage of dramatic shadows in your works.

Photo credit: Kevin Kirschner

Figure 5-18: Use flash fill (left) to enhance features of a subject outside.

Fences are a wonderful source of shadows. Wait until the sun is bursting through the slats and shoot a photo that conveys a feeling of movement and perspective, as shown in Figure 5-19.

Shooting at noon, dusk, and dawn

Because you can't always have the sun exactly where you want it, you need to master how to shoot at the times of day when sunlight isn't exactly optimal. At noon, for exam-

Photo credit: Leonardo Faria

Figure 5-19: Shadows cast through fence slats create strong contrast.

ple, light is very intense. And because it's directly overhead, you can get some unwanted shadows on people's faces from a hat or their glasses (or even their nose!). Conversely, when shooting at dawn and dusk, light can be a bit anemic and sometimes throw off the color you want. However (you could see this coming, right?), you can always take a less-than-optimal lighting situation and turn it to your creative advantage. Here's how.

Shooting at noon

The open container of (sugar-free) jelly beans in Figure 5-20 shows how colors can really pop in bright sunlight. I moved this object outdoors with sunlight shining directly on it. Photographed with the sun beating down on my back, the color of the jelly beans stands out dramatically against the highlights and shadows of the tray.

Figure 5-20: Place colorful objects outside for vivid photographs.

Be careful to keep your own shadow out of the photograph. That takes some maneuvering of your body so that you also don't distort the perspective of the object while you're attempting to photograph it from the middle, and so that its horizontal plane stays horizontal within the frame. Of course, keep in mind that while most photos will be judged by these rules, art photos can and often do break the rules of horizontal and vertical planes.

Shooting at dawn or dusk

Shooting when light is soft can be a little tough. However, the softness during these times of day can be exactly the message you want to convey, as shown in Figure 5-21, a shot of early morning. With some clouds to help diffuse the fading daylight, shooting at sunset is nothing but the very definition of drama.

Photo credit: Mark Salad

Figure 5-21: Shoot at dawn for added softness.

Glare and flare

Glare and flare are two banes of any photographer shooting outdoors. For example, when you shoot something reflective, like glass, smooth plastic, or water (see the following section), glare is sure to pop in uninvited, as shown in Figure 5-22.

Figure 5-22: Glare can be a neat or unwanted effect.

✔ **Glare:** If you want the glare, great. Hey, it's your art. To avoid it, though, really study the image in your viewfinder. Avoid shooting shiny surfaces, and don't use flash when shooting something through plate glass, like a storefront window (see Figure 5-23).

✔ **Flare:** Flare is a bit different of an animal. Caused by a diffraction of light rays (that's enough science for me), you can get unwanted beams of light or sometimes a halo or white outlining effect on a subject. Hmmm. How can you use these anomalies to your creative advantage? Check out Figure 5-24 to see how cool exploiting flare can be.

Photo credit: Kevin Kirschner

Figure 5-23: Shoot windows without flash to prevent glare.

Sometimes contrast can be compromised when a halo appears throwing the whole picture out of whack. Halos are not a good effect if too large and in the wrong place.

Photo credit: Jonathan M. Wentworth

Figure 5-24: Flare beams add flair.

Shooting glare on water, ice, and snow

Shooting water — or things on water, like animals, boats, and skiers — can be tricky. Water is shiny and it moves. Not a great combination for a subject.

Stick with me, though, to see how you can turn both minuses into great art photos.

When a lot of light reflects off water, your camera's light meter can be tricked and read for that bright light instead of exposing for your subject. Maybe that's not what you want — or is it?

What you have here is an exposure see-saw, when the shutter speed is quick, the aperture widens to make up for the difference in light. Sometimes, though, water glare can be downright pretty, becoming the subject of the photo.

Water glare gives you a shimmering effect by the water's reflection from the sun beating down on it. No question about it, water glare is one of the most thrilling items of photography, as shown in Figure 5-25.

Photo credit: Kevin Kirschner
Figure 5-25: Exploit the effect of water glare.

And don't forget about the glare from frozen water! Snow and ice can also provide you with some outstanding art opportunities.

If you don't want the glare from ice, do a spot read in a midtone area of your shot. That way, you won't overexpose from the light your camera reads from the reflective surface. Figure 5-26 (an image from the National Oceanic and Atmospheric Administration [NOAA]) is well exposed but offers enough glare to be compelling.

Throw a stone in a still pond and then shoot the resulting concentric ripples for a great art shot that shows motion through the use of a pattern of contrast and glare.

Photo credit: National Oceanic and Atmospheric Administration

Figure 5-26: With the proper exposure, you can control glare.

Weather and atmosphere

Another adage: Everyone talks about the weather, but no one does anything about it. Well, in digital photography you can do something about the weather, albeit not a lot — and not without compromising pixels.

Every weather condition affects the picture you take. Every speck of dust and every cloud (see Figure 5-27) affect the picture you take. It's just a matter of the weather you have to work in and what you want from your camera and your resulting print.

Get a variety of images at different exposures — bracket your shots — in iffy weather. Read more about this in the earlier section, "Bracketing."

- ✔ **Sunshine:** Read about shooting in bright light in earlier sections of this chapter.

- ✔ **Fog, mist:** Fog can cause your subjects to be underexposed. That is, you'll have trouble seeing the details within them. But Figure 5-27 shows that morning fog can add mystery to a photo as well. (Thanks to NOAA for this image; `www.photolib.noaa.gov`.)

Photo credit: Right: National Oceanic and Atmospheric Administration

Figure 5-27: Clouds and fog over landscapes are mysterious.

✓ **Rain:** Rain gives you some great opportunities to shoot for glare and flare, especially at night, and even added dramatic color. Figure 5-28 shows that despite the inherent grays and drabness, rainy or wet conditions can still offer you opportunities to bring in some reflective color.

Photo credit: ©Irene Tejaratchi

Figure 5-28: Use the grayness of a rainy day to bring color alive.

✓ **Clouds:** Clouds truly can be your ally with some breaks and puffs here and there, when you find dramatic ones against a clear blue sky, or when a storm approaches (as shown in Figure 5-29). Also, don't forget how light can paint clouds at sunrise and sunset.

Figure 5-29: Use clouds to bring drama to your photos.

Augmenting Natural Light

As kind as the sun can be, providing you with lots of wonderful light to expose your shots, sometimes Ol' Sol needs a little help, like when it's overcast. Or, sometimes Ol' Sol gets a little help when he didn't ask for it, like when you're shooting something brightly lit during the day, like a carnival. Here's how to make the best of each situation.

Using flash fill

As I discuss earlier (refer to Figure 5-18), you can use flash fill to help remove shadows on the subject. When conditions are hazy or overcast, or you're shooting a subject in the shade, flash fill can also be used to help add light to provide details.

Shooting bright lights in daytime

Your camera's light meter can get fooled by intense light emitted from bare light bulbs, like twinkle (holiday) lights on Christmas trees or the wonderfully gaudy lights of a carnival. When you shoot these during the day (like the photo in Figure 5-30), take care to make sure that your exposure is accurate. Watch out, too, when you're shooting at a sports field — sometimes those giant floods kick on while you still have available light.

Photo credit: Kevin Kirschner

Figure 5-30: Expose carefully when shooting lights during the day.

Composing a Shot Indoors

In This Chapter

▷ Setting your digital camera for indoor light

▷ Blurring images to create movement effect

▷ Discovering when to take an indoor picture with a flash

▷ Using indoor light fixtures to make art shots

▷ Seeing one-point perspective

Shooting indoors is inherently more difficult than shooting outdoors because you don't have optimal light — and what light you do have is often garish and harsh (creating sharp unintentional silhouettes) or has a color temperature that can give you unnatural tones (like how people turn green when shot under fluorescents or orange when shot under tungsten). And, after all, light is what drives photography. In this chapter, I show you tricks and tools for how to take that disadvantage and turn it into an artistic opportunity.

Finding the right type of light for your indoor shots is like performing a science experiment. Remember when you had to write a hypothesis in the form of a question and then answer that question? In an experiment with indoor lighting, your questions might be, "How do I light my object or scene so that my shot is clear and natural looking? Or interesting? Or have movement?" You can make dozens of hypotheses (questions) about using natural or man-made lighting — or both — to create a unique scene or present an object from either a traditional or a new viewpoint.

Start by thinking about the tools at your disposal (your camera and flash) and then factor in the world around you (man-made or natural ambient lighting). Next, determine whether the lighting that you're using answers your questions. Finally, consider the results: Did you get the results you expected, or were your results better than you could have hoped for?

This chapter takes you through the process of asking — and more importantly, answering — the questions involved with taking indoor art photographs so great that people clamor to buy them.

Setting Up to Shoot Indoors

When you shoot indoors, you (understandably) have less light than what is available outdoors. To compensate for this — without using flash — you need to adjust your camera's ISO speed. You also need to know when to choose manual over automatic exposure settings and also how to work toward achieving good white balance.

ISO speed

To compensate for shooting with not-always-optimal available light indoors, you need to adjust your camera's ISO speed. In terms of a digital camera, ISO could be called *sensor sensitivity*. Strange but true. With film, you have *film sensitivity* — that is, how sensitive the film is to light. These standard film ratings are set by the ISO (International Standards Organization). You might also see ASA film ratings, but ISO and ASA are similar.

The lower the ISO number, the less sensitive film is to light. Thus, 100 ISO film needs more light to capture the same shot than 400 ISO film does. The same holds true when shooting on a digital camera. All you really need to know in terms of the settings on your digital camera are the 100, 200, 400, and 800 ISO settings. Some cameras go lower and higher. However, when you set ISO lower than 100, you can get a lot of blur if you don't use a tripod. Shooting at ISO settings above 400 (or 800 for some cameras) can produce *digital noise* (unwanted red, green, and blue specks in the image) or *luminance noise* (undesirable light specks in the image). Digital noise is generally most evident in areas of shadow and solid color. When using your camera's flash, the ISO is usually set to either 100 or 200, depending on the model.

Figure 6-1 shows a picture at various ISO values. Note that the higher the ISO, the more noisy the image becomes.

If you have a tripod, use it and shoot using a lower ISO and a slowed shutter speed. If not, brace the camera on a stable surface and use a slightly higher ISO. If neither a tripod nor a stable surface is available when shooting in low-light situations, you need to choose between possible blurring (low ISO) or noisy shadows (high ISO).

So, what's the setting verdict for taking pictures of stuff inside? That's one of the easiest tricks in photography, digital or film. Simply set your ISO speed at 400 (or buy 400 ISO film for your film camera and then digitize your prints/negative/positives).

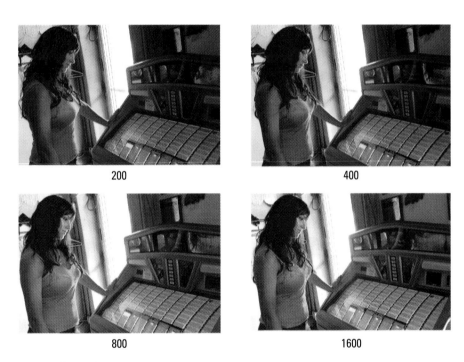

Photo credit: Kevin Kirschner

Figure 6-1: The same shot taken at different ISO values without flash indoors.

Manual versus auto settings

Determining the proper setting — manual or auto — to use when you shoot indoors without a flash all depends on whether you shoot with a tripod:

- **Most shots indoors come out great in auto mode without a flash, but only if you use a tripod.** In auto mode, most cameras default to low ISO values. If you want special effects — such as blur from movement — you need to use a tripod and you also must keep your shutter open longer than what your camera would in auto mode.

- **If you hand-hold your camera, set your ISO values high (greater than 400).** Many cameras allow you to change the ISO and yet still shoot in auto mode.

White balance

When you take a photo indoors without a flash, the color of the light you're shooting is enhanced, sometimes greatly. Figure 6-2 shows a golden hue that happens automatically (due to the color of the lights) when you take a picture without a flash indoors (with 400 ISO to reduce blur). Many digital cameras automatically correct this when they're set to indoors, but maybe you don't want to — to gain that artistic edge. (You can read more about white balance in Chapter 8.)

Figure 6-2: Use non-white light to your advantage.

Taking Indoor Pictures without Flash

The simplest scenario when shooting indoors is to just shoot — no flash, no nothing. Just shoot and go. You can get some decent shots that way, using only what light is available.

Photographing light as it is — flickering, glimmering, glistening, raining, shadowing, frightening, trickling, and twinkling — with all indoor light or outdoor light coming indoors in all its lit glory sometimes is best done without the help of your flash. Take a look at Figure 6-3. I took this photograph (with no flash) inside a subway station, using only the lighting there. (This photograph also offers an example of using the vanishing point to create visual interest.)

No flash? Indoors? No worries. With today's digital photo technology, you can indeed take a picture indoors without a flash. At higher ISO speeds and under the right circumstances, you don't need a flash. The *right circumstances*, mind you, have to do with the availability of light. Eye the light around you, seeking some for your picture when you don't plan on using a flash.

Figure 6-3: This passage leads to a point in the center of the shot.

When filming indoors, set your digital camera no higher than 400 ISO to find a compromise between graininess and blur.

Using available light only

So why not just use a flash instead of moving around the camera and yourself and/or your object, seeking out available light? Although flash as fill light can be your friend, flash light can also be a little obtrusive and difficult to control. For example, flash light sometimes interrupts what you're photographing, smacking it with a big white splash in just the part that you wanted to show up clear. This will happen without a doubt when you film shiny, plastic, flat surfaces with dark colors, or when you shoot through glass.

Trust me, though; it's okay to shoot indoors without a flash. To get great shots indoors without a flash, you just have to position yourself and your subject to make the best of indoor lighting. For instance, in Figure 6-4 (taken without a flash and obviously indoors), the little girl is lit with natural light coming through a window to her left. Because I didn't shoot directly into the light, the girl is evenly and softly lit, illuminating her perfectly and giving nice, soft colors suitable for a little girl.

Figure 6-4: The available light in this picture provides soft illumination.

In Figure 6-5, again, only available light is used. The young woman is positioned next to half-closed blinds so that she is lit by the natural light while shadows caused by the blinds also add a slightly dramatic effect.

Photo credit: Rebekka Guðleifsdóttir

Figure 6-5: Manipulate available light for a slightly dramatic effect.

Intentional blur

When shooting indoors, you can use a seeming disadvantage — not much available light in which to shoot — to your advantage. For example, without enough light, moving subjects can be blurry. Hmmm. Take that information and turn it into an art photo opportunity.

Indoor photography has gotten much easier with the advent of digital photography. You can shoot on the spot without having to go out and buy film. (See the earlier section, "ISO speed," for more information about exploiting ISO speeds.) You also set your digital camera to the correct ISO without having to change cameras (like with film) or wait till one roll of an ISO film is done before changing to another. Before you read on, though, I want to take a moment to discuss blur. Blur is an oft-spurned element of photography that is usually left to the professionals. I can't think of any logical reason for this except that maybe people thought the pros had better control over the beast.

But blur is not such a wily beast; you can tame it under the right circumstances. This is not new stuff, either, but it is as modern as photography. When the 19th century came to an end, photographers began shooting images not to solely copy real life but in an attempt to change it, following literature and other visual arts in taking the viewer away from what was thought of as real to the artist's subjective world — real and otherwise. In the late 19th and early 20th centuries, photographers began using blur as a tool to create their art. Figure 6-6 shows a blurred image that was produced at a low ISO in low light and shot in auto setting. That's one of the easiest, but not most effective, ways to produce controlled and artistic blur.

Photo credit: Kevin Kirschner

Figure 6-6: Blur is easy to create in low light.

Blur is like poetry: Its interpretation can be left to your viewer. Basically, you just create it — either you plan for it, let it happen intentionally, or have it happen by mistake. However it happens to be created, you can be sure that each time blur is created, it always sparks curiosity:

- **Make blur a strong element in your art photos.** Blur makes scenes anonymous, adding mystery to people and/or scenes. If either a part/person or the entire image of an image is blurred (as in Figure 6-7), you sense added thoughtfulness, such as the passage of time among life's fleeting moments.

Photo credit: Kevin Kirschner

Figure 6-7: Blurring part of your image can add mystery and/or thoughtfulness.

- **Create blur as an intended effect in your images.** Sometimes you just don't have enough light indoors to create a clear image, no matter what you do. However, if your subject moves in real life anyway, blurring it in the photo can make it look like it's moving.

✔ **Create blur by panning your camera.** If you pan just right, you can get a clear picture of your subject, which I discuss further in Chapter 11. Or you can just swing your camera following your subject to blur it, as in Figure 6-8.

Photo credit: Kevin Kirschner

Figure 6-8: Pan your camera while you shoot to create blur.

Don't think that you can clear up a blurred shot in Photoshop. The technology isn't there yet although it is getting better. The Smart Sharpen filter in Photoshop CS2 can do a very good job with some slight blurring, but severe blur is not something you can edit away.

Taming available bright light

A picture can be a big disappointment if your subject comes out too light. This happens sometimes when you're filming a person within a bright background. Your camera's light meter probably calculated the shot. The *light meter* is the device inside your camera that evaluates how much light is in a scene so that your camera's sensor can produce a properly lit picture, unlike the one shown in Figure 6-9, which is too light.

Photo credit: Kevin Kirschner

Figure 6-9: Subjects can come out too dark in uneven, ambient light.

Sometimes, though, the sensor can't calculate it accurately because there's too much light around the subject. If you're photographing in an automatic setting and don't want to fool around with your camera's setting, move closer (or zoom in) to the subject so that there's little or no background, like in the photo shown in Figure 6-10.

Adjust your exposure compensation for more light to go to the sensor. Most high-end and midrange digital cameras offer a feature called *exposure compensation.* To give your subject more light, you need to *overexpose,* or add more light to your shot: You need to adjust exposure compensation to the positive values that your camera displays. Negative values underexpose your shot, which is a concept that I discuss further in Chapter 8. (Keep in mind, however, that when you're talking about digital images you plan to manipulate in Photoshop,

Photo credit: Kevin Kirschner

Figure 6-10: In ambient light, subjects look better when you zoom in.

overexposure is more damaging than underexposure. The reason for this is that after pixels are "whited out," no information is available. True, moderately underexposed images produce more grain when you correct them in Photoshop, but at least you have some information to work with.)

When you photograph a person in a bright background and you overexpose your shot, it evens out the available light that's there. And although certain reflective backgrounds, like glass, will blast with white, this effect can be quite undesirable.

The flashes on many prosumer and dSLR cameras do a great job in filling in uneven ambient light. I suggest using it inside for portraits of people.

Taking advantage of color imbalance

What at first sight might look like the wrong hue or tone in a photo might not really be wrong at all. Sometimes the tones and hues produced by indoor light can be mesmerizing, bringing the viewer to what looks like the future (very white light) or the past (light with a mustard tone). Fluorescent light appears white and gives that futuristic-looking effect shown in the left image in Figure 6-11. Tungsten appears yellow in the right image of Figure 6-11. For more about color imbalance, check out Chapter 8.

Photo credit: left, Patrick Spence; right, Kevin Kirschner

Figure 6-11: Fluorescent and tungsten lighting can give color imbalance.

Augmenting Indoor Light

Finding fascinating light indoors is not that hard. After all, light is everywhere, but sometimes there just isn't enough to properly expose a shot. What should you do? The obvious answer is to shoot with a flash. Filming without a flash usually yields better results because using ambient light provides a total lighting effect that is more even. However, using a flash is not a panacea to low-lighting blues because a flash can travel only a short distance.

A traditional rule of photography is to not mix light — that is, indoor and outdoor — in the same picture. In traditional portrait and landscape photography, combining light sources is probably not a good idea because it can cause your camera's light meter to read parts of your picture in error. However, sometimes mixing light in an art photo — augmenting indoor light — can create a distinctive effect. For more about light and light temperatures, see Chapter 8.

Figure 6-12 shows how a camera's light meter has no trouble reading the yellow light (tungsten). However, the other light within the frame is misread as pure blaring white that looks like the film and/or sensor has been burned.

Photo credit: Kevin Kirschner

Figure 6-12: When you mix light, your camera can make errors reading one or the other.

Comparing shooting with and without flash

Your camera's built-in flash can leave white blotches on your image. Sure, you probably can take out these flash blasts in Photoshop later, but that's time-consuming. The best solution to this problem is to either move the image to better light or to use a tripod.

If you have a situation where you don't have enough light (or where you're not sure whether you have enough light), take two photographs — one with a flash and one without a flash — as in Figure 6-13.

Each exposure has its own merit:

- **With flash (left):** The subject is clear and evenly lit.
- **Without the flash (right):** The subject is lit more dramatically, without background shadows, and looks a bit more natural.

Photo credit: Kevin Kirschner
Figure 6-13: Left, shot with flash; right, shot without flash.

Combining indoor and outdoor light

In Figure 6-14, the light peeks from outside in the top of the picture, giving the viewer a sense of a way in and a way out. A couple of things about the light in this shot makes it interesting:

- ✐ The reflection from the indoor lights sink into the floor, mixing brown tones with yellow, which is a good color match.

- ✐ The outdoor light in the back of the photo is natural, contrasting the indoor light in color and intensity.

- ✐ The outdoor light provides a background for the moving man — one that brings the image of him forward, propelling him in the direction that he is moving.

Figure 6-14: Mixing light can create an interesting effect in an art photo.

Here's another way to combine indoor and outdoor light. Figure 6-15 has been taken from inside a truck. The camera is inside a truck, using the light coming through the windshield. This light creates excellent *back light,* meaning that the subject (the dashboard scene) is lit from the back. Also notice the *fill light* — the light coming from the windows on either side. Fill lights, well, fill the front and back to reduce shadow. The front light here is very subtle and smooth (coming from the rear window), just where the sun is peeking through, creating an almost perfect lighting situation for a dancing hula girl. For more about fill lights and back lights, see the later section, "Adding extra light sources; studio set up."

Figure 6-15: Hula girl lit from all sides inside the cab of a pick-up truck.

Using whiteboards

You need to use whiteboards (or reflectors) when you're shooting in a room with only one or two fluorescent or tungsten lamps. Notice the difference when you use a whiteboard (left image in Figure 6-16) compared with not using one (image on the right in Figure 6-16). Whiteboards are easy to make. Because a whiteboard can be made out of any type of board that is white, you can find something to use in almost a dozen sizes at any office store. Styrene boards are great stuff to use to make reflectors. Just cut your whiteboard in two, hinge the pieces, and tape it together so it can sit on a table like an open book.

When you photograph in many offices or stores, you won't need to use a whiteboard because these places already have lots of fluorescent lights that offer you enough light to take a good picture. And if you can't obtain a whiteboard when photographing in a poorly lit area, you can use other flat, reflective items in place of a whiteboard, like a regular ol' umbrella (yes, opened) or even a tray.

Adding extra light sources; studio set up

Sometimes the available light indoors or reflective devices are just not enough light for your needs. When that happens, you might have to resort to adding light sources for your shoot.

Although not the route many digital photographers are going to take while photographing scenes and objects, professional lighting such as that done with portable fluorescent lights and stands offers some good concepts about how to create different effects in your photographs.

Photo credit: Paul R. Wright

Figure 6-16: Using a whiteboard boosts the lighting effect.

A photograph of a hula girl earlier in this chapter (refer to Figure 6-15) shows you how light from all around an object — the back, the front, and the sides — can create a good picture without shadows and with softened controlled light. In contrast, Figure 6-17 shows the placement of lights in a studio or for a TV production — ideas that you can use by looking around at the light you have available:

- **Key light effect:** This effect is achieved when you place your object directly in front of a strong light source, with no other light around it. Using only a key light produces harsh shadows if the surface isn't flat. If it is flat, it could produce great color. (See Chapter 8, where I discuss getting great color in your photographs.)

- **Fill light effect:** Place your object near a weak light to get a *fill light* effect. For example, if you place an object on the side of a 60-watt lamp (or to the side of the sun at dusk or dawn), and that is the only light source, you get a mysterious effect, or even a spooky one. The subway picture earlier in this chapter (refer to Figure 6-2) uses many fill lights.

- **Back light effect:** Place a light behind an object to get a *back light effect.* This produces almost the same effect as shooting into the sun, as I discuss in Chapter 5.

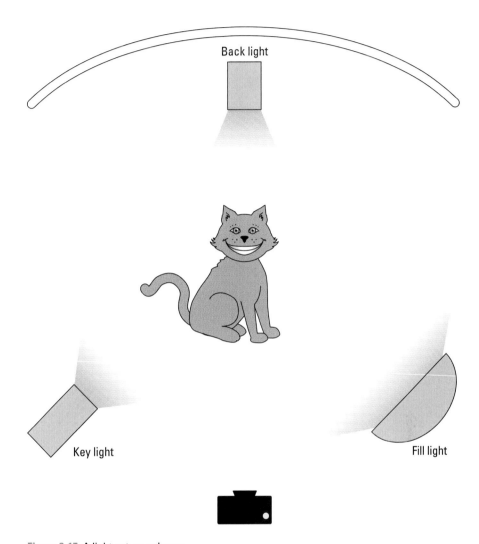

Figure 6-17: A light set-up scheme.

The images in Figure 6-18 show how using each of these lighting techniques can affect your shot.

You can use these light placements in combination inside your home and anywhere else by renting studio lighting. Studio lighting usually comes in kits, some with two lights and a reflector umbrella. Instead of using a fill light, the umbrella bounces the light off the key light.

| Key | Fill | Back |

Photo credit: Paul R. Wright

Figure 6-18: Consider extra light sources when shooting indoors.

Beginning studio lighting kits are available for purchase on the Internet and start at around $300. Type the keywords **"studio lighting"** into your search engine to shop.

Shooting Indoors with Flash

In the earlier section, "Comparing shooting with and without flash," I discuss how flash photography indoors is a viable alternative to lighting your subject, provided that your subject

 ✔ **Is close enough to the camera:** Your camera's flash spreads light only a few feet in front of you; this depth varies depending on your flash. The light that it spreads is white light and quite effective on human subjects.

 ✔ **Doesn't have a reflective surface:** If you're shooting from behind glass with a flash, you'll get a lot of light bouncing all over the place. You probably should think about that when taking a picture of a framed picture behind glass.

Many digital cameras will use a low ISO when your picture is taken with a flash so that your image is crystal clear. If you provide your own light, it automatically sets the ISO higher, resulting in a less clear shot. For more on ISO settings and auto mode, see the beginning of this chapter.

7

Photographing People and Animals

In This Chapter

▶ Taming moving subjects

▶ Photographing still objects around those in action

▶ Setting your camera for the best shot for subjects and actions

▶ Identifying symbols and metaphors for your subjects

▶ Panning your camera to catch action

▶ Setting shutter speeds in wildlife photography to control blur

*P*hotographing anything living usually requires that you establish some sort of relationship with the subject. When you work with human subjects, you have to put the people at ease. Some people appear perfectly natural for a picture, while others are like marble statues. Still others are in-between, needing encouragement anywhere from gentle prodding to full-fledged professional entertainment from you, the photographer. If you're lucky enough to have a subject who knows how to model, go with the flow and give input as to what you want, also.

Sure, sometimes you just want a simple portrait photo to record your visit somewhere — you know, with people posed, smiling, in front of an interesting building, monument, or fountain. Although these can be great shots that create memorable moments, they're probably not what you'd sell in an art gallery or put on display in a museum. Creating art portraits, though, requires a little fore-thought and creativity, whether you're on the road or in your own back-yard. As I show you in this chapter, you can create portraits of people by playing with backdrops, posing your subjects (or not), and showing folks involved in an activity to highlight their personalities.

You can use a lot of these same techniques when creating portraits of animals, too. Okay, getting some animals to smile is a little tricky (alligators are easier than butterflies), but here I show you some artful ways to capture Fido and Fluffy and wild critters, too.

To help move your portraiture shots from the everyday toward art photos, read about shooting with the art elements mentioned in Chapter 1 in your shots. As an art photographer, you'll probably have subjects in mind who are not your friends or family when you go on a photography exhibition — say, when you're traveling to another country.

Photographing People

When you think of photographing people, you probably have the standard smiling portrait/head shot in mind, kind of like what you expect for a yearbook. "Tilt your head a little to the left. Now lift your chin a bit. That's it, perfect! Now smile!" Not that anything is wrong with this traditional type of portraiture, but with a little creativity, you can create portraits of people and non-living "people" with a decided art photography twist.

Whether photographing humans or animals, the trick is to keep the technology as transparent as possible. You get the best shots when your subjects are as relaxed and natural as possible (see Figure 7-1); you can tell right away in any shot when the subject is uncomfortable. (Think about going to the dentist, and how he conveniently places those shiny tools out of your eyesight while he's doing his thing. Smart.)

Figure 7-1: Relaxed subjects make for a nice photo.

To help you be as nonintrusive as possible, try not to use a flash any more than you have to. Obviously, sometimes you need the extra light, but using a flash startles just about any subject. Remember, too, that your camera probably offers a red-eye reduction setting for the flash. Firing a preflash before taking the actual photo constricts your subject's pupils, helping prevent that spooky glowing red-eye problem.

The light from your flash dissipates the farther your subjects are from it.

When shooting groups of people, a flash doesn't always give you uniform illumination. Take a look at the picture shown in Figure 7-2. Because the subjects aren't the same distance from the flash, they're not evenly lit.

Figure 7-2: Subjects that aren't the same distance from the flash will be unevenly lit.

You can also reduce how intrusive you are (as a photographer) by getting closer with zoom lenses, which are helpful when filming athletes, people on stage, and animals. Most digital cameras have an *optical zoom*, which is a zoom made by adjusting your lens that yields no loss of quality of your image. This is the only zoom you want to use on your digital camera.

Don't use your digital zoom because you can do the same thing in Photoshop, which does a better job of interpolating the pixels when a picture is enlarged.

Traditional posed portraits

Probably the most traditional portrait is a *head shot,* in which you usually film your subject from a relatively close distance, capturing her from mid-chest-level up, paying attention to her face. However, before you begin to take a posed art portrait, pay attention to the background for your shot. There's nothing worse than a spot-on portrait with a jarring or junky background. (No one wants their portrait to end up showing a tree growing out of their head.) Of course, you can always use Photoshop to tweak an iffy background, but do what you can to get your shot right when you take it.

Second, decide how to light your subject (for more on lighting, see Chapter 6). Finally, work to pose and stage your subject. To smile or not to smile?

Optical versus digital zooms

Some digital cameras have *digital zooms,* which in essence are zoom effects that have nothing to do with your lens but everything to do with the computer chip that calculates how your image will look. It's a setting that permits you to go past what the optical zoom — the normal zoom that your lens performs and one that is more natural because there is no interpolation of missed points — would give you. You can get an extra magnification using this setting. You have to be careful with it, though, because when you use a digital zoom, you lose image quality.

Using a backdrop

Way back when, you had to buy expensive canvas to create a traditional drape backdrop for a portrait (see Figure 7-3). If you go that route, think about spending about $400 for a 10' x 10' canvas. To see what you can get in terms of cloth and canvas backgrounds, check out www.dennymfg.com or www.amvona.com. For something more unusual, consider using a mural or colorful prints as a backdrop.

You can, however, judiciously use a nontraditional background to add to the flavor of your portrait — for example, filming a race car driver in front of a back-and-white checkered backdrop or a quilting fanatic in front of a colorful coverlet.

Of course, you can create really cool backgrounds digitally (via Photoshop) by using your own photographs. Get creative with your backgrounds by shooting them separately from your subjects and then layering them into your photographs later in Photoshop. You can choose anything you've taken a picture of, from a medieval wall to glass blocks. However, the old-fashioned way (a backdrop) is still very effective and (in some ways) less work then manipulating an image on your computer.

Photo Credit: Mario Aguila

Figure 7-3: Use a backdrop to stage a portrait.

Who's smiling now?

Take the classic da Vinci *Mona Lisa* portrait. She's not smiling. The masters Monet and Renoir don't have their subjects smiling, either. So what goes with the not-happy face? The answer is technology:

- ✔ People have to sit for long periods of time while their portrait is painted. No one wants to (or can) smile for a couple of hours on end.

- ✔ When photography was new, exposures took several seconds or even minutes . . . not as long as sitting for a portrait, but you can't expect people to hold a realistic smile for that long.

- ✔ When exposure times shortened and people didn't have to pose as long, photographers started having subjects smile.

Smile for the camera

People look more friendly and less intimidating when they smile. And because photographers (usually) want their subject to appear in the best possible light (pun intended), they invariably asked posed people to smile when being photographed.

Even though more people smile in art these days (to see what I mean, check out the sidebar, "Who's smiling now?"), a good smile is one that's natural-looking and not forced. Artists, whether window dressers or masters of acrylics (a type of paint an artist uses), want natural facial expressions, including smiles, in their art. Sometimes all it takes is to say, "Smile," and then snap your camera to get your subject to smile naturally, as in Figure 7-4.

Figure 7-4: A natural smile complements the subject.

As you likely know, getting a true smile on your subject can be a little tough. Some people just plain freeze when being photographed. If you have a stiff subject who is ill at ease with being photographed, telling a joke or riddle to her can elicit a natural-looking smile.

For your more serious subjects

Face it, some people just don't want to smile when getting their photograph taken. Maybe they're not the biggest yukster around (think pensive novelists), maybe they're embarrassed about their dental work, or perhaps they're just downright serious folk who want to be taken seriously (think businessmen or politicians). And when you say, "Cheese!" or tell a joke to get people to smile, you can catch some unflattering laugh lines or crows' feet under the eyes, making your subject appear older than he wants to. Whatever the reason, insisting that someone smile who doesn't want to will give you a forced, unflattering portrait. Not what you or your subject wants. However, a non-smiling portrait doesn't have to be grim and boring. It can be dramatic, as in Figure 7-5.

When faced with a serious-natured subject, let his wishes dictate how you photograph him. If he wishes to appear a little gruff or dramatic, so be it. That is, after all, part of his personality, which is what portraiture is all about.

Photo credit: Mario Aguila

Figure 7-5: Use a non-smiling subject to create a serious and dramatic portrait.

And sleeping subjects make for excellent art photos. Of course, unless your subject is having a most wonderful dream, she won't be smiling. And not only is your subject relaxed and peaceful, but you can usually set your camera for a longer exposure in low light. (You can risk this longer exposure because your subject isn't moving terribly much.)

Personalizing a portrait

To help bring out your subject's personality — and get them to lighten up a tad — get your subject to do something or show you something that they love, like a hobby or an avocation (or vocation), like the young woman shown in Figure 7-6. If you don't know your subject well, talk to him to find out his interests: If he does yoga, ask him to assume the lotus position for a photo; if you come upon an artist working, ask her if you can take a picture of her doing her craft.

Photo credit: Matt Wright

Figure 7-6: Photograph subjects with objects that define them.

Depicting your subject's personality in the photo makes the photo more personal to that person — which obviously makes the photo more appealing. If the subject — or member of that person's family — finds a photo of himself or herself appealing, you are more likely to have a sale.

Incorporating items that symbolize something about that person's interests or hobby or getting multiple subjects to interact with one another can make a good photo even better, as shown in Figure 7-7.

Finding art in other features

Human portraiture doesn't have to be limited to faces. Any part of the human form is fair game to show a

Photo credit: Kelly Deriemaeker

Figure 7-7: Something unique about your subject enhances the photo.

miniportrait, or piece, of your subject's personality. Keeping these examples family-friendly, shooting facial features or other body parts is a great way to play with light and exposures, creating some fantastic art shots of curves and lines. See Figures 7-8 and 7-9.

Photo credit: Rebekka Guðleifsdóttir

Figure 7-8: Focus on just one body part to create an artistic "portrait."

Photo credit: Rebekka Guðleifsdóttir
Figure 7-9: Natural curves and lines add dimension and texture to a photo.

For art shots, consider honing in on these elements:

- Eye(s) and eyebrows
- Lips
- Facial lines
- Noses
- Hair and hairlines
- Hands and arms
- Legs and feet

Group portraits

When taking photos of groups, consider using the classic diamond pose. In a nutshell, the *diamond pose* involves posing subjects in groups of four, placing one person in the center, two others to the left and right of — and slightly behind — the center person, and finally the fourth directly behind the center person, but elevated (so that you can see person #4!). The four posed subjects make up the four points of a diamond: hence, the name.

For groups larger than four, start with the diamond pose and then cluster more diamond groups around that initial one until everyone fits in the frame. You might have to consider using a wide angle lens or shooting from creative angles (such as from above) to fit everyone in, but this gets easier the more large groups you photograph. Remember that you can always go with a closer shot when photographing groups (you don't always have to show everyone's legs, as shown in Figure 7-10) and sometimes a nice touch is to incorporate items that define the group, like sports equipment or musical instruments.

Photo credit: Kevin Kirschner

Figure 7-10: Arrange individuals as components of a whole for a group shot.

For a better composition, have your subjects stand or sit without space between them. They can be sitting adjacent or behind one another.

Candid portraits

Some of the best portraits are the informal — and sometimes unplanned — ones. As I mention in earlier sections, try to capture your subject involved in activities that interest her, keeping your eye alert to elements to incorporate in the shot to add visual appeal and depth. Remember that life is spontaneous and not all portraits have to be composed and set up, like the one shown in Figure 7-11.

Photo credit: Joshua Lennon Brown

Figure 7-11: Candid portraits can be great art shots.

Athletes can present you with great candid photo opportunities. Take advantage of showing them engaged in an action integral to the sport: serving in tennis, shooting close to the hoop in basketball, hitting the ball in baseball, and so on. (See what I mean by looking at the image in the nearby sidebar, "Drew Brashler: Sports photographer, full digital shooter.") Just remember to keep the focus on your subject. And don't overlook the opportunity, circumstances and decorum permitting, to capture candid portraits of people when they're in less-than-optimal moods. A photo capturing the torment of an angry toddler speaks volumes as does the angst of an athlete who didn't perform well.

Train your eye to capture action at its peak moment, when gravity is most defied. This lad flying from a swing seat (see Figure 7-12) will always be airborne now in this simple candid portrait.

Figure 7-12: Candid portraits can capture action.

Set your camera beforehand for action shots to help you shoot faster. Get as close to your subject as you can, keeping your f-stop low (big aperture) — as low as you can go on your camera (f/4.5 or lower).

Drew Brashler: Sports photographer, full digital shooter

Mesa, Arizona-based freelance photographer Drew Brashler looks through the lens of his Nikon for action shots that capture goal-based players stoked at playing their game. He shoots with a Nikon D1H (a pro dSLR) and Nikon AF 50mm f1.8 and Nikon AF 80–200mm f2.8 lenses.

Comparing shooting film versus digital, Brashler says, "For action, film doesn't even compare in my mind. For basketball, I shoot off about 115 to 140 photos for one game. With film, to shoot that much, I would have to change rolls three or four times. And think about rewind times and loading times. You would miss at least one main play . . . probably two, if you weren't quick.

"Now think of developing costs. That's four rolls of 36 (exposures), $10 each roll for developing. That comes out to $40 plus sales tax. I'm a college student, do most college students have that much cash laying around each time a basketball game happens?? No, because I go to Starbucks!

"Then there is the LCD screen. Being able to look at your photos between plays is HUGE for the starting-out photographer." (This is called *chimping,* thanks to www.sportsshooter. com.) "Sports is all about timing. With an LCD screen, you can look through your images and find out whether you need to hold back before pressing the button or be quicker at pressing the button.

"Finally, the last thing is turnaround speed. Every newspaper and *Sports Illustrated* have had their photographers switch to digital. One of the main reasons is the turnaround speed. With digital, you can shoot up until 30 minutes before a newspaper deadline to e-mail the photos to the office and have the photo editor edit the photos and turn them in for press. You can't do that with film: With film, you have to process the film, and then make prints and scan them, or just scan the negatives."

Photo credit: Drew Brashler

TRY THIS Use the *burst* series of pictures, a setting available on some point-and-shoot models. (Normally, point-and-shoot models aren't as fast at shooting pictures as their dSLR and SLR counterparts.) The burst gives you the option of taking a certain number of pictures (dependent on model) in quick succession (less than 2.4 frames per second. A Nikon D2H can shoot 8 frames per second (fps), which is great for sports photographers who want to get all of the action in a short period of time. First set the camera and then press the shutter halfway down to set the autofocus and exposure for all the pictures in the burst. Then press the shutter all the way down and hold it to take several pictures quickly.

Candid portraits don't have to be of only one subject, either. An interaction between two people in a photograph makes the photo tell a story, even if the interaction is as simple as two kids holding hands. Figure 7-13 tells the story of two little girls holding hands in friendship.

Figure 7-13: Include more than one person in portraits.

Capturing portraits of inanimate objects

For a little whimsy, don't overlook the opportunity to capture portraits of nonliving people — including statues, mannequins, murals, and art work — as shown in Figure 7-14. You can even pair inanimate "people" with live ones for a wonderfully artsy juxtaposition of realities. See Chapter 9 for more on how to photograph statues in black and white. And one of this book's bonus chapters on the Web (see www.dummies.com) shows how to arrange photos of statuary in a cohesive photo set.

Figure 7-14: Capture the unique to create unexpected portraits.

Wildlife Portraiture

To capture portraits of favorite animals, the best place to go is to a zoo or an aquarium or a circus. But there are other places, too, from private farms to your own back yard, where wildlife abounds. Photo opportunities are different for each, and each carries some precautions you'll want to take before filming:

✔ **The circus**

- *What works:* Telephoto lenses (at least 105mm) and 400 ISO. Try to shoot when the lights are up.

- *Watch out for:* Avoid using a flash so you don't spook animals or performers. And remember that the effective range of your flash is likely only 10 or 12 feet.

- *Make an art photo by:* Filming a lion in a roar to show how big its mouth is. Or zero in on one lion in the cage while blurring the others for added dramatic effect. (See Chapter 11 for more about intentional blurring for an added artistic edge.)

✔ **The zoo**

- *What works:* Use a tripod for steady shots. Use telephoto lenses (at least 105mm) and 400 ISO.

- *Watch out for:* Waking nocturnal animals. Avoid using a flash so you don't spook animals. Also watch out for flash glare when shooting in front of plate glass exhibit windows. (And, must I add — don't go beyond the exhibit barriers!)

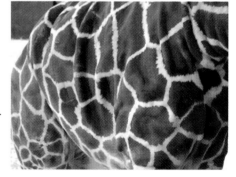

Photo credit: Timothy K. Hamilton

Figure 7-15: Zoom in, and an animal portrait becomes a study in texture.

- *Make an art photo by:* Shooting a giraffe up close so that the "animal portrait" is also a study in texture and pattern, as in Figure 7-15. Other ways might include shooting at night with longer exposures, shooting wide angle, or capturing comfy sleeping animals.

✔ **Out and about (your own backyard, on the street, in a park)**

- *What works:* Everyone has animals in their yard or at the local park. If you're a city dweller, you likely have horse police patrols or pigeons on the roof. Time permitting, use a tripod for steady shots. Use telephoto lenses (at least 105mm) and 400 ISO.

- *Watch out for:* Be quick on the shutter draw. Critters move fast, so be alert. Set your camera to auto mode after every shot. Don't try to handle animals you don't know or know much about. Squirrels are indeed cute, but they pack some nasty teeth. Avoid using a flash so you don't spook animals.

- *Make an art photo by:* Capturing animals in black-and-white (as shown in Figure 7-16) to evoke emotion, or a pet doing a trick (for an example, check out Figure 7-18 in the upcoming section, "Pet Portraiture").

Photo credit: Cole Rise

Figure 7-16: B&W portraits of animals are compelling.

Pet Portraiture

When you create portraits of animals, remember that safety comes first — especially if you're in the wild, photographing animals in their habitat. If an animal you don't know senses that you're uncomfortable or frightened of it — for even one moment — the charm can go very quickly.

If Fido is a black blur tearing after his fave Frisbee (or postal carrier), show off his speed by blurring the background during an action scene, like when he's running (as shown in Figure 7-17). When you capture

Figure 7-17: Pan your camera for blur.

something fast-moving with the action setting on any camera, the aperture tightens, so that everything is clear. That's not what you want for this effect. Rather, to blur the background, manually set the shutter speed to 1/30 second in your camera's Tv mode, the mode that lets you set the shutter speed while your camera sets the f-stop. (Note that the Tv mode might not be available on non-dSLR cameras.) Then move your camera to mirror the animal's direction and speed (panning) while you make the exposure.

If Fido is the type of dog who loves to jump high in the air after a toy (like a Frisbee), photographing him clearly with a blurred background may require that you take many shots. It's great fun though to see your pet gliding through the air with the greatest of ease. See Figure 7-18.

Photo credit: Kristi Foster

Figure 7-18: Watch Fido fly.

Remember, too, that not all pets have personalities that are action-oriented. Take a look at Figure 7-19, which you might consider to be "pet as still life." And as I mention in an earlier section about filming sleeping animals in a zoo, don't overlook the opportunities a sleeping pet gives you. Except for an occasional twitching leg, you're guaranteed that Fluffy will be still. You can also do some wonderful up-close studies of their fur.

Figure 7-19: Catch them at rest.

Goin' bananas

The cute primates eating banana pieces are on top of a cab on the way back from the ruins in Angkor Wat, Cambodia. Photographing them did indeed get dicey. They made themselves quite at home inside the car, making the photographer more than a little nervous. As cute as any animal is, wild animals are just that — *wild.* Photograph with care, not petting nor feeding nor handling wild animals.

Shooting for Color in Art Photography

In This Chapter

▷ Understanding the relationship between light and color

▷ Discovering how your camera handles light and color

▷ Mastering f-stop settings to achieve maximum color

▷ Trying advanced color techniques

*A*fter cracking groggy eyes in the morning, you notice rays of dusty light sweeping across your bed. You watch as the tiny specks of debris scatter about, floating aimlessly. You cough. Outside your window is a bright red cardinal among maple leaves, motionless for the moment. You grab your camera and snap. You captured the bright red bird in all its grandeur. It flies away. You are happy with your shot, and you go back to sleep. Later, when you upload your picture to your computer, you find that the crimson bird is now maroon with blue tones, and the green of the maple leaf background is olive brown. The bird doesn't even look like a cardinal. What went wrong?

Taking an art photo is more than just snapping pictures of flowers or birds. Shooting for explosive color — from cool blue hues to melting reds — is one of your major goals. Then you can take that color to its brightest, boldest, softest, or smoothest image in your shot (all the way, even, to setting your shadows and colors in Photoshop).

In this chapter, I give you the lowdown on shooting photos in color — bright vibrant colors — from the basics of understanding color to more advanced techniques that you can implement to take great photos. As Paul Simon says, "Don't take my Kodachrome away."

The techniques presented here are a guide for creating something worthy of wall space at your home or at someone else's, a spectacular framed print for a gift or to sell. Or maybe a high-resolution JPEG submission to your favorite travel mag or one of the dozens of new photography and literary publications making their way to newsstands and bookstores everywhere.

Discovering How Light Makes Color

Simple light and color principles form a basis for producing a wide range of photography, from aesthetically appealing shots to those of outrageous pop — ones that people pay dollars, euros, and yen for (pun intended).

Color comes in three *primary* shades: red, yellow, and blue. On a printed or painted picture, these colors' reflection of light on white paper to your eye offsets the colors to yellow, cyan, and magenta. Combining two primary colors — say blue and yellow — results in a *secondary* color: in this case, green. Mixing a primary and a secondary color forms a *tertiary* color. Blue (primary) and green (secondary), for example, make bluish-green (tertiary). Figure 8-1 shows the added colors of *tints* (made by adding white to colors) and the *shades* (made by adding black to them).

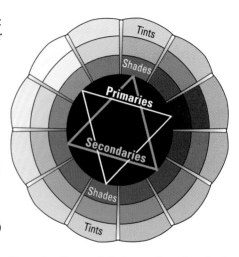

Figure 8-1: Tints and shades on the color wheel.

Different types of materials and objects reflect different wavelengths of light. And the wavelength of that reflected light defines the color. Understanding color is critical to creating good shots because, after all, photography is all about writing with light.

This short exercise can help you see how light changes color:

1. **Place an object under ample light.**

   If you need, augment the light, such as setting a dimmer switch to maximum intensity.

2. **Take a picture of the object.**

3. **Dim the light a little, watch what happens to the light reflected from the object, and take another picture of the object.**

4. **Repeat Steps 1–3 a few times.**

5. **Compare the pictures to see how the different light changes the appearance of the object.**

   The object changes its hue or tone as the light varies. When the room darkens, black is added to the color. Red, for example, changes to maroon.

Figure 8-2 shows comparative pictures of a toy snake, each taken in manual mode at a shutter speed of 8 seconds and an f-stop of f/16. (For more about shutter speed and f-stops, see Chapter 5.) Before each shot was taken, I reduced the amount of available light by turning down the dimmer switch in the room. Notice the change of tones in the colors.

Figure 8-2: Diminishing light causes color shades to shift in tone.

Light and color, which are both fluid and manageable most of the time, are the elements that make or break a good photograph. Throughout this section, I explain what you must know about color, how light affects color, and some basics about using color to make wonderful photos.

Keeping an eye on color

Look at the colors around you while waiting in line at the grocery store or sitting in traffic. Ask yourself the following:

↙ Does the color of the object tell a story?

↙ Has the color of an object faded to a shade you've never seen before?

↙ Has someone painted something a color so bad that it's good?

↙ Do the colors you see provoke an extended emotion or feeling that you wouldn't normally associate with that object?

If you answered yes to any of these questions, quick, grab your camera and take a picture of it. It could be an art photo.

The mood mix

How would a cowboy look dressed in green? Or a sea adventure movie preview blaring on a movie screen in pink? Colors come in all kinds of hues and tones, from primary colors mixed with white (the pastels) to blazing primary colors that pop artist Keith Haring included in his graffiti. Each makes you feel something and each makes an association with your viewer, joining the two of you in what you know about color.

Greens and blues are cool and calming. Grays and browns are dull and uneventful (but they match well with other colors). Reds and oranges are warm and inviting.

And wait — that's not all. There are light colors, the pure ones, that make you feel happy. Haring's colors, bright and medium-toned, can give you goose bumps from an invigorating mix of primary red, green, and blue. And don't forget the feelings evoked by the dark tones of the big maroon pencil you used when you were six and the deep navy blue of the mid-ocean, which can be cool and peaceful.

If you're thinking about art to use indoors — framed digital prints — think of colors and mood. Use warm colors (coral and orange and yellow) to add comfort to a cool, dark place. If you live up north, make lots of art with warm colors. People will love you for it in the winter. If you've got lots of sun (say where I live in the desert), go with some chilling blues. And if you love Keith Haring, let out your inner child and paint your digital pictures (like the one here), leaving your inhibitions behind.

Positioning yourself and your camera

Choosing objects to photograph in color requires that you be selective about how and where you aim your camera. To balance ambient lighting, you might need to shift your body position, sometimes dancing about the object to get the right light. As you move to the left or right or up or down, the object takes on different hues because light bounces off it in a variety of directions.

In your effort to capture the world around you as a work of art, your goals are to eliminate glare, iron out streaks, and minimize shadows. Especially when shooting outdoors (more on that in Chapter 5), you must move around an object to find the light that's just right. Do a few stretches and then follow these steps:

1. **Choose an object that you want to photograph.**

   Don't get stumped on this one. Just select something with color (like the yellow tables in Figure 8-3) or get anything colorful that you can carry outside.

2. **Focus on the object where the light is greatest and snap a shot.**

   You might find yourself bending and contorting your limbs in positions that you're not used to.

3. **Photograph the same object in the same light/location but now focus on different light intensities around the object.**

   If you find that a lot of light on the center of the object doesn't give the enhanced color effect that you want, move the object (or yourself) to experiment.

4. **Notice where the light falls to help you choose the best color exposure.**

Figure 8-3: Shooting from different angles causes subtle color changes.

Sometimes (like when photographing the cardinal I describe earlier), you have but a small frame of opportunity to catch the subject's color. You must be quick, simply taking your camera from your nightstand and snapping a picture. To achieve optimal color exposure, set your camera to a general automatic mode (which I discuss further in Chapter 5) in case a photographic moment presents itself on short notice.

Using complementary and contrasting colors

You have millions of ways to mix colors to create a mood. For instance, take the bright colors of fast-food restaurants. The colors that corporations use to sell fast food make you hungry, so you buy more food.

In order to make sense of color in a photo, apply what you know or see around you. Look for complementary and contrasting colors, both in man-made objects and in nature. You don't want to precisely match colors, like the dreaded bridesmaid syndrome of dyeing shoes to match the color of a dress.

Complementing or contrasting color is more on the order of choosing a color range (family) or of finding a snippet of color in two things: like black shoes that go with an ensemble of black-and-white houndstooth. The boy's shirt in Figure 8-4 complements the other earth-toned shades surrounding him. Think of choosing colors in a photograph in the same terms as picking out clothes for an outfit that you want to wear, or perhaps you want your children to wear for a big family event.

Figure 8-4: The colors here work because they match.

Nature provides rich opportunities for capturing color. Think about how and why they look good. The colors in the photo shown in Figure 8-4 complement each other because the boy wore a seasonal color, perfect for taking art photos of him at the pumpkin farm. After selecting certain objects to photograph, soon you'll discover that keeping within a range of colors is better than having your viewer take in a helter-skelter range picked randomly from several objects that happen to be near each other.

Also, while training your eye to work with color, notice how it sometimes tricks the human eye. Figure 8-5 compares the contrast effects of different color backgrounds for the same red square. Red appears more brilliant against a black background and somewhat duller against the white background. In contrast with orange, red appears lifeless; in contrast with blue-green, it exhibits brilliance and depth. Notice, too, that the red square appears larger on black than on other background colors.

   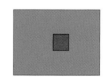

Figure 8-5: Background and foreground colors contrast differently, creating perceptual differences.

If you are color-blind, don't let that stop you from taking art photographs. Think of it this way: People (designers and your potential subjects) have taken the time to do your color-matching work for you. Fashion designers mix colors to match the latest trends. They know what they are doing. They're trained in color theory, so that if you take a close-up shot of your Aunt Bea in her new Chanel blouse, the color choices have already been defined in the clothes themselves.

Sign makers, architects, and artists spend a lot of time making sure that the colors they use work together. For example, the sign in Figure 8-6 contains a mix of vibrant color, wonderful by itself. The color of the photo, however, is enhanced by the magnificent blue sky behind it (thank you, Mother Nature!).

To see what I mean:

1. **Find a candy package in a colorful wrapper.**

2. **Set your (digital) camera to its highest resolution, as discussed in Chapter 2.**

3. **Put the package under a lamp, position the package for the light that you want on it, and take a picture of the package.**

Figure 8-6: Contrasting background and foreground colors create perceptual differences.

4. **Take other pictures of the package from different angles and under different light sources.**

   My candy company of choice uses a striped background on the wrapper — one that, when snapped as a close-up and printed out at high resolution, literally glows on your (or someone else's) wall.

Figure 8-7 shows two shots of part of a candy wrapper: one shot under tungsten light (on top) and one shot under a fluorescent light. I shot these at different angles to enhance the color differences between the two.

Start capturing fantastic color with close-ups of objects:

   ✔ A window display at a local shop

   ✔ A sports player in uniform

   ✔ A billboard

   ✔ A cluster of flowers

Figure 8-7: Angle and light source create different color shades.

How Your Camera Interprets Light and Color

When you prepare your camera for taking a picture, you control the *exposure,* or how much light is cast on the film (with a film camera) or on the sensor (with a digital camera).

A shining sun, bright and unobstructed, is necessary to get the most color on film or your digital camera's sensor. If you set your camera to aperture-driven auto settings (see Chapter 5) so that the shutter speed is automatically determined by your sensor, you do lose a bit of creative control regarding shooting for color. To maximize color on a sunny day, you need to factor in

- **ISO/ASA:** How sensitive the film/sensor is to light; often called the *film speed.* Film speed is a measure of light sensitivity. When using fast film speeds, you can take a picture inside with less light (with the result of a loss of color). A slow film speed allows objects to get "soaked" — that is, *saturated* — with light and color. (Although ISO and ASA are similar, ASA value is based on an American standard and ISO on an international standard.)

  The film speed for a digital camera is a measure of how much light it needs to take a well-exposed photo. (Obviously, a digital camera doesn't use traditional celluloid and emulsion film, per se, like an SLR or a view camera does.) Usually, film speed for a digital camera is stated as an ISO equivalency (light sensitivity expressed in the terms used to rate the same characteristic in film). ***Bonus:*** When you set the ISO for a film camera, you are stuck with that setting for the entire roll of film. For a digital camera, however, you can change the ISO for every exposure if you want.

  - *Low ISO:* A low ISO setting (50–200) generally produces better, cleaner images, but the pictures can be dark if not shot in bright sunlight or with a good flash. Images are also more susceptible to blurring because of the slower shutter speeds required when using a low ISO setting.

  - *High ISO:* Higher ISO settings (400–1600) can produce better-exposed pictures in low light but also introduce more electronic *noise,* or pixel distortion, which can make your image look grainy. Noise has been significantly reduced in high-end digital cameras when you shoot at high ISO; when you change ISO settings, there's no longer a discernable difference between high and low ISOs in some shots.

Figure 8-8 shows pictures taken with a Canon 350 dSLR camera, handheld indoors without a flash at ISO settings of 100 and 1600. Notice that the picture on the left in the figure is clear — and on the right, blurry. Low ISO settings are more sensitive to camera shake.

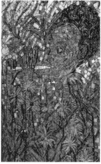

Figure 8-8: Use a high ISO to eliminate blur in low light.

TIP

For a clear, colorful shot, set your camera to a high ISO indoors. At settings such as 1600 or 3200, you can shoot in dark cathedrals — or even in a cave lit by flashlight. However, you can expect a *lot* of digital noise when shooting at such high ISO settings.

✏ **Shutter speed:** This is the actual amount of time that the camera's shutter remains open. The longer the shutter is open, the more light that falls on the sensor or film. (When the shutter is open too long and too much light enters the camera, the image is *overexposed* and looks pale and washed out. When the shutter isn't open long enough and not enough light enters the camera, the image is *underexposed* and appears too dark.)

✏ **f-stop:** A measure that indicates the size of the lens opening *(aperture)*. The value of an f-stop is inversely proportional to the opening of the lens. Smaller values such as f/2.8–6.3 mean that your lens is open wide, letting in more light in a given amount of time (the shutter speed). Larger f-stop numbers, such as f/18–36, create a smaller aperture, thus letting in less light at the same shutter speed.

REMEMBER

As you take more and more pictures using aperture-driven auto settings, keep these points in mind (and see Chapter 6 for more information):

✏ Have your camera preset to the *Av mode,* which is a feature that lets you set the f-stop number and automatically maintain correct exposure as the camera adjusts the shutter speed. Set your f-stop to around f/6.7 to f/8 (a moderate setting that will give you decent depth of field) and begin shooting. Use a lower f-stop to keep the subject in focus while gently blurring the rest of the image. Use a higher f-stop to keep the entire image in sharp focus. See what I mean in Figure 8-9.

✏ Choose a position to shoot where the background of the shot is the least cluttered and offers good contrast with the object itself.

When in Av mode, the smaller your aperture is set, the longer your shutter has to stay open so that at very high f-stops (say, f/36), you get blur very easily because your shutter has to stay open longer than your subject can stay still.

Photo credit: Kevin Kirschner

Figure 8-9: Widening your aperture decreases depth of field.

Setting ISO speed for maximum color

The first thing that you do as a film photographer before a shoot is decide what kind of film you will use: That is, choose the film's sensitivity to light. You can purchase film with speeds from ISO 100 to ISO 800 at just about any drug store around the world. Films with higher and lower ISOs are available at specialty camera shops. Although digital photographers have a wider choice in ISO settings (some digital cameras have lower and higher settings than are commonly found with film), they can also set their ISO settings to many of the same values used for film.

For the brightest, boldest colors, shoot with traditional high-resolution film and scan those images or shoot with your digital camera set at a lower ISO value.

Setting your digital camera to a film speed greater than ISO 400 or shooting with film that's over ISO 400 and scanning the prints or negatives/positives sometimes results in *noise*, unwanted specks of red, green, or blue and undesirable light specks in shadows and areas of solid color.

Noise isn't always bad. In fact, sometimes it's preferred to achieve a certain effect, as shown in Figure 8-10, which features a shot of a French town taken through a plane window on the way to Paris. Here, noise makes the photo look almost like a pointillist painting.

Figure 8-10: Noise comprises tiny dots that can appear at high ISOs.

Setting white balance

Color exists in various proportions in any lighting situation. Its hue, tone, and intensity depends upon *ambient light,* or lighting that seems to come from all directions (rather than from a single source) and fills a scene, shedding light on the objects you're photographing. Your camera measures ambient light with a value known as color temperature. Essentially, *color temperature* is the blueness or orangeness of the light that you see.

Color temperature variances can be corrected by covering your lens with a filter, offsetting odd-colored tones that are created by ambient light. For example, with a conventional film camera, you need to use a *skylight filter*, one that reduces the blue tones that occur at high color temperatures. While your digital camera likely has both automatic and manual white balance settings, you may still find the need (or desire) to use photographic filters in front of your lens. Your white balance choice may include Daylight, Shade (or Cloudy), Fluorescent, and Incandescent (or Tungsten). Generally speaking, you'll leave your camera set to Auto, but there may be times that you want to use an *incorrect* white balance setting for special effects. You might, for example, make a snow scene bluer by taking the photo with white balance set to Incandescent/ Tungsten. Or you might want to make an indoor fireplace or candle scene seem even warmer and cozier by shooting with white balance set to Daylight.

Knowledge of color temperature with respect to your white balance settings can ensure that you get the optimum color results because ambient light has a color temperature value. Different light sources emit light at different color temperatures, causing your picture to lean either to a red or blue hue. A high color temperature shifts light toward blue (as in Figure 8-11), and a low color temperature shifts light toward red hues (as in Figure 8-12).

Figure 8-11: When color temperature is high, more blue light exists.

Figure 8-12: When color temperature is low, like in a production, more red light exists.

Tweaking white balance settings also enables you to deceive your camera into giving you results that will enhance your images. Toying with your white balance settings can turn deserts into icy retreats, prickly and cold, or set the indoors afire with a global warming–like result — color science that makes art "art."

Take some time and play around with your camera's white balance settings adding warmth (by increasing reds) or coolness (by increasing blue) when you're photographing in daylight. You'll need only a little while to determine your favorite settings to fool — I mean, set — your camera. Figure 8-13 illustrates the relationship between sources of light and color temperature, showing how the color temperature changes with different ambient light around your subject/scene.

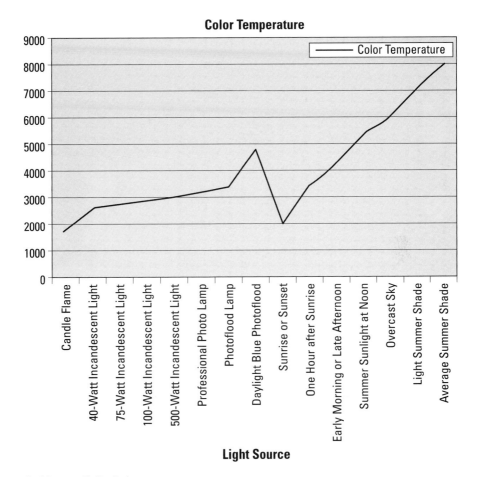

Color Temperature

Excel chart created by Matt Bamberg.

Figure 8-13: Low color temperatures (indoors) appear with red hues; high color temperatures (outdoors) appear with blue hues.

If you set the camera to a shade white balance while taking a picture in broad daylight, your digital camera adds more red tones into the scene. Check the Kelvin color temperature chart (refer to Figure 8-13) to see that overcast conditions are about 6000° K. Light shade conditions are about 7100° K. Therefore, setting your white balance to Shade adds more red tones than setting your camera to Overcast when you shoot in daylight. Some digital cameras allow you to enter the Kelvin temperature for your white balance so that you have maximum control over the amount of red or blue tones that you add to your shot.

The Auto White Balance (AWB) mode on your camera uses its sensors to calculate the white balance for the image. Usually, the Kelvin (K) temperature range for AWB is 3000–7000° K. Using AWB normally provides a good image albeit with some color temperature distortion that you see with film — for example, the same blues and reds as seen in Figures 8-11 and 8-12, respectively.

Warmer light of sunrise yields to the cooler light of midmorning. After twilight, when light dims, conditions for shooting change fast. Now is when your ISO should drop to capture better color in your shots.

If you're shooting where shadows abound, or perhaps the sun is in front of you, you'll need to manually adjust your camera's exposure or you may have trouble with your images when you go to edit. Lackluster colors, washed with black, are likely to appear. These are colors that won't budge from stubborn hues; they're unmanageable and easily pixilated, even when you're using the best tools that Photoshop has to offer. The pink Cadillac in Figure 8-14 isn't done jus-

Figure 8-14: Dark hues hide colors.

tice in this shot. Because the camera adjusted itself to avoid overexposing the sky in the background, the subject of the photo is too dark. Manually setting the camera to a larger aperture and a slower shutter speed could have produced a lovely photo.

For the most natural color results in a picture taken with a digital camera, set the white balance indoors to your digital camera's indoor (incandescent or fluorescent) setting. If you're shooting outdoors in the shade, set it to the Shade/Overcast setting.

Setting your digital camera to automatic is your best bet because if you go to photograph a crimson cardinal outside your window without having changed the white balance from your last (indoor) shot to either automatic or daylight, your picture will be a throw-away.

The film for a traditional camera and the sensor for a digital camera are optimized for daylight color temperature. Whether you use film and then digitize your negatives, or shoot a picture using the sensor on a digital camera, your picture will edge to one hue or the other (blue or red) as your light source varies unless the white balance setting is adjusted, either automatically or manually.

Experimenting with settings can create interesting effects — effects that people might just buy and hang on their walls. If you've made a mistake but find your image looking good, don't dump it. It could be a valuable print. Fortunately, when you manipulate your image in Photoshop, tweaking your picture to normal color levels is fairly easy — and by *normal,* I mean the levels that your eye would see.

The beauty of simplicity in color

Santorini, Paros, and Mykonos are Greek beach-bumming heavens, but you can also find a photographer's paradise in Greece. A mix of the Greek summer sun, the ubiquitous stucco walls, and the soft Mediterranean colors combine for some of the greatest photo ops in the world. Add in smooth arches and a couple of beveled edges, and you're almost in photography heaven. What finishes it off is the blue sky that curves through to perfect the composition.

A photographer's job is to capture the beauty of the simplicity of colors around us — to make us aware of things we might not notice. So take the time to look around and see what others might not.

Using an f-stop to Enhance Color

I believe that good color photography begins with a bright sunny day. Some think that the best time to photograph is during fog because objects are muted and shadows disappear. However, direct sunlight on an object distinguishes its color, which produces a bold-colored image. Light, ever changing and unpredictable, is what makes or breaks a good color shot. Keep in mind that some people — that is, your potential clients — buy bold and bright colors. (That's not to say that there isn't a market for black-and-white photography or even color images with more subdued colors, but the bold and bright shots are easily marketed.)

To use the sun to your advantage and produce photos with eye-popping color, go outside on a sunny day. With the light behind you (move a little if you cast a shadow over your subject), take several photos of one object. I feel that the best light for a color art photo is direct sunlight on the object being photographed, as in Figure 8-15. Whether you're shooting billboards in Havana or flowers in your garden, each will make a unique photo when the sun hits your subject directly. If the sun isn't where you want, move around the object until you see it reflecting the most light. If the object is small enough, move it in front of you with the sun at your back. If you're in a hurry — say if the object is borrowed from a shop after asking the owner for permission to photograph it — use the same f-stop setting each time. ***Hint:*** Using f/6.7 is excellent for flat objects that have direct sunlight on their faces.

Figure 8-15: A bloom directly in the sun makes a great subject.

For more about shooting photos outdoors, see Chapter 5.

Finding objects in direct sunlight and photographing them is a great way to make a set of images that contain bright colors. For more on shooting in shade, see the upcoming section, "Shooting colors in the shade."

Advanced Color Techniques

In traditional photography, your goal might be to create a print of realistic impression of what you see. In art photography, however, colors (like other subjects and elements) can either be exaggerated or subdued in a wide variety of ranges: You can underexpose to saturate color, shoot in the shade, or even use pollution to your advantage.

Underexposing your photo to enhance color

Heavy overexposure will lighten your print and move your colors to white. Underexposing, conversely, tends to work in an opposite manner, ranging from deepening colors to blacking out your entire photo.

All cameras, digital and film, rely on their light meter to measure the light around the lens and within the frame of your shot. For ordinary exposures, most cameras use an average of all the light that the frame has in it.

However, using an average of all the light in your frame sometimes just doesn't do the job of reproducing the bright colors in the frame. You have to help it along by using the *exposure compensation settings* that allow you to take in more or less light in your frame. When you reduce the amount of light that you let in the camera, you deepen the colors of the image. Tauntingly deep colors can attract potential buyers of your photos.

Play with these setting to see which work best for your shots. You can override how your camera exposes your film or the sensor to light. You can lighten or darken the image by using the EV (exposure value) compensation, using positive and negative fractional numbers in decimal form, like +1.0 or –0.5.

Decreasing the exposure by 0.5 (depending on the brightness of the sun) will do a much better job of saturating colors in your image than waiting to do it in Photoshop later.

You can never have enough flowers in your life, especially when it comes to fooling around with your exposure compensation settings. (Come to think about it, you can never have enough insects and butterflies and animals and light and color, too.)

1. **Find some flowers in your garden to photograph, making sure the flowers have the sun shining directly on them.**

2. **Set your camera to the Av setting with your f-stop set at your choice.**

   Remember that you're experimenting only with color enhancement and not depth of field.

3. **Set your exposure compensation at –0.5 to underexpose the shot so that the colors appear more saturated.**

4. **Take a close-up picture of the flowers.**

5. **Repeat at an exposure compensation setting of –1.0.**

Figure 8-16 shows how shots taken at different exposure compensations (0, –.66, and –1.33, top to bottom) bring out the color of flowers.

Figure 8-16: Change exposure compensation to deepen colors.

Some art photography provides viewers with a clear focus of an object or a part of an object, like this bridge in Hanoi, Vietnam (see Figure 8-17). The color red among the contrasting green background of foliage and water provides a clear focus based upon color. The f-stop was set high so that the picture has a clear foreground and background. The exposure compensation was set to –.5, making the colors appear saturated.

Figure 8-17: Underexposing the shot slightly helps saturate the red of the bridge.

The rules for shooting for color are changing with the new Raw formats that are available on dSLR cameras. Even if you didn't saturate your colors while you were shooting, you can later — in Photoshop — just as if you were shooting. In your software, you can simply increase the saturation value with a slider. For more about this, see Chapter 12.

If this morning's cardinal came back at noon and the sun was shining brightly on it, the chances are great that the red of his feather coat would scream loudly off of a printed page, almost pop-like. You'll be lucky if you get time to adjust your exposure compensation in time to photograph it in the deep reds that you would hope to get. If your specialty is photographing wildlife in deep colors, you might want to have your camera preset to your favorite exposure compensation setting.

In Av (automatic) mode, if your f-stop is high (for a clear background and great depth of field) in a lower light environment, you risk blurring your picture because your camera will automatically decrease the shutter speed.

Shooting colors in the shade

Tall downtown buildings, trees with wide girths, and very cloudy days — all casting shadows over your world — can turn photo opportunities from glamorous to pitiful. Shade can present a challenge when trying to capture color. However, you can use shade to your advantage, especially when contrasting bright and shadowed areas, such as you see in Figure 8-18. Also note in the figure that even the shady area has variations — some areas are darker than others.

Varying light, whether in sun or shade, can make a shot more interesting.

When the sun pours on the green, that's a perfect time to underexpose a shot by –0.5. When you underexpose, sunlit green won't be dull, but vibrant and verdant.

Figure 8-18: Shady spots can have mixtures of light.

When you make colors vibrant, however, watch out for the shadows and shady spots that abound because these will turn even darker when you underexpose.

Think of shade as a kind of mini-night: a time when color is blackened. Keeping your shutter open longer (a slower shutter speed) solves some of the light problems that you may have with shade. To fool the camera into exposing the scene a little longer, use your camera's Manual mode, keep the same f-stop, and slightly increase the time the shutter is open. Using a tripod will help to eliminate blur that tends to creep in when you make a handheld exposure with a longer exposure time.

When taking a photo that includes areas both sunny and shady, you should consider using your camera's *spot metering* mode (if offered). This enables you to designate which part of the image should be properly exposed. (With some cameras, you point the camera at the area you want the camera to consider for setting the exposure, press the shutter button halfway down, and then reframe the shot before taking the photo.) Remember, too, that when shooting a subject in the shade with a bright background, you can set your camera to fire the flash *(force flash)* to illuminate the subject. You'll hear the term "fill flash" used for this technique.

Although you'd generally avoid taking photos where the same object is half in the shade and half in the sun, always look for those special opportunities to exploit the juxtaposition of very different lights and how they create color.

Color and the atmosphere

Color changes according to the light available, which in turn is affected by environmental variables and atmospheric conditions, including pollution, haze/fog, the season, and time/temperature of day.

Generally, the more polluted the sky is, the less intense the sun will be. Not only is there less contrast from the surface of an object to a background of smog, but you also end up with pixel separation of the browns and blues when your picture is digitized and enlarged.

On a sunny day in an area with heavy air pollution, haze on the horizon is likely. You might find this to be distracting or even that it ruins what could be an otherwise beautiful image. The more the light is scattered by air pollution, the poorer your color saturation can be.

Although mastery of your photo editing software can salvage quite a few marginal (or even potentially great) photos, you want to shoot under the best conditions possible for the subject you're capturing. When given a choice between hanging out until the light is right or spending hours in Photoshop correcting an image, sit tight (or chill out) until conditions are perfect. And then take lots of photos with a variety of settings to ensure you have the best shot possible.

9

Crafting a Quality Black-and-White Art Photo

In This Chapter

▷ Why you should consider black-and-white (B&W) photography

▷ Shooting in B&W

▷ Noticing the differences between film and digital camera images

▷ Mastering shadows, midtones, and highlights

▷ Using lighting to make great B&W images

E ver been to a gallery or a museum exhibit that shows only black-and-white (B&W) photographs? B&W photography shows happen all the time from small coffee shops in small towns to big shows in big cities — shows such as the photography of Garry Winogrand, who photographed the streets of America throughout his lifetime during the last century. (See the sidebar on Winogrand's work later in this chapter.)

And although digital photography does affect how black-and-white images look, this newer technology won't kill its kindred and traditional B&W art form because there are more ways than ever to compose, capture, and manipulate those subtle shades of gray into images that mesmerize and captivate. Of course, you can always convert an existing color shot to B&W (see the "Manipulating a color image to become B&W" section, later in this chapter), but when you want B&W, shoot in B&W.

Shooting B&W is a serious form of art photography. Some people tend to dismiss B&W as boring or somehow less artsy because — face it — there's no color! However, there are plenty of markets for your B&W art photos, from galleries to museums to photojournalism to portraiture and architecture shots. In this chapter, I give you the basics of B&W digital photography and printmaking, whether you're shooting film or digital.

Why Shoot in Black-and-White?

So you think that B&W is boring? Sure, who wouldn't rather have a color TV than one in B&W? Who wouldn't rather look at color photos than plain ol' B&W? And hardly anyone bothers to film movies in B&W anymore.

Still, B&W has never gone out of vogue for certain practical applications, such as capturing architecture and architectural detail (see Figure 9-1), products for publications, and photojournalism. And from an artistic perspective, using B&W can afford you very dramatic prints, especially in portraiture (including when shooting sculptures) and when capturing shadows.

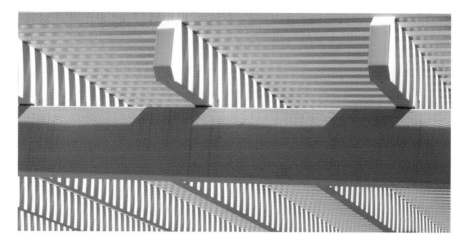

Figure 9-1: B&W is the workhorse for filming lines, light, and shadow.

After all, to shoot in B&W is to master light and shadow — which is what photography is all about. In short, to shoot in B&W is to shoot with an art focus of drama (see Figure 9-2). Also, using B&W can lend a warm feeling of nostalgia.

B&W images can comprise many shades of gray. Read more about grays in the upcoming section, "Understanding the 256 shades of gray."

From an educational standpoint, mastering shooting in B&W is the training ground for serious photographers. When you shoot in B&W, you train your eye to read light and not be so distracted by the additional layer of color in our surroundings that you automatically and unconsciously process. Study the great photographers of yesteryear and today — Ansel Adams, Alfred Eisenstaedt, Alfred Stieglitz, Dorothea Lange, Henri Cartier-Bresson, and Diane Arbus, to name only a handful — to see how they were masters of B&W.

Figure 9-2: B&W portraits can be shot with an art focus.

Digital black-and-whites and your friendly neighborhood museum curator

Most modern art museums do accept digitally manipulated images, but only if there's a certain "wow" factor. Brilliantly colored nighttime prints (in which the shutter of the photographer's camera has been left open) or prints for which the photographer risked life and limb to obtain (climbing tall buildings for unusual perspectives, for instance) seem to forever attract curators. Museum curators and high-end gallery owners accept digital photos in the context of larger art pieces and installations — say, a video made up of elaborately connected digital images.

You can create the building blocks of more elaborate works and use B&W as your colors of choice, but getting into a museum requires that you use your imagination to create prints that work together with other media and/or multimedia — from collages to MPEGs (files of moving pictures on the computer).

Check out the Digital Art Museum's Web site at `dam.org` to view the latest in digital art forms. Many B&W digital photographs by the artists on this site are part of larger art installations and multimedia projects. (This Web site also gives viewers an excellent overview of the history of computer art.)

A brief B&W perspective

B&W photography is an aberration in art history. Before the advent of the pinhole camera, visual art images — more specifically, paintings — in galleries or museums were in color.

At one time, though, B&W photography was modern — the technology of its day. It was even portable, although photographers had to lug around bulky equipment and make their own exposure plates (what we take for granted as "film" today). And the results were quite exciting for the times, allowing everyday folks to see images of faraway and exotic locales as well as being able to obtain affordable portraits and other photographs, as shown in Figure 9-3 (compared with the luxury of a painted portrait). Too, the advent of a portable camera launched photojournalism.

With the growing acceptance of photography as an art form throughout the 19th century, some came to find that the B&W images were actually more artistic and intellectually challenging than paintings, in which viewers didn't have to imagine nature's colors.

With the advent of color film, though, B&W fell out of favor with some. People wanted this new technology and the more realistic images intrinsic to color photography. Naturally, because color processing was more costly and because color photo technology was new, B&W photography was considered by some as a poor man's photo option.

Figure 9-3: B&W was the start of photography.

Shooting architecture

Towering buildings, old forts, walls of steel and glass . . . man-made structures of our modern world stun in real life — and can in photographs, too, if you take a few steps when setting your camera before taking architectural shots in B&W.

1. **Set your camera.**

- *Av mode:* This is aperture priority. Set the aperture to f/16 or higher.

- *A-DEP:* The automatic depth of field mode is on the knob of the Creative Zone on a number of SLR and dSLR cameras (see Chapter 11). The A-DEP setting allows you to use multiple focusing points within the frame to keep everything in focus. It uses a very fast shutter speed on the order of the inverse of several thousand seconds ($\frac{1}{2000}$–$\frac{1}{4000}$) and wide aperture openings (f/4 to f/6).

2. **Set your lens or zoom factor so that your frame contains what you want and no more.**

   For example, if you want to show a towering building like in Figure 9-4, either use a *short* lens (a lens whose focal length is shorter than the diagonal length of your camera's sensor) or a *fish-eye* lens that captures the entire structure (and possibly some framing by other structures nearby), or set an adjustable lens to a wide angle setting. For details about how different lenses are calibrated according to the size of your sensor, see Chapter 2.

Figure 9-4: Modern skyscrapers become art in B&W.

The wide angle on an adjustable lens is when you "zoom out" so that the lens is set to the smallest focal length.

Shooting things of an architectural nature don't always mean filming tall buildings. Just train your eye to look for structural details in all sorts of situations. To get your creative juices started, peruse the database at www.archinform.net to see literally thousands of images of international architecture, originally emerging from records of interesting buildings and their details from past to present.

To see how different the same piece of architecture looks in color compared with B&W, see the juxtaposition in Figure 9-5 of a color and a B&W image (converted to grayscale in Photoshop, in this instance, for the sake of comparison) of the same architectural shot. (Nice juxtaposition, too, of old and modern architectural styles.) Both give a different effect and feeling.

Figure 9-5: The same shot looks very different in color versus B&W.

- ✓ The color photo reveals the warm hues of sepia along with the creation of finer detail in the art scenes on the walls. You're more likely, in this picture, to focus on the content of the murals.

- ✓ The B&W image is less distracting and gives greater focus to the architecture — especially to the melding of the shade and light (from the huge skylight) from the bottom to the top of the picture.

When shooting architecture, with its strong straight lines, watch out for vignetting and line distortion — unless, of course, you want to exploit those effects for an artsy twist to a shot. These effects are caused by the

curvature and structure of your lens that can either be prevented or elimi-
nated (or welcomed):

✐ **Vignetting:** Some lenses create *vignetting,* whereby the sides of the shot are
darker than the interior, like a fading vignette-matte effect of an old-time
photo. Some, um, less-expensive lenses have this problem. You can switch
to a lens with better optics (say, from the lens that came with your SLR
or dSLR camera as part of a package to one of Canon's L series lenses).

Vignetting is an easy fix in Photoshop CS2. Shoot in Raw format (see
Chapter 18) and fix the vignetting with a slider bar when your Raw
image is opened. And to research lenses with vignetting problems,
search online for equipment reviews and specs.

✐ **Line distortion:** *Line distortion* is the subtle curvature of a line that should
be straight. You can get shift lenses for your SLR or dSLR cameras (about
$1,300) that straighten out lines caused by lens curvature. Photoshop CS2
also has a cure for this ill — the Lens Distortion filter, which repairs quite
a few kinds of distortions.

When shooting a building, first study it in a variety of ways. Shoot so that
everything in the photo moves to one vanishing point or to one direction as
the viewer looks across the frame.

Shooting architecture as architecture is often best done at dusk and dawn
when the light is softer and the shadows are less harsh. (For dramatic art
photos, on the other hand, you might want to shoot architectural details with
harsh shadows.) The time of day in which you shoot architecture changes,
which in turn affects the look of your B&W photograph. A picture taken in the
noon sun can provide more detail. In contrast, a picture taken at dusk can
have more shadow — providing more contrast perhaps but also a little less
detail in any small objects in the shot. Finding the perfect time of day for
shooting in B&W is an experiment in light and shadow. You'll know when you
get it right, and the results might surprise you.

Photographing at dusk when the sun is still above the horizon can be a disaster, especially when long shadows from nearby trees are cast over your
architectural subjects. Figure 9-6 shows how late afternoon shadows can
distract from the subject in a B&W architectural photograph.

Although the weather and the time of day (not to mention the time of year)
can affect how your picture comes out, adding to and/or taking away from
the focus of your structural subject, your perspective also involves some
calculation.

Figure 9-6: Shooting late in the day can create undesirable shadows.

Figure 9-7 shows a picture that is divided about a third of the way so that everything moves to two vanishing points — one to the left, and one to the right. From these two points, you can tilt your camera in any direction so that the vanishing points move up or down into the corner and/or top of the frame. For more on composing a shot using the vanishing point, see Chapter 1.

Figure 9-7: Shoot from different perspectives.

You can tilt the canvas of your B&W and color images with minimal loss of sharpness in your photo by choosing the Image⇨Rotate Canvas option in Photoshop. This is a great help when you are cropping your photos. See Chapter 12.

The picture in Figure 9-8 was taken at night. The shutter was set to stay open for one-half second using the Tv mode (shutter priority) of a digital camera. The aperture of the camera was set automatically using the light available to determine how wide it would be for the half-second it was open. The picture didn't blur because the camera was set on a minitripod on top of a newspaper stand. For more about night photography, see Chapter 10.

Figure 9-8: Avoid blur by using a tripod.

Photoshop has a feature for turning an image into a pen and ink style, like architecture drawings. You can read about this technique in Chapter 15.

You've probably heard the old "stop and smell the roses" expression. I like to apply this to architecture, especially the little stuff that comes attached to a fence, gate, or door, or the bigger stuff that forms patterns like that found in iron work. So when you're looking for subjects to shoot in B&W, don't forget architectural ornamentation — and get up close to capture all the detail.

Shooting portraits

Creating B&W photos gives you experience in working with enhanced shadows, highlights, shapes, and forms without having to think about color. Some subjects are a natural for B&W photography, such as the portrait made of the stone figure shown in Figure 9-9. You can see the weathering in how B&W captures its texture: You can almost feel the statue's roughness. The camera's depth of field and the subtle blurring of the background produces a totally photographic phenomenon that's not seen as clearly in any other art medium or in person. It is this depth and texture that brings emotion to the viewer.

Figure 9-9: Capture texture in B&W photography.

Take a look at the lighting in the following photos. The lighting affects how the shadows, midtones, and highlights come out in your photograph, each being different and dependent on how you expose the shot. (See Chapter 6 for more information about lighting with studio lights.)

- **Flash, indoors:** Flash inside creates bright light on a face. The light from the flash and the ambient lighting mix leave a shadow in the background. The fix for this might be not using the flash and upping the ISO speed to ISO 400 (see Chapter 7). The left image in Figure 9-10 shows the powerful effect that an in-camera flash has on lighting up the face of your subjects.

- **Flash fill, outdoors:** Using flash fill outdoors when your object is standing with his or her back to the sun is a good technique to keep the face more evenly lit, augmenting enough light to prevent muddy tones. See what I mean in Figure 9-10 (right image).

- **No flash, indoors:** Try to get away with using no flash inside for a more natural picture. Move your subject near an outside window or some decent light to take the shot. You can also place your subject so the light reaches his or her face from different directions so that you emulate the studio lighting described in Chapter 6.

Photo credit: Kevin Kirschner

Figure 9-10: Use flash for front lighting and flash fill for outdoors.

Famous photojournalist: A look at press photographer Charlie McCarty

Thousands of photojournalists with AP and dozens of news organizations throughout the world have risked their lives covering war, famine, the World Cup, and the NFL, capturing not only pain but glory and achievement. These people are the achievers themselves, speaking about the world through their photographs and news stories. Take Charlie McCarty, who with his camera and flash strung around his neck, documented the world in storytelling photographs until he was 80 years old. (He died in 2004.) And yes, he won a prize — in 1958, from the National Press Photographers Association, for a photograph of an incident among teens during the civil rights struggle in the South. A man and his camera: one picture worth an era in words that communicated the uneasiness of the times.

Many times photographers stay away from severe shadow — shadows so dark that they surround the subject by black. However, these kinds of shadows can enhance the physical features of a subject.

Portraiture doesn't have to be formal and composed. You can look for opportunities for more candid shots, too, like the woman with child in Figure 9-11. Get a model release from your human subjects! See the following section for more on that.

Shooting for journalism

Photojournalism is a classic innovation of photography as functional art. If you've ever seen the news on TV or online or read a newspaper or magazine, you've been touched by photojournalism. Who can forget the gritty B&W newspaper photos of the Vietnam War? Who doesn't remember that even-earlier poignant kiss of a sailor returning home and happy to be there? Good photojournalism can transport you to a time and place instantly with its historic spontaneity and realism.

Figure 9-11: Capture an informal shot when your subjects are relaxed.

Being a successful photojournalist is a matter of balancing preparedness, timing, and luck. You've got to be at the right place at the right time with your camera. Take a picture of an event that soon will be history, and you've got yourself an image of merit — a document that over time becomes more interesting.

To develop your own photojournalistic style, first try to emulate the best photographers — and shots — in this field. You can search for the works of Dorothea Lange, Margaret Bourke-White, and even Matthew Brady. Also peruse the grand photo mags, like *Look* and *LIFE*. Train your eye to notice what they did and develop your own style from there.

Here are places where you can find these snappable, historic events:

- **In your own backyard:** You can be anywhere when an event happens, even your own home, say, when a lightening bolt strikes the tree in your front yard and the tree goes up in flames. If your target is to sell to local publications, these are the kinds of shots you want to be prepared for.

- **When traveling:** Suppose you witness a protest march. What a great opportunity to snap pictures of the marchers or something artful that accompanies them or is installed by them. Figure 9-12 captures a peace march anchored by the classic Robert Indiana sculpture in the foreground. (Of course, remember to find out what the protest was about so you can make note of it.) Save the picture, bring it home, write an article about what you saw, and submit (and submit, and submit again). If it's an interesting enough shot and your writing is good, chances are that an Internet site, newspaper, or magazine will buy it from you.

Figure 9-12: A 1960s art piece anchors a 1960s-style protest.

Here are some thoughts to keep in mind if you're considering trying to sell photojournalism shots:

- **B&W or color?** Although many publications prefer B&W images, shoot color. It's a simple matter to convert a color image to grayscale, but converting grayscale to color means hand-painting the image.

- **Facts, facts, facts:** Be sure to document the date, time, and location of your photojournalism shots. If you sell shots to a publication, those editors need this information.

- **Model releases:** When you capture people who are recognizable in your shots, you need to get their names and have them sign a model release form, which gives you permission to market their likeness. That's not to say that you have to get release forms for every person in a large crowd — just when it's obvious that a person is a deliberate subject of your photo. Images of public figures — like politicians and celebrities — usually don't fall under this rule. However, if in doubt, get permission. And you can always consult a publications lawyer for more advice. You can get printable release forms here:

  www.dpcorner.com/all_about/releases.shtml

- **Simultaneous submissions:** Some publications only accept submissions that you haven't sent to other publications for consideration or that have not been previously published. And some publications might want only one submission at a time from any one person. So, before you send your work to a publication, find out its policies on these issues and adhere to them.

- **Timeliness:** Many times you'll think that you're the first person who's captured a certain photograph or reported a journalism-worthy event. Do some research before submitting your pic and/or writing. Google has a good News search: Type in a few keywords associated with the event to see whether it's been written about yet.

Capturing Black and White

You can use many methods to get any image — those that are a hundred years old to those of today — using negatives and positives of all shapes and sizes, prints, and digital (Raw, TIFF, and JPEG) files — all printed clearly and at high resolution in B&W. Pretty amazing stuff when you think about it. (Read more about digital file types in Chapter 2.)

Creating a B&W image

Creating a B&W print requires no magic wand: You can

- **Shoot with B&W film on a nondigital camera.** Black-and-white film is probably still the best medium for the genre. The light coming onto the film can create natural sepias with realistic-looking grains that develop when the film is mixed with chemicals.

- **Shoot with your digital camera set to B&W mode.** For what it is, it's good but can get to look a little like plastic.

- **Take a color image and tweak it in Photoshop to make it appear B&W.** You can either desaturate your photos or scan them in grayscale mode.

Remember, too, that a digital camera actually captures a color image when set to B&W. If you shoot in the Raw file format, you can easily restore the color later in Photoshop's Camera Raw plug-in.

B&W film

Not to insult your intelligence, but shooting in B&W on a nondigital camera requires using B&W film. This gives you a negative or a positive (film type depending) to enlarge to make a print. Just like color film, B&W film has an ISO rating (how sensitive it is to light; see Chapter 6 for more on ISO ratings).

Scan a B&W print or developed film to create a digitized image that you can tweak in an image editing program and then make copies. (See Chapter 3 for more on scanners and slide attachments.) In the upcoming section, "Getting the best quality image," you can read more about using B&W slide film for great results.

Shooting B&W on a digital camera

Obviously, digital cameras can't use B&W film, but they do have a setting with which you can shoot in B&W. The B&W mode in many cameras is among many menu items (described in Chapter 12). In some cameras, it may be hard to find without that handy roadmap, the User Guide. For example, the B&W feature on a Canon Digital Rebel XT, can be found within a setting called Parameters.

So what's better for B&W: film or digital? As a comparison, here are two images, shot at the same time and angle: one on film and one that's digital. (Okay, both are technically digital now because the film image was scanned.) But there are differences, as you can see in Figure 9-13. On the left is a B&W film image of a Spanish-style staircase taken in the P (that's *point-and-shoot mode*) of a film (Canon Rebel) camera and then scanned with an HP Scanner. On the right is the same image taken with a digital camera (a Canon Digital Rebel), again in the P mode. The film image has a somewhat broader tonal range, with darker shadows and brighter highlights, while the digital image shows better detail in the shadows.

Figure 9-13: B&W film versus digital comparison.

There are at least a dozen parameters at work when you look at images printed on a computer or in this book that can make the two different — and those parameters aren't always because of the digital versus film format itself. And of course, there's always the factor of personal preference. So rather than declaring one medium superior to the other for B&W photography, let me caution you to remember that the quality of your digital art photos, whether originating as pixels or on film, depends on two things: the settings you use when capturing the image and the post-capture processing you do in your image editing software.

Don't forget that when you capture in the Raw file format, all the image's original data is still part of the file, including color. Using Photoshop's Camera Raw plug-in (or other Raw-capable software), you can always return to the original image, as captured in the camera, complete with full color (even when the camera was set to use its B&W feature).

Manipulating a color image to become B&W

You can manipulate digital B&W digital images so that they look like B&W film prints. Sometimes you might need a B&W shot for certain types of publications, like catalogs or newspapers. Or, you might want to convert a color image to B&W (see the earlier section, "Creating a B&W image") to invoke a sense of nostalgia and time past.

Face it, the past sells. And B&W is an important piece of the past. From deco to retro, people like to have a piece of the past. Imagine an image of a woman wearing an apron in a 1950s-style kitchen or a man outside in a bathrobe picking up the newspaper, waving happily at the neighbor in front of a 1920s Craftsman home. The old days become new again for younger folks, and the old days are relived by older folks. Figure 9-14 shows a B&W shot of a modern building — a photograph that was shot this century but looks like it was shot decades ago because of the architecture and its lack of color.

Figure 9-14: Make modern photographs appear vintage.

For the deepest grayscale tones, choose the Channel Mixer option in Photoshop. Knowing how to do this is a must for anyone who loves B&W photography. Here's how you do it:

1. **Open your image in Photoshop and examine each color channel individually.**

   Open the Channels palette and click on each channel, one at a time, to evaluate what it offers to the final grayscale image. Which channel has the best detail in the highlights? Which channel has the best detail in the shadows?

2. **Choose Layer➪New Adjustment Layer➪ Channel Mixer, click OK, and then select the Monochrome check box.**

   After you click OK in the New Layer dialog box, click the Monochrome check box (in the lower-left corner of the Channel Mixer dialog box; see Figure 9-15) to give your image a grayscale appearance.

3. **Move the slider bars to tweak the black and white in your image.**

   Using the information you gleaned from the Channels palette in Step 1, balance the sliders

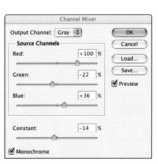

Figure 9-15: Make a grayscale image here.

to produce the best possible tonal range for your image. Increase the values of the channels that have good detail in the highlights and shadows, and compensate for their added contributions to the image by reducing the value of the third channel. Finding the perfect mix of channels is a balancing act — and of course, there can be different combinations that provide equally pleasing results.

Generally you start with a properly exposed color image; the values of the four Channel Mixer sliders should (ideally) total about 100. (Multiply the value of the Constant slider by three before doing your math — that slider is applied to all three color values.)

Figure 9-16 shows the original image of corn (color) and the change to B&W.

Figure 9-16: The same source image, shot in color and converted to B&W.

4. **(Optional) Flatten your image by choosing Layer⇨Flatten Image.**

Remember that the value of using an adjustment layer in Photoshop is flexibility. Unlike using an adjustment command, an adjustment layer lets you change your mind. If you don't flatten the image and you save it in Photoshop's PSD file format (or another format that supports layers), you can reopen the image and change your adjustment. If, for example, you find that your printed image is too dark in the shadows, you can simply reopen the image, reopen the adjustment layer (by double-clicking it in Photoshop's Layers palette), and change the sliders. If, however, you're quite happy with the image as is, feel free to flatten the image.

Getting the best quality image

Whatever your reason for capturing and printing in B&W, you want to start with the best image possible. You won't get a quality print from a so-so image. You can't serve hamburger and pass it off as filet mignon, you know. Here's how.

To create a great print, you need to start with a great image — a quality image, that is. You want the best quality image that your camera can capture whether you shoot with B&W film (and scan those images) or with a digital camera set to B&W. For the highest-quality photographs, follow these pointers:

✔ **Film:** Shoot with B&W slide film and scan the positives.

Scanning from a positive (a slide), rather than from a negative, gives you better results because your scan doesn't need to be inverted (swapping black and white). Although this isn't nearly the problem for B&W film that it is for color, you're still likely to be happier with scans of B&W slides than with scans of B&W negative film.

You can read about scanning images in Chapter 3.

✔ **Digital:** Shoot in B&W mode.

• *dSLR:* Shoot in *Raw format,* the highest resolution format with set standards that relates directly to the sensor on the camera. See Chapter 3 for more about Raw format, dSLRs, and how to set your camera to shoot Raw.

• *Non-dSLR:* Shoot in highest photo quality mode that your camera dictates for non-dSLR. Most digital cameras capture images using a high-resolution JPEG format that's convertible to a high-quality TIFF format — one that can print images at 8" x 10" inches without pixilation.

After you make changes to a JPEG image in an image editing program, I recommend that you save in another format. Resaving as JPEG can degrade the image quality through recompression. (It's safe to open and close a JPEG as many times as you want — it's only the process of compressing during saving that causes problems.) TIFF is a non-lossy file format that is an excellent choice for digital photos.

a. *Choose File⇨Save As (or click the Save icon in the program).*

b. *In the Save As dialog box that opens, click the list for choices of file type (usually JPEG).*

A drop-down menu appears.

c. *Choose TIFF from the drop-down menu.*

d. *Navigate to the location in your computer or to the location in your external hard drive where you want the file saved and then save it.*

Understanding the 256 shades of gray

A B&W photograph comprises shades of gray that add definition and depth and detail to the image. Figure 9-17 shows a chart depicting shades of gray in 5-percent increments from darkest to lightest (including the background color, which is the 50% gray sample). The chart includes a total of 21 shades of gray.

The image of a hibiscus flower (in Figure 9-18) shows the range of gray that makes up a typical B&W photo. There are 256 distinct shades of gray in the photo.

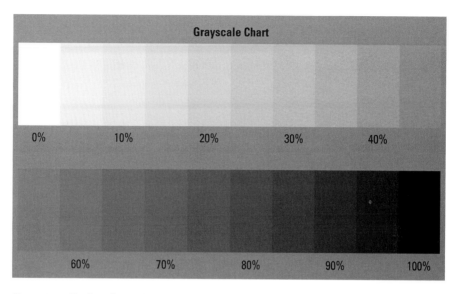

Figure 9-17: Shades of gray, from black to white.

Digital cameras set to 8-bit color offer 256 shades of gray from pure white to pure black. If you're shooting in Raw, your camera can capture in 16-bit color — twice as much digital data is used to record the image, producing a much greater number of subtly different shades of gray. Depending on how much processing and editing you do, and depending on your printing device, you might see no difference between 8-bit and 16-bit grayscale prints.

Figure 9-18: Many shades of gray define B&W photos.

Landscape shots can provide a natural scene containing clear highlights that contrast with the midtones and shadows in the image. (A good B&W photograph has many contrasts between light and dark tones.) The photograph in Figure 9-19 shows dimension using B&W:

Figure 9-19: Landscapes offer interesting composition tones.

- **Foreground:** White salt. Also note the salt bags, the face of each covered in a shadow. See the following section for more on shadows.

- **Contrast:** Two objects in the middle ground — one dark and one light, which provide good contrast — that is, broad differences between the darkest and lightest parts of the photo.

- **Background:** Light clouds above shadowed mountains in the background, providing more good contrast in gray tones.

To enhance tonal difference in your B&W shots, assess the tones of your subject and then choose a background that is different. If you're shooting something with a lot of highlights, choose a very dark background, as many product photographers do. See how effective this can be in Figure 9-20.

Figure 9-20: Flowers, in B&W, contrast with an almost-black background.

When shooting outdoors with B&W, look for great tones that nature throws your way, especially when it comes to moisture-bearing entities, like clouds, fog, haze, and steam. What's murky when shot in color can often be brought out as a very interesting highlight. Clouds can be your friend, either filtering harsh sunlight or cutting across the sun, giving you dramatic shadows. Fog and haze can provide wondrous midtones or spectacular highlights when side- or backlit. (For more on light sources, see Chapter 5.) And don't forget to look for steam — from a train, a geyser, a heating system, a tea kettle, or hot lava hitting the ocean.

Your lighting source and direction help define how many highlights and shadows your shot will have.

Defining highlights, midtones, and shadows

In B&W photography, distinctions are also made in the gray tones of various colors by how dark or light they are. These distinctions become even more important in B&W because these tones are in essence the "color" of the photo. By knowing what highlights, midtones, and shadows mean, you can

✓ **Tell whether you have a decent print, exposure, or onscreen image.**
 When I pull a B&W image onscreen, I look for clarity in the distinction of grays. Take, for instance, the picture of the Spanish architecture on the left in Figure 9-21. Check the contrast in two spots within the frame. You can see, for example, that the tiles on the roof are distinguishable from one another because each has a different shade of gray, and the place where the mountain meets the sky also differ by a couple of shades of gray, indicating good contrast.

Figure 9-21: Good contrast means having a balance between many tones.

During the evaluation of your photos and/or when you are tweaking them in Photoshop, pick out a few spots and evaluate the contrast in each. In many photos, one area can have really good contrast, while another area does not. Not a good thing in architectural or landscape photography.

✔ **Understand how to manipulate an image in an image processing program.** If, indeed, one part of an image has better contrast than another, you can tweak the image using a number of options:

> In Raw format, use the Temperature, Tint, Exposure, Shadows, Brightness, and Contrast sliders in Photoshop's Camera Raw dialog box.

> If you shoot JPEG or TIFF, adjust your image by using Image➪ Adjustments➪Shadows/Highlights or Image➪Adjustments➪ Exposure.

✔ **Add *depth* (the capturing of shading and light to give the illusion of dimension) to your image when shooting and when editing it.**

- *To add depth when shooting:* Look for spots with a foreground, middle ground, and background. Experiment with your f-stop (see Chapter 11) so that you can blur your backgrounds to make your subject stand out so you can see its sides in perspective.

- *To add depth when editing:* Tweak the exposure, brightness, and/or contrast sliders when the image is in Raw format so that the contrast is natural looking with no large areas of white and/or black. See a before/after example in Figure 9-22. Doing this also corrects what you've done to your image previously. **Hint:** This feature works especially well when there's no color in your image.

Figure 9-22: Tweaking the contrast adds depth to your image.

TECHNICAL STUFF

Hi, ho, silver!

Museum and gallery curators refer to B&W photographic prints as *silver-gelatin prints*. Silver — an ingredient that ends up in the final print — is one of the materials in the process that makes a photograph come to life. A standard B&W photograph is produced in a darkroom, on photographic paper that's coated with gelatin and compounds containing silver — hence, the name. The cost of a silver-gelatin print isn't prohibitive despite its chemical composition.

So what do these terms mean?

- **Highlights:** Just think of going to a hair salon to have *highlights* — lighter shades — added to your hair. Figure 9-23 shows how dramatic highlights can be during late day in summer. Shoot to where the sun was after dusk to get beautiful silhouettes with highlighted backgrounds on partially cloudy days.

- **Midtones:** These are the tones that make up the middle shades of gray. When shooting barren landscapes devoid of sky, you can get a photo composed mostly of midtones, as in Figure 9-24.

- **Shadows:** Unlike the silhouette you cast on the sidewalk on a sunny day, the shadows in your digital image can include objects themselves. If your subject is between you and the light, the term *shadow* in photography refers not only to the shadow on the ground cast by your subject but also to the dark tones of the subject itself.

Figure 9-23: Capture highlights for drama.

Figure 9-24: Capture B&W midtones in landscapes.

Look — really look — at your surroundings in terms of identifying dark areas, light areas, and in between areas of B&W tone. Train your eye to read light and not just color.

Just like you can divide any photograph into thirds, horizontally or vertically, also pay attention to the tones of your photograph, from light to middle to dark. You can use a histogram to analyze and tweak your image's exposure:

1. **Choose Layer⇨New Adjustment Layer⇨Levels to create a layer in Photoshop to which these changes will apply.**

2. **Click OK in the next dialog box.**

   Your new layer is called *Levels 1,* as shown in the Layers palette. (Choose Window⇨Layers to see the Layers palette.) Also, a window like that shown in Figure 9-25 appears. This is your Levels adjustment dialog box, which includes the *histogram* (a map of the tones of your image).

3. **Click and drag the white and dark slider bars on each end so that they match up with the beginning and end of the curves. Then slide the middle point toward the area where the curves reach up the most vertically and click OK.**

   As you make changes, keep an eye on your image to be sure you don't overdo it.

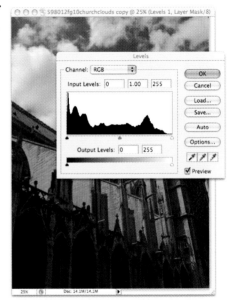

Figure 9-25: The "mountain range" shows the distribution of tonal values in your image.

The B&W world of Winogrand

Study the B&W photography of Garry Winogrand (www.getty.edu/art/collections/bio/a1834-1.html), who photographed the streets of America throughout his lifetime during the last century. In 1959, his photographs of street scenes and landscapes in Los Angeles and New York City captured everything from convertibles among skyscrapers enshrouded in haze to the long shadows of girls in miniskirts among offbeat surroundings depicting the good life, the desperate life, and an often bigger-than-life life.

Printing for best quality

After you compose your image and have a digital image to work with, it's time to make a print. Yeah!

You've walked the walk. Now it's time to talk the talk — the photography talk, that is. You got hold of a good printer, say an Epson Stylus Photo 2200, and now you're ready to take your show on the road.

The print of choice for museum quality is a silver-gelatin print. Digitally speaking, though, your silver-gelatin print is going to look better on some papers than others. I use enhanced matte because it's inexpensive, takes to the ink very well, and looks great behind glass. New papers come out all the time from rag to fine art to canvas. Try www.inkjetart.com to get all the latest about new papers and their compatibility with your printer and any special settings you might have to use. For more about printing the final product, see Chapter 17. To read about print mountings and framing, hop to Chapter 18.

You can name your B&W prints by the type of paper you use and/or the type of print process you've used to make them.

Julius Shulman: Creator of an eternal future

Architectural photographer Julius Shulman selected the best middle-of-the-last century buildings and homes — architecture by well-known architects, such as Richard Neutra and Frank Lloyd Wright — to capture on film. He has become well known for studying the components of the architecture he has shot. His iconographic photography not only teaches us about modernism though a wide angle lens but also about the futuristic optimism of the era's architecture. His photographs, set in reality of steel and glass, were so fine tuned that even today, they set the standard for the future.

Shulman photographed architecture by talented architects. (He met Richard Neutra in 1936 by showing him photographs that he had taken of Neutra's designs.) He studied the materials that he photographed: how the mid-century wall-to-ceiling glass reflected desert light, and when and where shadows from posts and beams made or broke a photograph.

By understanding the architecture in your community in the same way that Shulman did (by identifying buildings and homes you like and that are significant styles coveted by professionals — an arts-and-crafts home or an Edwardian), you can look at these and other similar structures that interest you. Scout them out and watch the light that shines upon them. Sometimes you'll find that dark shadows are beautiful at noon, repeating and perhaps falling in patterns opposing and/or juxtaposing the structure that cast them. Choose an architectural hot spot of beauty and look at it at different times of the day; then pick up your camera when the light is right and photograph it in B&W.

David Glomb, architectural photographer

With a rebirth of interest in modern architecture, a home-building boom, and new renovations of inner city neighborhoods, the media buzz has put architecture in the bull's eye of public interest. With home improvement first on everybody's list these days, taking pictures of a well-done home in the latest modern style has become big business, too. Magazines such as *Dwell* and *Architectural Digest* contain the works of the best-known architectural photographers.

One of these architectural photographers, David Glomb (photographer for the book *Palm Springs Modern)* makes his job evaluating light and shadow. "Shadows and light work for you or against you," Glomb says. "It's all in artistic interpretation. Every situation has its own unique characteristic."

Glomb shoots digitally when evaluating a location. He still prefers to use film, but uses his Canon a lot for producing his images for Web sites like Architecture Week (www.architecture week.com). His favorite camera is a Mamiya RZ 67, an electronically controlled 6 x 7cm film format camera that's an industry standard.

Night Art Photography

In This Chapter

▶ Eliminating blur in your nighttime photos

▶ Taking a clear photo at night without a flash or tripod

▶ Understanding film speed for nighttime shooting

▶ Shooting nighttime flash photos

▶ Identifying the modes and settings for nighttime photography

▶ Reading night light for spectacular shots

*P*icture the light of a lantern under an arch, stone tombstones lit by the moon, or the streaming red lights of a police car slicing the night sky. Images of the night have mystified and intrigued artists throughout time, especially with the advent of photography. After all, you have to have light to create a photograph, and nighttime is well, dark. However, with the tricks and techniques I show you in this chapter, you can tame the night and capture the denizens of the dark — at least in a photo. Not only can you capture what the night truly holds, but you can also use low-light situations to your creative advantage to craft shots that are fantasy-like, just like the magic of the night itself.

Taking a Shot in the Dark

Understandably, shooting at night has inherent problems — namely, the lack of available light. Without adequate light, color tones shift, becoming overly muted and neutral, as shown in Figure 10-1. To compensate for the low light, you can tweak the following settings by themselves or in combination, but each can introduce more problems:

✒ **Use a wider aperture.** This reduces your depth of field but allows more light to reach your camera's sensor.

✒ **Use a slower shutter speed.** Subjects are more easily blurred (unless you use a tripod or otherwise support the camera), but, again, more light reaches the sensor.

✔ **Use flash.** This can create uneven illumination and washed-out areas in your shot, but it provides the light necessary to capture the image.

✔ **Use a higher ISO/ASA.** This results in more noise/grain. Most of the time, you'll want to resist the urge to use an ISO setting higher than 400, even at night.

Photo credit: David Helán

Figure 10-1: Night photos are often filled with muted tones.

The art photographer that you are, however, will not be thwarted by such limitations. Right? Take all these tethers and turn them into creative advantages. The night is full of too many wonderful events and views to avoid simply because not much light is available.

Here's how to take a con of nighttime shooting and turn it into a pro, just like you (pun intended):

✔ **Use a slightly longer exposure time to show action.** A long exposure (longer shutter speed) captures "marching ants," neon lights, or a kid with a sparkler or fireworks drawing crazy scribbles of color in the night, as shown in Figure 10-2.

Figure 10-2: To shoot fireworks, use a tripod to get an unblurred shot.

When your camera must remain steady during a long exposure time, a tripod or other support is necessary. And tripods don't have to be giant, cumbersome beasts, either. Look for small, inexpensive collapsible ones that are very portable. ***Bonus:*** Small tripods are great for placing your camera near ground level so that you can shoot upward and with a long exposure, like the image shown in Figure 10-3. This shot, which I took in Manual mode, wouldn't be possible handheld because you'd get blur from camera shake. Read more about tripods in the later section, "Seek nighttime landscapes," and about Manual mode in "Creating a blur-free, flashless night photo."

Figure 10-3: Because this was taken with a tripod, this shot is blur-free.

Tripods aren't always necessary in night shooting, however. In the next section, "Creating a blur-free, flashless night photo," I discuss ways to shoot at night without a tripod.

✏ **Use a much longer exposure time to show motion.** A long exposure turns car lights or lighted amusement park rides into ribbons of color, as shown in Figure 10-4.

Photo credit: Roger Vail

Figure 10-4: Amusement park rides make great night photos.

✏ **Use a series of shorter exposures over time to show progression.** A series of shots like this can show the moon dancing across the night sky, as shown in Figure 10-5. See the sidebar, "Putting the moon to bed," later in this chapter, for more about this technique.

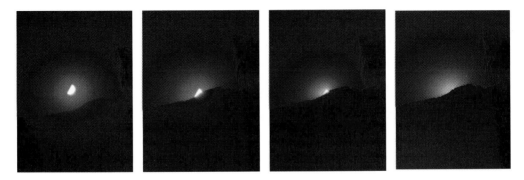

Figure 10-5: Follow the moon to bed.

✏ **Take advantage of soft, ambient lighting:** Look around for natural night lighting — streetlights, the moon and stars, or a lamp's soft glow, as in Figure 10-6.

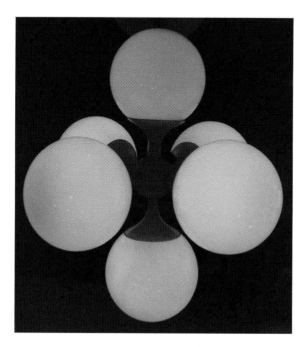

Figure 10-6: Look for ambient night lighting.

When you can find the perfect ambient night lighting, your camera's flash will ruin the effect. Don't use flash unless absolutely necessary. You might have to override your camera's default setting to disable the flash when shooting in the dark.

Creating a blur-free, flashless night photo

Once upon a time, taking pictures at night meant that you absolutely had to have a flash; if you didn't use a flash, you definitely needed a tripod. Back then (oh, sometime in the last millennium), the standard film speed was ISO 100. Fast black-and-white (B&W) film (400 ASA) appeared on the scene in the 1950s, and 400-speed film hit the market in the mid-1970s. Those faster films certainly helped with low-light and night photography exposure needs, as did even faster films that followed.

To photograph at night with a film camera and then scan the negatives, positives, or prints later, you should use film with an ISO rating of 400 or higher. If you set your camera to a low film speed (say ISO 100) or load it with 100 B&W/color film, you will get handheld blur when shooting at night, no matter how steady you are.

The higher the ISO speed, the noisier (digital) or grainier (film) an image will be. Using ISO 400 film gives you far less grain and more clarity with night pictures than ISO 800 film. When shooting digitally, the difference in noise between an ISO setting of 400 and ISO 800 is even greater for most cameras.

Figure 10-7 shows a pair of neon signs. The top image was taken with ISO 200 film. Because of the longer shutter speed required by the slow film, the image is somewhat blurry — an error that would put off many potential buyers. In comparison, the neon sign on the bottom was shot with a faster film — ISO 400 — resulting in a clearer shot.

Blur in nighttime photos has to have a specific focus, such as to show motion. If not, blur looks like (is) a technical error. When shooting neon signs as historical photos (and these images are marketable, by the way), you should have no blur because it would have no purpose. Blur serves a purpose only when it's indicating movement or time or when giving photos a mysterious quality.

If flashless night photos are your goal, you can achieve them without blur. The first thing to do in order to take a good night photo without a flash (and maybe without a tripod) is to scout out areas with enough light. After you find a good location with abundant streetlights and well-lit buildings, you're ready to practice. For example, shooting architecture and cityscapes at night gives you some pretty remarkable shots using only the light that's available.

Figure 10-7: Use higher ISOs at night to eliminate blur when you're not using a tripod.

Because buildings, gates, and bridges are usually well lit (and dramatically lit, too), they offer some great opportunities to shoot without a flash, as you can see from Figure 10-8.

Figure 10-8: Get handheld shots with no blur when ISO is set to 1600.

1. **Set your camera for the available light.**

   • **ISO**

   Load a film camera with ISO 400 film; set your digital camera to ISO 400.

   • **Exposure control**

   a. Set your SLR or dSLR camera to Av mode, the manual mode in which you can set your f-stop and your flash won't go off automatically.

   If you're using a point-and-shoot digital camera, turn off the flash first.

   b. Choose an f-stop of 8.

2. **Look for an object that has sufficient light around it.**

   Figure 10-9 shows St. Petersburg, Russia, at night, which is lit by ample amounts of ambient nighttime light. This image is scanned from an ISO 400 film negative.

3. **Press your camera's shutter release halfway to let your camera perform its autofocus chore.**

Figure 10-9: Use available nighttime light.

As dusk approaches nightfall and you find yourself losing light quickly, you'll have to reset your camera at some point because the auto modes don't do all that well with variable light, like the light you get at night. You also need to watch out for surrounding light sources — flood lights, street lights, and car lights.

Here are the basic exposure controls on your camera that can help you successfully shoot at night:

✓ **Shutter priority (Tv on most cameras):** This is an exposure mode that lets you control the time that the shutter of your camera remains open, while your camera automatically sets how wide the aperture opens to let just enough light in to give you a good picture. You can experiment at many different shutter speeds to get a different effect. If you want to turn car lights into ribbons of color, as in Figure 10-10, you would set shutter priority to a longer exposure time.

Figure 10-10: Choose shutter priority and use a longer exposure to capture traffic at night.

Don't be confused by what your camera's LCD screen or viewer is reading in terms of shutter speeds. $\frac{1}{250}$ is displayed as 250 on most cameras, whereas $\frac{1}{60}$, a smaller number but longer exposure, is displayed as 60.

✓ **Aperture priority (Av on most cameras):** This exposure mode lets you control the size of the aperture in your lens, while your camera automatically sets how long the shutter remains open to give your picture adequate light (exposure). When photographing at night, you don't want your lens open too wide because you'll get *white out* (when too much light hits your sensor or film causing a blazing white shadow to sweep across your frame), especially if your shutter is open a long time. This mode's great for close-ups of neon signs, but Tv is a better mode for everything else that dances in the night with less light.

Your camera's indicator light can help you get your light right. Don't shoot if it's red or blinking red. Wait for the green light as you look through the viewfinder and press your shutter halfway down. Then, press the shutter button all the way down to take your picture.

✓ **Manual mode (M on most cameras):** This mode lets you control both the aperture and the shutter speed, giving you nearly complete control over your exposure. After setting up the camera and switching to Manual mode, press the shutter button halfway down to autofocus and let the camera evaluate the existing light. In the viewfinder, you'll see (on most digital cameras that offer a true Manual mode) the small exposure scale, indicating whether your selected f-stop and shutter speed will produce an underexposed, normally exposed, or overexposed image.

Remember that *under* and *over* are relative terms when shooting at night. Some midrange digital cameras offer a Manual mode that doesn't let you set specific values for the aperture (f-stop) and shutter speed, but rather presents you with the exposure scale and lets you choose to underexpose or overexpose the shot.

✔ **Metering:** This is when your camera measures how much light is available in a portion of the frame of your picture. On some cameras, you'll get a green light indicating your shot is a go when you've got your settings set and have your finger pushing halfway down on the shutter release. The light meter of your camera works the same, whether it's day or night. But if you're using long shutter speeds and not using the shutter priority mode (which is all you can do on some point-and-shoots), your exposures will vary widely from too dark to too light to just right. But, hey, you've got a digital camera and you can keep trying until you get it right. Your camera should have a choice of metering zones.

When you set both your camera's aperture and shutter speed manually, *bracket* your shots — that is, take shots at progressive shutter speeds — until you get the exposure you want. Your camera might offer exposure bracketing as a setting. You can, for example, set the bracketing to take three shots at predetermined exposure intervals; then press the shutter release three times.

Night dreaming

Folks like art that takes them to a different place and time. Night photos can change a viewer's mood, perhaps even transport the viewer to an anywhere-but-here mentality. Okay, so it's not nighttime in Paris everywhere in the world, but when people look at a picture of nighttime in Paris, their thoughts can drift to being somewhere else, perhaps sipping coffee in a café in Paris at night. If Paris isn't someone's idea of a nice place to be, try Rome, New York City, or a late-night stroll in a plaza in Venice, as shown here.

Neon, neon, neon

If you dig neon like I do, here's the skinny on crafting some great night shots. Photograph any neon sign — or any neon for that matter, like the amusement park rides you see in this chapter by Roger Vail (we.got.net/~rvail/index.html), close up by setting your camera to Aperture priority mode, with an f-stop of 8 and an ISO speed of 400. The general auto setting will set your f-stop in this range, too, but you need to turn the autoflash off. These are good settings, but look around and if there's other light around you'll have to adjust a bit lower, say to f/5.6. Or you can up your ISO setting to 800 or higher (which risks adding too much digital noise).

Using fast film and high ISO settings

To be able to exploit wider aperture settings when shooting at night, pull out the fast film or set your digital camera to a fast ISO speed. Fast film and/or high ISO settings on your digital camera let you take night pictures without using your flash, which means you get more of the natural light from the surroundings in your picture.

If you have a dSLR, select the Av mode and choose an f-stop of f/6.7 or f/8. (For more about Av, see Chapter 9.) If you're using a digital point-and-shoot, set your camera to night mode or auto mode and set the ISO speed to 800. If you're using film, load it with ISO 400 or 800 film. In Figure 10-11, you can see the difference between shooting at ISO 80 and ISO 3200 on a dSLR.

Figure 10-11: Top: Clear image shot at low ISO. Bottom: Detail is lost at high ISO.

For a cool, grainy, mysterious effect, choose a setting above ISO 800 on your digital camera. Anything grainy, smoky, and/or empty (like empty chairs or shots with no subjects or one subject alone) will create a feeling of isolation, long considered a mainstay of humanity in many works in the art world. (For more about ideas for interesting photos, see Chapter 4.) As of this writing, Canon has a dSLR that you can crank the ISO up to 3200 (wow). See in Figure 10-12 how using a high ISO (1600 for this shot) introduces some artsy noise, which makes the picture more grainy and adds to the isolated effect.

Photoshop offers a variety of filters that you can use to reduce unwanted noise or grain in your image — and others that you can use to add noise or grain. Photoshop CS2 includes the powerful Reduce Noise filter, which works wonders on both *luminance noise* (light colored specks in your shadows and areas of solid color) and *digital noise* (specks of red, green, and blue scattered throughout the image). Of course, if you don't like digital noise in your images, it's generally easier and more effective to simply use a tripod and a lower ISO (perhaps 200) when shooting at night.

Figure 10-12: Use a high ISO for intentional noise.

Shooting with a flash

So when's the right time to use your flash at night for art photos? My advice: Take advantage of your flash *only* when you are capturing objects close-up.

Figure 10-13 shows that a flash was used to take pictures (really portraits) of Tikis in Honolulu. There was little light around for this shot so the flash provided almost all the Tikis' illumination. Sure, it's harsh light — bright and concentrated — but it can be a helpful art photo creation tool, creating a pretty cool effect, especially on the Tikis, which are made to look a little sinister in this instance.

Figure 10-13: Use harsh flash for an effect.

Here's another great way to be creative when shooting at night with a flash. You know those wretched red and green demon eyes you get when shooting people and animals with a flash? Take advantage of those night eyes and be aware of opportunities to capture animals of the night, like owls, frogs, or a cat on the prowl, as shown in Figure 10-14. (If your backyard is a bit short of wildlife, check out your local zoo.)

Photo credit: Victoria Archer

Figure 10-14: Sometimes green-eye is good.

Your camera's flash is a blessing when you're shooting in almost total darkness. Don't be afraid to use it if you need to, but keep in mind its limitations. (It reaches out only about 10 feet in front of you.)

Other Nighttime Art Opportunities

After you get a little practice (and confidence) shooting at night, here are some other great ways to think about photography in the dark.

Light your subject from beneath

Anything lit from beneath shows drama. If motion is involved, so much the better because your longer shutter speeds will exaggerate the motion to create some nifty other-worldly effects. Look for fountains as good examples of this, as in Figure 10-15. And don't forget how well lighted fountains photograph in B&W, too; read about B&W photography in Chapter 9.

Figure 10-15: Shoot fountains lit at night.

Shoot the moon

Here's a subject that's available most nights: the moon. Sure, it might hide beneath a cloud or change size, but photographing the moon — especially when it plays with the tiny droplets of water vapor illuminated by the clouds, as in Figure 10-16 — can provide you with some pretty stellar shots. (Get it, stellar?) If you can capture the moon reflecting off water or turn it slightly blue in Photoshop (more about that in Chapter 15) or by attaching a color filter to your camera (more about that in Chapter 11), you're on your way to a money shot.

Figure 10-16: Capture the (blue) moon with your own style.

How much light does a full moon give? Not a lot. A handheld digital camera exposure when shooting the moon will have blur unless

- The moon is on the horizon, big and full, and you're zooming directly into it so that it fills most of the frame.
- Other lights are around — bright ones — and a lot of them.
- You use a tripod.
- You use very fast film (above ISO 800) or set your digital camera to that ISO equivalent or higher.

Figure 10-17 shows two shots of the moon — one at ISO 400, which is a fairly fast film speed but still not fast enough to eliminate the blur from the moon high in the sky with minimal ambient lighting from a few neon signs. The second shot shows the moon captured with better sharpness (photo courtesy of NOAA).

Photo credit, right: National Oceanic and Atmospheric Administration

Figure 10-17: The moon clear and not-so-clear depends on how you shoot it.

Be quick when shooting the moon:

- When the moon is at that perfect place — the horizon — it doesn't stick around all that long.

- The amount of light from the moon decreases rapidly as it rises from the horizon to the sky.

Putting the moon to bed

When the moon comes up and out, wolves howl (that is, if you live in the outback). You'll do some howling, too, when you discover the photo ops that this celestial body offers as seen through your lens. A few tricks of the trade are in order here, as the moon, whether it's a sliver in the sky or half or full, is a fascinating little rascal:

- Check out a Web site (www.shetline. com/java/moonphase/moonphase. html) that offers a moon phase calendar so that you know when to shoot. There's nothing worse than wanting to shoot the moon and finding out it's not out there yet (what astronomers call a *new moon*).

- Watch where the moon moves in the sky a few days before you shoot. Look for where

it rises and sets and scout out a space where you can catch all of that in glorious detail. If the weather's good a day or two later, return to that same spot to shoot it.

- Use a tripod, press your shutter halfway down to get it in focus, and then move your camera (still holding down the shutter release halfway) to where you want it. Shoot at a lower f-stop and with your lens set at a focal length of 90mm or greater. Use your camera's timer or a cable release for the clearest shot.

Tip: If you're shooting the moon going to bed, be quick, as it settles into the horizon in seconds. If you want a series of shots of the moon slipping down, shut off your timer and snap a picture every two or three seconds.

Making an instant tripod

Many times you won't have a tripod with you at night. In that case, you have to make do. And there's not always a flat appropriate-height surface close by (like a ledge or a car). Here are some tricks to help you to steady your camera when you make your body the camera's tripod:

↙ Hold only your camera (put all your bags, and so on, down).

↙ Keep your arms (elbows) close to your body.

↙ Lean against something stable, like a wall or a tree, if possible.

↙ Keep your legs some distance apart.

↙ Press the shutter release button slowly with your index finger, moving it very slowly.

↙ Press the shutter release after a long exhale — that's when your body is most still.

Remember: Even if you don't have a tripod, you can improvise with what's around you. Look for a stable and level place to set your camera when taking a photo: newspaper stands, walls, street fixtures, crates, or tables.

Seek nighttime landscapes

Landscapes at night offer a different take on a standard shot, as shown in Figure 10-18. For sharp nighttime landscapes, experiment with the higher aperture range that your digital camera offers: that is, f/16 or f/22. Don't forget to make the moon your ally when shooting at night, too, both for the light it provides as well as being an important element when composing your shot.

Figure 10-18: The moon is your friend when it comes to composing shots at night.

If you want a clear shot without graininess in your image, bring along a small tripod when you're shooting at night. Think of this three-legged beast as your assistant who holds your camera steady so you get no blur.

1. **Set your camera on either a tripod or another surface that's steady (like a ledge or a rock).**

   Make sure your tripod is stable and relatively level. Double-check through the viewfinder that your image is level and adjust the tripod accordingly the best you can.

2. **Take your shot via the camera's timer or use a cable release so that you don't shake the camera when pushing the shutter-release button.**

Use reflections

Always look for water where there are lights. Water, with its inherent reflectivity, gives you a double chance to show off the beauty of the night, as in Figure 10-19. This amusement park ride delights twice over: once with its bright neon lights and again with its water reflection.

Seek out shadows and weather

Shadows at night can be harsh and egregious, making for a good opportunity to create a study in lines and patterns. Look for lit wrought iron gates and fences or heavily backlit scenes like in the left image of Figure 10-20. Look for weather nighttime opportunities, too. For example, get out and shoot at night (with ambient light, like from a streetlamp) when it's snowing — you'll get some great blur, especially when using slower shutter speeds. Lightning at night is very dramatic (see the right image of Figure 10-20), but I'm not encouraging you to put yourself in harm's way.

Photo credit: Roger Vail

Figure 10-19: Show off the night with reflections.

Photo credit: left, Leonardo Faria; right, Kevin F. Leroux

Figure 10-20: Strong shadows and lightning at night provide great photo ops.

Achieving Creative Results When Shooting

In This Chapter

▶ Identifying the modes and settings on your digital camera

▶ Adjusting your focus and light metering for more interesting shots

▶ Making flowing water look like silk

▶ Taking pictures with long shutter speeds

▶ Using camera filters in your photo art

*I*n Hollywood, you think of special effects as Jurassic Park stuff or maybe Harry Potter zooming about, playing a game of Quidditch. In magic, a special effect is pulling a rabbit out of a hat. In math, a special effect is that the digits of multiples of nine add up to nine. In traditional photography, you might think of a special effect as water flowing in a stream, looking as if it were billows of steam. Special effects, really, are what you want them to be. After all, they're what's inside your head — what ultimately comes out when you set and focus your camera on something — anything, invented or otherwise.

My definition of special effects (as I use this term in this chapter for the purposes of creating digital art photography), however, encompasses using particular measures — tweaking camera modes, using time lapse, employing video techniques, and so on — while shooting photographs that achieve certain creative results. Using these techniques are the sort of special effect this chapter covers. If you want to add Jurassic Park dinosaurs to your photographs, you have to use Photoshop.

Tweaking Automatic Modes and Settings to Achieve Creative Results

Capturing an image of a unique home at dusk, your best friend up close with a blurred background, a gorgeous landscape, a flower, or a tennis player on the court requires only a simple move of your camera's modes. In this section, I show you how to take the traditional uses of these modes and then bend the rules to create some fantastic art shots.

Digital cameras are a funny lot. Some come with all the nuts and bolts you could possibly need to take a shot that's not only interesting but also mind-boggling. Others come with an odd assortment of stuff that can take comparable shots after you fool around with them to see how they work.

Take, for instance, the point-and-shoot models — yes, some are very powerful (5MP or more) — that have no manual modes. (*Manual modes* allow you to change the f-stop or shutter speed yourself in the little knobs at the top of the body, within the menu on the LCD screen. These controls open your photographic world so that you can use a multitude of aperture openings and shutter speeds without the limitations of the point-and-shoots. For more on f-stops and shutter speeds, see Chapter 6.) Tweaking with a point-and-shoot, where everything is preset, can be done but only by tricking the camera — say, setting your shutter speed to stay open for a second but being limited to only shooting in a dark space. Remember that if the shutter is left open for a long time, no matter what your aperture is, your exposure will turn to white because of too much light.

So the modes do it for you, right? You really don't need anything but the auto settings to be a great photographer? Well, in some ways, how well they really do work is pretty incredible. But much of the time, you want more — more setting choices, that is — especially the more you photograph.

With film and digital point-and-shoot cameras, you have many automatic settings from which to choose that do affect your *f-stops* (how wide your lens opens) and *shutter speeds* (how long the shutter stays open).

Every time you set your camera in an auto mode, it calculates an f-stop and shutter speed.

You can set both your shutter speed and your f-stop manually using the M mode. When doing so, you'll also want to refer to the camera's light meter to make sure that the exposure is correct. Your camera will use the EV — the exposure value — to let you know if there's too much or too little light. Then you can adjust the f-stop or shutter speed to get the exposure that you want.

REMEMBER

On some point-and-shoot models, the only way to adjust the shutter speed is via choices within a limited set of values that are controlled as a setting. They can't be adjusted as a mode (by turning the knob on the body of your camera). Most camera modes are on the external portion of your camera. Look for a knob (as shown in Figure 11-1) with tiny pictures of each mode drawn on it. Sometimes this portion of your camera is called a *programmed image control zone*.

Figure 11-1: This knob shows the camera's settings.

You can tweak any of your digital camera's settings for special effects, but first you have to introduce yourself to them. The following list describes the modes on your digital camera, explaining how you would traditionally use each and giving you hints for tweaking those modes to achieve a different type of effect:

- **Auto (A):** Use this mode in places with good lighting, sun or shade, during the daylight hours and in shots with little or no action. Put masculine shadows (for a masculine effect) over subjects by shooting into the sun.

- **Portrait:** This mode is perfect when you want a clear shot of your subject's face up close. Figure 11-2 shows a woman photographed in portrait mode. Soften the look of animals by shooting them up close in portrait mode.

Photo credit: Kevin Kirschner

Figure 11-2: Use portrait mode to take, um, portraits.

- **Landscape:** When you're shooting to the horizon, with lots of distance to cover and you want it all to come out sharp, use the landscape mode.

- **Close-up or macro:** For those times when you want one or two objects in focus and everything else in the background/foreground blurred, the macro mode is your friend. You can teach botany with this handy feature on many camera models. Figure 11-3 shows clearly a flower's stigma, style, anther, and filament.

Figure 11-3: Use macro mode for tight close-ups.

✔ **Action:** This mode uses higher shutter speeds to stop action with little or no blur. Figure 11-4 shows a pitcher in action. Action mode will give you a shot that isn't blurred when you're moving, also.

Photo credit: Kevin Kirschner

Figure 11-4: Use action mode to stop action.

✔ **Night:** This mode will come in handy when you're photographing a scene at night without a flash. Remember to keep the camera very still to avoid a blurry photo — this mode generally uses a slower shutter speed. Figure 11-5 shows the added effect of wet streets shot at night. Shoot at night when the streets are wet for extra-glimmery photos.

Figure 11-5: Use night mode to take advantage of low light.

This list briefly describes the main settings that you need to tweak to achieve great effects when shooting:

✔ **Exposure compensation values:** Increases or decreases the exposure, making the image lighter or darker. Generally use the *default* setting (what your camera automatically has when you turn it on). For stained glass indoors backlit by bright sunlight, drop it down by –1 EV for bright colors, as shown in Figure 11-6.

Figure 11-6: Adjust exposure compensation values.

✔ **White balance:** Compensates for the temperature (color) of the existing light to prevent an unwanted color tint to the photo. This is something Photoshop can also do. Many models of digital cameras have a white balance setting for different types of light, both indoors and outdoors. See Chapter 8 for a description of what the settings do. A camera set at automatic can sense each of the light types — fluorescent, tungsten, and sunlight — but you can set to the daylight mode inside with fluorescent lights on and get no correction, that is yellow, in your shot.

✔ **ISO:** Increasing the ISO setting alters the sensitivity of the camera's sensor to capture more light quickly — crystal clear if you set it low (100 or 200) with a greater chance of blur in low light, and grainy if you set it high (above 400). If you shoot for special effects, anything goes here; you just have to experiment. Use high ISO speeds like 1600 to pick up reflected color that happens in low-light situations.

✔ **Color:** Some cameras offer a choice between sRGB and Adobe RGB as the color space, and some also offer faux sepia and black-and-white (B&W) settings. Use Adobe RGB if you'll be working in an image editing program; sRGB if not. Shoot into the sun at dusk in black-and-white mode for mysterious shadows and wild light, as in Figure 11-7. Chapter 9 covers shooting in B&W.

Figure 11-7: Use the color setting to shoot in B&W.

✔ **Focus zone:** Uses the designated area of the image as the point for autofocus. Adjust the focus point if the subject is off center in the frame. Use low f-stop settings to get a focused off-center subject and a blurry background.

✔ **Exposure metering setting:** This changes how much light your camera uses for a shot. Most digital and film cameras use the lighting throughout your whole frame. Some digital camera models let you reset this so that only the light from the center (or just a spot in the center) is used. For example, use this for a clear shot of the moon. Set your camera to center-weight at night and put something moving and well-lit in the center of your frame — it will look as if it's wrapped in cellophane. The flag (taken at night without a flash) in Figure 11-8 was shot with the focus zone set for center-focus, the gathering place for all the light.

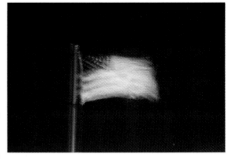

Figure 11-8: Use a center-weight exposure.

Playing with Light

You can trick the light meter of your camera to enhance your photo by giving it better color and more depth. Usually your camera assesses what it sees in terms of light while you press your shutter halfway down. If you keep holding it, the camera will remember the first place you took the reading.

You can press your shutter halfway down to set the autofocus and exposure, and then point your camera in another direction while you keep holding the button halfway down. You might, for example, set the camera while aiming at a brightly lit area, and then actually shoot while aimed at an area more dimly lighted, thereby producing an underexposed photo.

To create a special effect from how your camera perceives light, press the shutter halfway down in one place and move to another place to shoot a picture, like this:

1. **Set your camera to auto mode.**

2. **Turn off the flash.**

3. **Sit by a window.**

4. **Point your camera out the window so that your entire frame is in daylight.**

5. **Press the shutter release halfway down.**

6. **Point the camera inside the room to where there is some color or a little light (less than what was out the window).**

7. **Press the shutter button all the way down.**

Congratulations! You just messed around with your camera's light meter.

Experiment with the light meter and the settings and modes (see the preceding section) in as many ways as you can to see what your camera can and can't do. The images in Figure 11-9 show that by focusing on a spot in the shade and then moving your camera to shoot your composition as you want it framed, your image is brightened up significantly. The image on the left in Figure 11-9 is not as bright as the image on the right.

Figure 11-9: Play with the light meter to brighten images.

Come Get 'Yer Effects Here!

In the previous sections of this chapter, I explain how to manipulate your camera's settings, modes, and light meter (tools used generally to achieve a "good" photograph) to achieve artsy effects your viewers will find unexpected and wonderful. But there are other ways to capture special effects while shooting photos — including using time lapse and special filters. I show you some of these tricks in this section.

Double exposures

Double exposures are a funny lot. Love 'em and have your camera snapping two or more shots on the same frame of film. A *double exposure* occurs when your film camera takes two pictures without advancing the film.

Figure 11-10 shows a double exposure shot at dusk without a tripod of birds flying out of a palm tree. To combine multiple digital images to create a double exposure, you have to use an image editing program, such as Photoshop. See Chapter 13 for more about combining images digitally.

Figure 11-10: Combine two image imprints within the same shot.

In order for the frame (which was exposed to light twice because the shutter opened to take the two shots that were imprinted on it) not to be overexposed — that is, turn white — set your exposure compensation to –1 (see Chapter 9).

You can also take triple exposures and more. It's best to do this at dusk or at night, though, because one frame can only take so much light before it turns white.

Panoramic shots

A *panorama* is generally constructed from multiple images taken side by side (or up and down) that are then stitched together in the darkroom or digitally. Figure 11-11 shows a sample panorama. There are film cameras available that specialize in panoramas, rotating the lens to expose a long strip of film, but when shooting digitally, you need to combine exposures in an image editing (or dedicated panorama) program. I recommend using a tripod and manual exposure when capturing frames to use in a panorama, and allowing at least 15 percent overlap on each side for proper alignment.

Figure 11-11: Use a wide angle lens or zoom to 100mm or more to grab a vast area of land and/or sea.

Panoramic shots are not only landscapes (horizontal) but can also be vertical shots, like architectural and sculptural elements. For more about panoramas, see Chapter 13.

Reflections

Reflections offer your viewers two ways to see the world: the real image and the one that's reflected. The distortion of a subject can vary, depending on the reflective material. You've probably seen reflections on water, from the almost mirror effect it can produce in the right light when there is no wind, to interesting distortions on a sea of light chop. Other materials reflect light, too, as shown in the coffee pot in Figure 11-12.

Second on the reflection front is the reflection of glass. To be sure, there are the ins and outs of light bouncing through, around, and among glass windows, doors, and panels. Last is the glory of reflection, that of a string of mountains reflected on the water in Figure 11-13.

Zooming while shooting

Zooming while shooting can be a tricky proposition, but the effects are unreal — literally. Figure 11-14 shows the sense of motion created by zooming with the shutter open. (Don't look at it too long, or you'll get motion sickness.)

Photo credit: Rebekka Guðleifsdóttir

Figure 11-12: A chrome coffee pot offers interesting reflections.

Figure 11-13: Nature reflections are peaceful.

To engage in zoom play — that is, moving your zoom in (and out if you want) while shooting — you gotta be quick. Set your shutter speed to at least 1/30. To do this, shoot in Tv mode and set your shutter speed by cranking the dial on your camera.

Figure 11-14: Zoom while shooting for wild effects.

Intentional lack of focus

Have you ever tried to turn off your autofocus? Seems like we've become so enamored with it that we forget that we don't have to use it. Experiments conducted by creating blur can create results that are much like a soft pillow. Matching a pillows' softness in Figure 11-15 are the toddler's eyes and face that are just slightly out of focus. Soft focus can be an extremely flattering effect, especially as we age. You might also want the camera to be slightly out of focus to create a great background into which

Figure 11-15: Slightly burred features speak softly to the viewer.

you can drop another image. Take a slightly blurred photo of a building, crop out everything except the blurry building, and *voilá!*

Intentional underexposure/overexposure

You can read tons about how to properly expose a shot. However, you can create some really cool shots by breaking those standards — purposefully under- or overexposing for a great in-camera art effect.

- ✒ **Underexposed:** Compare the two shots shown in Figure 11-16. On the left is a photo that would be good had it been properly exposed. As it is, the detail in the image is lost because of a lack of contrast. On the right, however, slightly underexposing the image allows the subject to remain a dark mystery and prevents the sky from becoming featureless white.

- ✒ **Overexposed:** Compare the two images in Figure 11-17. On the left, overexposing has reduced the detail in the photo's subject, the hotel, and allowed the sky to become a featureless void, neither of which makes this a particularly compelling image. On the right, overexposing minimizes much of the detail of the house in the background, allowing the detail of the subject, the foliage, to remain prominent. (You might also find that when shooting greenery, slightly overexposing helps you capture more detail.)

Figure 11-16: Sometimes underexposure hurts (left), and sometimes it helps (right).

Photographing in the direct sun with long shutter speeds will make your photos look as if they've been hit by a snowstorm (which washes out the subject).

Figure 11-17: Overexposing can eliminate detail (left) or highlight part of an image (right).

For a special effect, slow down the shutter speed (on dSLR or SLR cameras) so that the lens stays open for almost one-half second. This can produce some interesting effects.

Making flowing water turn to silk

Shots that have flowing water turn to silk — on rocks, over bumps and curves, and through tunnels — are the shots that are always popular. To get flowing water looking like flowing velvet, you need to film in low light:

- At dusk or dawn
- In fog or in winter
- When the sun is low on the horizon
- In a shady spot

Take a walk to a fountain during one of these days and bring your tripod. You'll find an adventure in shutter speed awaiting you.

dSLR models and SLR models offer time exposure using the Tv mode, as I explain here.

Load your SLR film camera with ISO 100 speed film or set your dSLR camera to ISO 100 or 200.

1. **Find a place by a body of moving water that's flowing with bubbly excitement where it's shady — or better yet, at dusk when the sun has just fallen below the horizon.**

2. **Frame your picture.**

   Set your camera on a tripod and compose the image.

3. **Set your camera to Tv mode, the shutter priority mode.**

4. **Set your camera to a slow shutter speed — say, ¹⁄₆₀ of a second.**

5. **Set your camera's timer so that the camera doesn't shake when you try to push the shutter button.**

   Look for the little clock icon/button at the top of your camera.

6. **Release your shutter and wait for the camera to take a picture.**

7. **Reset your camera to a slower shutter speed — say, ¹⁄₃₀ of a second.**

8. **Repeat Steps 4 through 6, using a slower shutter speed each time, until the flowing water looks like velvet.**

   The result is shown in Figure 11-18, which was captured with a shutter speed of 0.6 seconds at f/22.

Use low light when filming anything with your shutter speed open longer than ¹⁄₆₀ of a second.

Figure 11-18: Find a shady spot, and you can make flowing water look like velvet.

For art photos that are correctly exposed, rather than calculating a shutter speed *and* an aperture, let your camera do some of the work by choosing the Av or Tv mode. You select an aperture and the camera picks an appropriate shutter speed (Av) or you select your desired shutter speed and let the camera determine the best aperture (Tv).

Using filters

Camera filters help make a better picture when you are shooting during the day because the sun's glare can affect both the color and the details of your subjects and backgrounds. dSLR and SLR cameras have a ring around which you screw the filter onto your lens.

There are dozens of types of filters, each with a specific function:

- **UV/skylight:** Ultraviolet (UV) filters get rid of the haze and UV light that your sensor or film picks up but that you can't see. This is the most common kind of filter that most professionals have with them at all times.

- **Polarizing:** These filters reduce the sun's glare. They also help if you're shooting through glass. These filters give improved clarity and color balance to your photographs. Figure 11-19 compares an image taken with a polarizing filter (on the top) and no filter (on the bottom).

Figure 11-19: Compare using a polarizing filter (top) and no filter (bottom).

- **Neutral density:** These filters reduce the amount of light that gets to your lens. In the earlier section, "Making flowing water turn to silk," I discuss how there's a period around dusk where the light is just right so that you can keep your shutter open a bit longer. Using this filter blocks out some of the light so that you can keep your shutter open longer — long enough for water to turn to silk in broad daylight!

- **Close-up filters:** Also known as a magnifying glass that you can attach to your lens, close-up filters are pretty nifty and cheap, but the quality can be dicey, with blur and whatnot.

- **Color conversion:** These filters stop certain wavelengths of light from reaching your film or sensor, thus changing the color in your entire photo. These are actually colored glass that you put over the lens of your dSLR or SLR camera to change the color of your photo.

  Yellow: Yellow works with the sun's color to make your shots look more vivid (see the leftmost image in Figure 11-20). If you live near L.A. (like I do) or some other hazy metropolis and you want a landscape that frees up some of the yellow haze, this filter will help.

  Blue: Blue enhances the sky and/or water to the way they'd appear in a dream. Use the filter to let the blues from the lens soak in to both sky and water by looking for rays of sunlight striking directly on water and shooting so part of the sun's reflection on the water is evident (center image in Figure 11-20). This causes a part of the water to turn yellow and white, adding more tones of color to the enhanced blues that are everywhere else in your shot.

  Red: A red filter heats up your environment, kind of like if you were living on an angry red planet. The rightmost image in Figure 11-20 shows the Mars-like landscape that a red filter can provide.

Color conversion filters can be improvised by using transparent or translucent Mylar or plastic — the same stuff that some report covers are made from. You can get this stuff at an office supply store.

Figure 11-20: Photographic filters change the actual light that hits your camera's sensor or film, unlike filtering later in Photoshop.

✔ **Special effects:** These filters come in all types of configurations and colors. There are pop filters of bright red, blue, and green that you can use separately or together. There are also *soft-diffused* filters, which change the light to create effects such as fog.

Diffusion: Pictures taken with diffusion are usually used on shots of women, but you can use them on anything you want to soften. For instance, you can soften even the hardest metal and dark colored subjects taken at midday with a diffusion filter.

Use a woman's stocking over your camera lens for a similar effect to a diffusion filter.

Infrared: An infrared filter gives images a surreal, other-worldly quality, as shown in Figure 11-21. The filter itself is really dark — to block all visible light — so when you use film, it has to be a special film that can record the image. To see whether you can shoot infrared with your digital camera, point a television remote control at the lens, press and hold down the shutter button, and take a picture. If you can see the light in the photo, you can probably take infrared images with an appropriate filter (such as a Hoya R72). You can tweak your digital camera by bumping up your ISO setting to 800 or above and bumping up your exposure compensation to at least +1 EV. If your camera doesn't offer that level of control over the settings, try the Night Portrait mode for the longest exposure.

Photo credit: © 2005 Robert Contreras. Reprinted with permission.

Figure 11-21: Use an infrared lens for an other-worldly quality.

Star: This type of filter makes it look as though points of light radiate outward from any light source in your shot. A star filter makes any scene more glittery and glamorous, as shown in Figure 11-22.

Figure 11-22: Make your photos glitter by using a star filter.

Part III
Photoshop Art: Using Software to Enhance or Create Art Photos

The 5th Wave   By Rich Tennant

©RICHTENNANT

CLAY

"I couldn't say anything – they were in here with that program we bought them that encourages artistic expression."

In this part . . .

This part covers all things Photoshop. For the lowdown on repairing or jazzing up old photos, Chapter 12 is your guide to Photoshop tools and techniques for restoring faded color and eliminating the ravages of time, like creases, scratches, and dust. Peruse Chapter 13 to see how to use Photoshop to merge images into a single, giant photograph. Chapter 14 presents Photoshop layers, which are a great tool for creating digital art photography. And because Photoshop offers so many creative and tempting filters, I dedicate a whole chapter here to them (Chapter 15).

Adding New Life to Old Photos

In This Chapter

▶ Spotting the artistic value of old photographs

▶ Using Photoshop touch-up tools

▶ Creating sepia tones in historic photos

Climb into a time machine by going up into your attic and pulling down those dusty old photos. There's gold up in them thar attics. What you can do in Photoshop with the old photos you find — tweak them for color, repair them, make them sepia tone, and so on — is nothing less than putting your relative's (or someone else's unknown relative's) past into the present and making it crystal clear. In this chapter, I cover auto and manual tweaks as well as adjustments to black-and-white (B&W) and color photos.

Taking an old photo and scanning and repairing it saves its life and can extend its life far into the future. Paper and film fade and are fragile. Conserving old photos helps ensure that these histories and precious images are around for generations to come.

Using Automatic Adjustments to Refresh Older Prints

Retro-based art — including photographs — is a saleable commodity because lots of folks want some piece of the past. Although recycling formal portraits is good, snapshots are just fine, especially if they contain nostalgic elements.

After you pull out your old photos and scan them, you can use the following Auto commands in Photoshop to try to refresh them and make them more clear and colorful. You can find these tools via Image➪Adjustments. These adjustments are one-size-fits-all; that is, you don't have any sliders or options to mess with.

✔ **Auto Contrast:** Use this option when you want to adjust contrast only — that is, make dark pixels darker and light pixels lighter. It does nothing with the color of your image but can really liven up a B&W shot. Figure 12-1 shows the improvement you can get with some images using the Auto Contrast option.

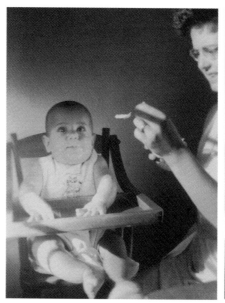 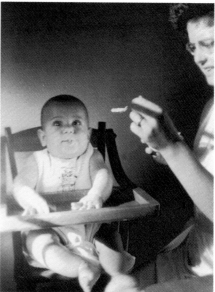

Figure 12-1: Try using Auto Contrast to improve the tonal range in your photograph.

✔ **Auto Levels:** Use this option to cut away some of the pure white and pure black that your photo might have from under- or overexposure. After that, it readjusts the blackest black and whitest white of your photo to even out the contrast. The best part of this command is that it also works on color photos, working especially well with those that have good uniformity of color (lots of shades) so that Photoshop can find the shades to make each shade distinguishable from the other. (See the upcoming example of using Auto Levels.)

✔ **Auto Color:** Use this command when you want to neutralize your mid-tones. Say you have a red cast over your entire print: Using Auto Color removes the excess red. Use the Auto Color correction to specify shadows and highlights that you want to reduce.

- *For B&W conversion photos:* Choose Enhance Monochromatic Contrast.

- *For color:* Choose Enhance Per Channel Contrast.

  For more about color tweaking with this tool, see "Using Manual Adjustments for Fine-Tuning."

You can also have Auto Color find dark and light colors as well as keep what you set as a default mode.

Over the years, age can flatten colors in a print. You've undoubtedly seen the yellowing effect that really happens fast with newspaper. With photos, it happens slower (the paper is better), but the deterioration still results in a yellow midtone. Photoshop can sense the plethora of yellows and fix this imbalance by adding blues via the Auto Color command. Mind you, I'm not talking about repairing damage here (later sections deal with that) but rather fading and color shift.

Whose photo is this?

There are many laws governing the world of photography telling us about the *fair use* of an image after it's produced. In a nutshell (and not substituting for consultation with a legal professional), regarding photos, fair use refers to the rights a photographer has and the details of permissions that someone else — who wants to use and/or reproduce the photo in question — must agree to that protects the rights of the picture-taker. If you have any questions about the old photograph(s) you have in hand, discuss them with your attorney. Although this issue can get complex, here's some general information that can help you decide whether you want to use a photo as saleable art:

- **A photo you didn't take:** If you have a photograph you bought at an antique store or found rummaging through your old photos that's decades old and has no identifiable subjects (or if it's a photo of yourself taken by someone else), the original owner of that photo is not likely to be able to identify it (or

would even want to). Use these photos at your own discretion and/or talk to a copyright lawyer if you're considering selling it or publishing it.

- **A photo that you took of someone else:** The same rules apply for old photo portraits as for current ones: You need to have the subject sign a release. If you've got photos of deceased relatives that you or someone in your family photographed and that you want to publish and/or sell, you should contact all the estate heirs of the relative to get permission.

- **A photo taken before 1923:** If you've got a photo that was taken before 1923, it's pretty assured that you can republish it or sell it regardless of who's in the picture or who took it. Again, this is not set in stone, and there are situations where this may not be the case, so talk to a copyright attorney.

See the improvement after using the Auto Levels adjustment on this vintage photo, as shown before (left) and after (right) in Figure 12-2. It looks great now because the yellow is gone and there's more contrast in the midtones. (Take a look at the browns in the hair in both pictures, and you'll see more shades of brown and more detail).

Figure 12-2: Period photo before and after using Auto Levels in Photoshop.

If you don't like the results of your tweaking, choose Edit➪Undo (or press ⌘+Z/ Mac or Ctrl+Z/Windows) and try again using a different command or technique.

Using Manual Adjustments for Fine-Tuning

You can also tweak parts of your picture manually to fine-tune specific areas of an image. To the rescue come Photoshop's Dodge and Burn tools. Use these tools to lighten, darken, and refine details in an image. Photoshop also has filters that you can use, such as Despeckle (Filter➪Noise➪Despeckle) and Dust & Scratches (Filter➪Noise➪Dust & Scratches) to minimize grain in an old photo.

Dodge

Use the Dodge tool of the Tools palette to lighten something dark in a photo. You can choose to lighten midtones, highlights, or shadows. Too, you can choose the exposure you want by typing in a value in the Exposure box at the top of the Photoshop window. (It appears after you click the Dodge tool of the Tools palette.)

When you click and hold down the Dodge tool, a drop-down menu presents you with a couple of other tools: the Burn tool and the Sponge tool. Read about them in upcoming sections.

Finding an old B&W surfing photo from the '60s is a jewel from the sea, but tweaking it carefully using all aspects of the Dodge tool is indeed a surfing safari. I do that in these steps, to show you what you can achieve with this handy tool that makes dark areas lighter:

1. **Choose a picture to tweak and study it, pinpointing the areas where you want to see more highlights.**

   For example, look for areas with too much black shadow, like that under and around the surfer's body in Figure 12-3.

Figure 12-3: Use the Dodge tool to lighten dark areas.

2. **On the Options bar, select a brush tip size that's appropriate for the shadow area you need to lighten.**

   For this example, I use a master diameter of about 75 px (pixels).

3. **Create a duplicate layer by choosing Layer➪Duplicate Layer.**

   Creating a new layer keeps your original from getting messed up, which enables you to go back to the original image layer, should your corrections go horribly wrong. For more about layers, see Chapter 14.

4. **To begin, choose Shadows for Range and an exposure of about 20% if your photo is too dark.**

5. **Brush over the dark spots of the picture. Rub (click and drag) around the dark spots until you see more distinction among the shades.**

   If you see a little too much white, don't worry because you'll correct that in a later step. Or if you go way overboard, fade what you did by using the Edit➪Fade command. In the surf photo, I use all size brushes and switch options often to get the maximum contrast between the surfboard and water, and the water and white caps. I'm looking for drama here, maximum splash with lighter gray tones and good distinction between water and surfer/surfboard.

   Feel free to change the brush size and switch back and forth from shadows to highlights to midtones in the Range drop-down menu. And use different exposures by typing in different values in the Exposure Value box next to the Range options.

6. **Open your Layers palette by choosing Window⇨Layers.**

7. **Slide the Opacity tool until you get an image you like (one with more highlights to cancel out the dark shadows and increase the distinction among shades, or *contrast*).**

The results in Figure 12-4 are easy to see because I chose a photo that had many areas of darker tones that needed slight lightening.

Figure 12-4: Using the Dodge tool can really liven a vintage photo.

In Photoshop, some command names (in a menu) are followed by ellipsis points. This just means that when you select one of these, a dialog box opens requesting that you choose some manual options. But just over a dozen of Photoshop's filters do *not* have ellipsis points after their names in the Filter menu. Photoshop automatically applies those filters to your image with preset values.

Burn tool

The opposite of the Dodge tool, the Burn tool darkens. With the Burn tool, which is also found in the Tools palette, you can darken highlights, midtones, and shadows and also change the exposure of the tool while you work. All these options are located on the Options bar and appear after clicking the Burn tool from the Tools palette.

On the left in Figure 12-5 is a faded image of a plane, faded especially where the plane has been damaged (see image on the left). By using the Burn tool, I can darken the damaged parts of the plane so that they have better contrast among the tones (see image on the right).

Figure 12-5: Improved a faded image (left) with the Burn tool (result, right).

Smart Sharpen/Unsharp Mask commands

Tweaking using the Unsharp Mask filter (Filter⇨Sharpen⇨Unsharp Mask) or the Smart Sharpen (Sharpen⇨Smart Sharpen) filter — new in Photoshop CS2 — requires that you set values that cause the pixels to change color so that your picture loses some of its blur. For the finest distinction of the edges, choose Lens Blur from the Remove drop-down menu of the Smart Sharpen dialog box. Unsharp Mask is the choice for sharpening in Photoshop CS, but it doesn't let you control the sharpening of the highlights and shadows individually.

Sponge tool

The Sponge tool (located on the Tools palette) changes an area of your photo's color saturation. You can saturate the color or desaturate by any percentage (called the *flow* in the menu bar).

Figure 12-6 shows marching cadets in red (and leaves a viewer nostalgic for old Kodachrome film). The picture, scanned from a positive, was taken in the '60s. The only part of the picture I want to change is the bright blue car in the background (image on the top), which I can do with the Sponge tool. Wiping the car with the Sponge tool desaturates it so that it blends in better with the gray tones of the building in the background (image on the bottom). Using the Sponge tool provides the perfect tweak for an interesting picture — not too much so as to destroy its integrity and period-feel, yet enough so that the car doesn't distract as much from the marching cadets.

Figure 12-6: A small tweak with the Sponge tool keeps a photo's integrity while improving it.

Dust & Scratches filter

Choose Filter➪Noise➪Dust & Scratches to quickly remove scratches and creases. You can use this tool to rid your photo of light scratches, dust specks, and slight folds. It does a fairly good job of eliminating the pesky little dots that sometimes cover your old photos. The Dust & Scratches dialog box (see Figure 12-7) shows the Radius and Threshold values I set for a picture of secretaries. At high radius values, the image starts to blur, so I moved the sliders while looking for the least amount of blur in the picture where most of the small scratches are removed. Compare the two images (the image on the left is the original) to see that after all is said and done, the Dust & Scratches filter does a pretty good job of removing the little beasts without compromising your picture much.

Figure 12-7: Use the Dust & Scratches filter to eliminate most small imperfections.

Blur tool

The Blur tool is located to the left of the Dodge/Burn/Sponge tools. The Blur tool, um, blurs. By that, I mean that the Blur tool is great when you want to smooth out an edge in a picture that contains a copied and pasted element or an area that has received a bit too many tweaks that you want to smooth out. You can blur with any size brush or strength when the normal mode is selected. I use it most often to smooth out where one object meets another in a picture — areas that can look unnatural after tweaks with other Photoshop tools.

Color Balance

The next feature I use is the Color Balance adjustment (Image➪ Adjustments➪Color Balance), which uses sliders that move from cyan to red, magenta to green, and yellow to blue. You have the option to tweak all tones — shadows, midtones, and highlights. In Figure 12-8, the cute pooches (Fido and Cody) could use a little bit of color balancing, and the grass could be made greener.

Figure 12-8: This picture could use a little color adjustment.

Figure 12-9 shows my color balance values — for shadows, midtones, and highlights — to color the dogs' world. I'm looking to get some green grass here, as well as some color in the old car in the background.

To merge the changes to the existing photo — to make them more subtle — I set the opacity in the Layers palette to 70%, as shown in Figure 12-10.

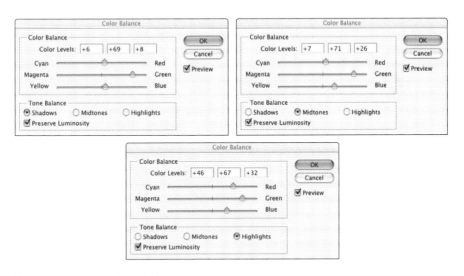

Figure 12-9: I rework the color balance to get more green.

Figure 12-10: Meld a new, tweaked layer with the existing background layer to make subtle changes.

The picture shown in Figure 12-11 shows an improvement in color over the *before* picture (Figure 12-10). The color balance only goes so far in adjusting color, however.

Removing a horrible shadow

Figure 12-11: Color balance tweaks change color tones only so much.

When you need to remove a horrible shadow — like that seen to the left of the secretary in Figure 12-7 — use the Magnetic Lasso tool and then the Clone Stamp tool to replace a dark blotch made with a crude flash. (See more on this in the section "Healing Damaged Photos.") The Clone Stamp tool copies pixels from one area (the *source point*) to another (the area that needs repair). Notice the bevels in the wooden wall behind the secretary: They're fairly even. To start, I click the Clone Stamp tool and select a source point by Option+clicking (on a Mac; in Windows, you Alt+click to define the source point) in a clean place on the wall at the meeting point of bevel and flat wall;

I then drag to the right (that's the area I'm painting over). In doing so, I am able to carry the bevel evenly all the way to the secretary's shoulder where the horrible shadow once was. Figure 12-12 shows the shadow removed from the area to the left of the secretary.

When you use the Clone Stamp tool, you can click and drag while holding the Shift key and moving the tool. When you do, you get a straight horizontal line if you move your mouse horizontally (and a vertical line if you click and drag up or down).

Figure 12-12: A click here, a click there, a little dragging, and the shadow is gone.

Healing Damaged Photos

Time takes its toll on all things, and old photos and negatives can suffer a lot of damage from water (mold or mildew), pests (mice and silverfish), and storage problems that cause damage (like when photos stacked in a box stick to each other). Many of the bigger challenges facing you come in the form of scratches, tears, and bends. Figure 12-13 shows just such a print. This print can be fixed with trusty old Photoshop.

Figure 12-13: You can fix this.

Using this photo as a model in the "Making the Corrections" section, I show you how to touch it up so that it's ready for printing. I scanned it first to have a digital image to work with. ***Note:*** Achieving good resolution from the very beginning — when you scan — can't be overstated. Resolution is important because the more information (that is, the higher the resolution) you have in an image, the better the detail; the better the detail you start with, the better the quality you have to work with. Think of it like bed sheets: The higher the thread count, the better and softer the sheet. Lower is thinner . . . and not as good.

Cropping before you fix

Sometimes a photo needs a little more help than just color adjustment. If your print has an area on its edge (not in the middle) that's damaged, as the image on the left does (see the lower-left corner), you can either cut out the damage with the Crop tool, as I do here in the following steps, or fix it by following the steps in "Making the Corrections."

1. Open the image you want to crop.

2. Select the Crop tool from the Toolbox.

3. With the Crop tool, select the area to cut out, and then click the Crop tool icon on the toolbar to initiate the crop.

If you want to save what you have at this point, just click Save. The image on the right in the figure shows the cropping in progress.

I use a Hewlett-Packard (HP) Scanjet type of scanner. It comes with a negative/ positive reader that is merely a long light table upon which you slide your negative/positive into and then set the mechanism into the scanner bed. That might be different from yours, although the basic steps are similar. If you come across something weird, consult the documentation that came with your scanner software or consult a copy of *Scanners For Dummies,* Second Edition, by Mark L. Chambers (Wiley).

Making the Corrections

Open the scanned image that needs a little love and cosmetic aid. Then use the tools in Photoshop to help correct whatever problem is at hand — a tear, a scratch, a bend. In this example, part of the emulsion of the print is gone, leaving the white stock of the print paper showing through. Not good. To correct this issue, I use the Clone Stamp and Healing Brush tools. ***Remember:*** You can find these tools in the Toolbox.

1. **Using the Lasso tool or another selection tool, click and drag around the area that you want to fix, as shown in Figure 12-14.**

   Selecting an area can be tricky. If you aren't familiar with using the selection tools, I recommend practicing doing so before trying this exercise or consulting *Photoshop CS2 All-in-One Desk Reference For Dummies,* by Barbara Obermeier (Wiley).

Figure 12-14: First select the area to repair.

2. **With the Clone Stamp tool, click inside the drop-down list in the Photoshop Options bar to pick a brush size for your cleanup.**

   You can also get the same window to appear by right-clicking (if you have a two-button mouse) or Control+clicking (for you one-button mouse users).

   Figure 12-15 shows some of the brush types you can select from and the slider bars to change the brush's diameter and hardness.

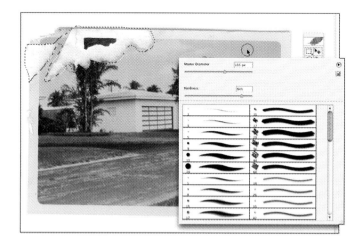

Figure 12-15: Choose a brush by texture; smooth for sky, textured for trees.

   You use the Clone Stamp tool to take pixels from an undamaged area in the photograph and replicate them in the damaged area you identify. You have to determine what brush size will cover the area you want to clone. If the damaged area is small — say, for example, a long sliver of an area along one edge of the photo — choose a smallish size (such as 20 px) to maintain detail. If a large portion of the photo is damaged, like part of the sky in Figure 12-14, less detail is needed, so a larger size (such as 80 px) is appropriate.

3. **Still using the Clone Stamp tool, find an undamaged area that's similar in color and texture to the area that you're repairing and Option+click (Mac) or Alt+click (Windows) to set the point (Photoshop calls it a *source point*) from which you'll copy (clone); then move your mouse over the area you want to fix.**

   You now have the good pixels with which you can repair the damage.

4. **Carefully color in the area, making sure that you copy only the area that you want to fix.**

   If you accidentally pick up some of another object, reset your clone point by pressing Option/Alt and clicking your mouse over an area that includes what you're cloning.

5. **Repeat Steps 2–4 with the Clone Stamp tool until you repair the entire area that needs fixing.**

   The whole process is a series of pick-up-what-you-need actions you achieve by constantly repeating Steps 3 and 4.

6. **Deselect the area that you had been fixing by pressing ⌘+D/Ctrl+D.**

   Select another area (or the same area again if you were adding a background, such as sky, and if you want something to go over part of that background, like a tree).

7. **Clean up the edges of the old selection area with the Healing Brush or the Spot Healing Brush tool (Photoshop CS2).**

8. **Repeat Steps 2–7 to repair any other damaged areas in the photo.**

   Use an appropriate part of the undamaged area to serve as the new source area for the Clone Stamp tool!

9. **Crop the picture.**

   The finished product is shown in Figure 12-16. In this step, you can choose to take away borders or insignias, names of places, and other specific details that old photos sometimes contain.

Figure 12-16: All touched up and ready for the Photoshop CS2 Smart Sharpen feature.

Old photos scanned at higher resolutions will print almost perfectly, even if enlarged several times. Find more about enlarging your photos in Photoshop for printing in Chapter 17.

Tweaking Color in the Digital World

In this section, I show you how to take an old picture and make its color even better by using Color Balance tools. Figure 12-17 was taken in the late 1950s, although most of the color in the picture has remained (fortunately); that means that the tweaks should be minor for an ideal picture (that is, if you want to make them at all). Although some people like old pictures just as they are — faded and yellowed (a nostalgia thing) — you might have to eliminate creases and folds, which you can take out with the Clone Stamp and Healing Brush tools, as shown in the earlier section, "Healing Damaged Photos."

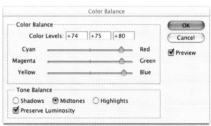

To tweak the color in the image shown in the "Cropping before you fix" sidebar, follow these steps:

1. **To adjust the color, choose Image⇨Adjustments⇨Auto Color.**

2. **To adjust the color more, choose Edit⇨Fade Auto Color and play with the slider bar until you get what you want.**

   I want to play with the reds at this point, deepening them a little.

3. **To adjust a particular color, choose Image⇨Adjustments⇨ Color Balance and play with the midtones.**

   Figure 12-17 shows the Color Balance sliders I set to get deep Christmas reds in the outfits of both Santa and the boy.

4. **After you finish with color balancing, you can finesse the rest of the image with the Clone Stamp and the Healing Brush tools.**

   The steps in the section "Making the Corrections" show you how to use these tools.

   The final picture after edits with the Clone Stamp and the Healing Brush tools is shown in Figure 12-18.

Figure 12-17: Adjusting your color balance to make up for faded colors.

Figure 12-18: This photo looks like it was taken yesterday (almost).

Enhancing Sepia and Other Tones

A photograph with a *sepia* tone is a black-and-white photograph that has tones of brown in it. Photographers can control the sepia toning with film in the darkroom, and you can, too, with your computer.

Figure 12-19 is a B&W photo that I manipulate to give it a sepia tone. To do this, I use the same tools using the Images⇨Adjustment⇨Color Balance command. Instead of playing with the midtones, I adjust the highlights because I'm looking to pick up more details in the background — the background is almost all light toned (contains only highlights). In the Tone Balance area, I select the Highlights radio button and adjust the three sliders, adding and taking away color until I get the effect I want. I choose not to check Preserve Luminosity because it gives my picture too much bright contrast.

Figure 12-19: Give a B&W picture like this a sepia tone.

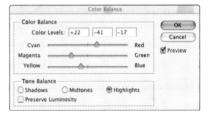

Figure 12-20: Tweak sepia tones here.

Here's what happens: I can make out some of the tree branches in the background, making the picture have more depth as I move the values of the sliders to those shown in Figure 12-20.

1. **For the top slider bar, I shift toward Red and away from Cyan (a mixture of blue and green).**

   The red tones brighten up the picture a bit.

2. **For the middle slider bar, I shift a bit toward Magenta.**

   This gives more detail.

3. **For the bottom slider bar, I play with Yellow and Blue and then decide to not change this (by clicking and dragging the slider bar to a 0 reading).**

   The slight red in the highlights gives a subtle brown tone, resulting in a nice sepia effect, as shown in Figure 12-21.

Figure 12-21: Adding reds helps deepen contrast and creates sepia tones.

The sliders in Photoshop's Color Balance dialog box can make any tone that affects the entire picture, turning it to shades of red, cyan, magenta, blue (see Figure 12-22), yellow (see Figure 12-23), or any combination of these.

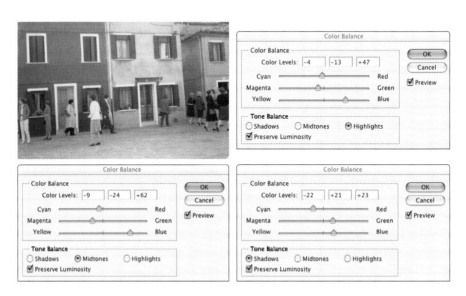

Figure 12-22: Adjust color balance to make an image more blue.

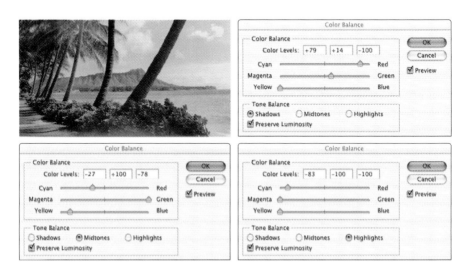

Figure 12-23: Adjust color balance to bring out the yellow in an image.

Enhancing Shadow, Highlights, Hue, and Saturation

There's nothing like taking a picture of a friend and finding it 30 years later in a box. It's a picture that says *wow* with color, especially if it's on a negative that you thought you'd never use. Even more exciting than snapping the picture today is finding an image that you snapped when you were a kid, and not just any image, but one on old Kodak 126 color negative film that scans onto your computer like it was shot yesterday. Figure 12-24 shows an image that was shot in the late 1960s on some very tough film.

Figure 12-24: Some of yesterday's film loses very little of its color.

Although this picture is pretty good as is because its color and contrast stayed in tact for over 40 years, you can get it to print with hues of orange that will soak the paper on which it will be cast. Here's how to set this up for a print out of paradise.

To enhance shadow, highlights, hue, and saturation in a photograph, take any photo with good exposure and follow these steps. (You need to experiment a little, though, with the values that you choose in each step.)

1. **In Photoshop, open the photograph and decide what repairs you want to make.**

2. **Choose the Clone Stamp tool, Option-click on a clean spot nearby, and then clean up specks of dust.**

   In Photoshop CS2, you can use the Spot Healing Brush tool of the Tools palette (looks like a Tootsie Roll with a dashed ring around the end of it). Photoshop calculates the surrounding colors and washes away the spot.

   For the Clone Stamp tool, I recommend a small brush setting to maintain detail. To do this, slide the master diameter bar to get the brush size you want. Because your brush size is going to be small, as are the areas you're correcting, you won't need to use the Healing Brush tool.

3. **Choose Image⇨Adjustment⇨Curves to deal with contrast, color — all the tones at once — and highlights, midtones, shadows.**

I recommend using the Curves dialog box here — instead of Auto Levels — because of the sweeping manipulations you can make simultaneously.

There's more to this dialog box than meets the eye. You can adjust each curve channel by channel. Add a point on the curve by clicking in the work area. Take away a point by clicking and dragging it off the work area and using the Eyedropper tool to reset your black, gray, and/or white points. (Say, if you click the picture with the black point Eyedropper in an area lighter than black, you get a very dark picture because you added lighter tones to the value from which Photoshop calculates pure black.) Last, as you click your picture, you'll see the values of the input and output changing. Those values are actually the tonal ranges as they're read from the curve. Yes, they're algebraic x and y coordinates, that in effect associate the tonal value from a point on the line to a point in your picture.

4. **Choose Image⇨Adjustment⇨ Shadow/Highlight to open the dialog box shown in Figure 12-25.**

This tool has to be one of Photoshop's most effective, lightening dark images and darkening light ones. The sliders in the dialog box work best on images where you have strong backlighting. Use them also to brighten shadows. To correct your lighting, move the Amount slider back and forth until you get what you like. Watch out for the hazy white that is created when you overdo it. The Tonal Width slider determines what values are included in "shadows" or "highlights" as you adjust. The Radius slider controls how large or small an area of shadow or highlight must be before it's adjusted.

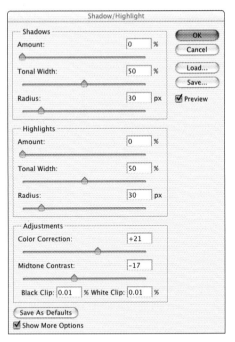

Figure 12-25: Lighten and darken here.

5. Choose Image⇨Adjustments⇨ Hue/Saturation to open the dialog box shown in Figure 12-26.

Figure 12-26: Tweak color here.

This dialog box — which you use to make adjustments to color — features sliders and also an Edit drop-down menu that shows the different colors that you can adjust: red, yellow, green, blue, cyan, and magenta. I make most of the values for each color in the positive range because the original picture lost color and became dark — so I give it color and make the colors lighter using these tools. I take away a tad of red to make the helmet bright orange. I up the saturation a little bit because during printing, I want more red and yellow ink to go to the helmet (and to the pattern in the girl's dress). That's all I want to tweak because the dark background of the fish and plants is appropriate for what the picture was intended to do — make the subject look like she's underwater.

Pushing curves adjustments to the extreme

Play around in the work area clicking back and forth from your picture and from the black and white Eyedropper tools for some pretty wild effects ranging from screaming oranges to flaming reds to comic book black (no gray tones here), as shown here.

Figure 12-27 shows the image after the tweaks. No more changes to this image are necessary in preparation for printing for some printers, such as a HP Photosmart (a printer series in which the colors are decided by the printer itself so that the range of colors you choose in Photoshop has only a nominal effect). The image might need more tweaks if it's printed on different printers. See Chapter 17 for more about printing.

Figure 12-27: An image after printing tweaks.

Combining and Manipulating Images

In This Chapter

▷ Merging files automatically in Photoshop

▷ Identifying color for use for picture backgrounds

▷ Using symmetry to create new pictures from photos

*Y*ou can think of Photoshop as an image processing program in either two or three dimensions. In two dimensions, Photoshop can take many photos and place them side by side in a collage or montage. That you can discover in this chapter. In three dimensions, Photoshop can meld one image on top of another to create three-dimensional effects that awe. (No, no *Twilight Zone* or *Sixth Sense* here, just old-fashioned photo layer manipulation that's been around ever since Photoshop introduced layers in version 3.) That you can discover in Chapter 14.

The fun thing about Photoshop, of course, is that you can manipulate images in all sorts of cool ways. Just like in most any other application, such as Microsoft Word, you can copy and paste images side by side in a new document or add them to an existing one. You can copy and paste tables, graphs, other people's pictures — even a picture of someone's kitchen sink — into Photoshop.

In this chapter, I show you how to position images using Photoshop's Photomerge. It can sew sections of a larger photo into one cohesive image. Think of a broad, panoramic landscape view that's difficult to capture in one shot. With Photoshop, you can take individual shots — sections, if you will — of that scene and seam them into one wide, complete image. And you're not limited to horizontal images, either. For example, in this chapter, I show you how to take pieces of a giant Tiki — a tall vertical image — and put them together to make a large, whole picture of the entire Tiki.

I also show you how to integrate backgrounds into photographs and how to cut, copy, and rotate images to create symmetry that makes the items in your photograph indistinguishable, but makes your photo itself interesting and unusual.

Preserving Detail

The very first thing — the most important thing — that gives you make-or-break prints is the fine detail in your image. Certainly there are images in which you'll use creative blurring techniques, but generally you'll want to preserve as much detail as possible. For more about managing the size of your file so that your image's detail won't fall apart to noise, and so that your image stays crystal clear from the time you take it to the time you tweak it to the time you print it, see Chapter 18.

Cropping an image can be done with the Crop tool, which is located in the Tools palette in Photoshop. Figure 13-1 shows the crop selection in an image of a sidewalk artist. I crop fairly closely (because in an image like this, you want the total focus to be on the subject). Using the Crop tool without specifying a new print size in Photoshop's Options bar pares down your image to make it more appealing to you and your viewer, improving the image's composition. It also cuts down your file size without compromising detail in the image, although you might have to resize the image later to fit specific print requirements.

Figure 13-1: A simple crop won't damage the detail in your image.

Cropping an image is one of the most important aesthetic decisions you'll make when you edit in Photoshop or other image processing software. Follow the same rules you would while shooting, such as the Rule of Thirds and other composition rules presented in Chapter 1.

You can check the size of your image (both pixel dimensions and print dimensions/resolution) in Photoshop with the Image⇨Image Size command. When Photoshop crops your image, it becomes a smaller file. Figure 13-2 shows the file sizes before and after the crop.

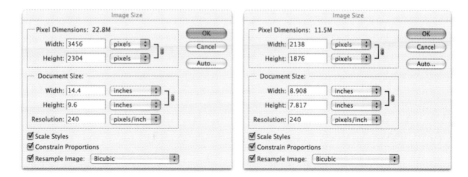

Figure 13-2: Find file sizes for a cropped image in the Image Size dialog box.

Making an Image Whole Again with Photomerge

You can take extra-tall things or extra-wide things and string them together to make a panoramic picture with Photoshop's Photomerge feature. Although a landscape shot piece by piece and stitched together in Photoshop has great appeal — and that is what most people use Photomerge for — you can do this same process on images of other tall and thin subjects, too, such as buildings, trees, sculptures . . . even clowns on stilts.

Using Photomerge to create one large, whole image of something you could never fit into one camera frame while shooting is easy. First, you need several photos of something large, either horizontal or vertical — a very tall tree, a landscape, or a building. For this example, I use photos of a Tiki, which is a very tall sculpture carved from a palm tree trunk. (See Figure 13-3.)

Because of its thin width with respect to its height, fitting it in one frame — even with a wide angle lens — would at best give me a mediocre medium shot of the Polynesian god. Instead, I snapped several pictures of it (it's an original, carved in the '60s

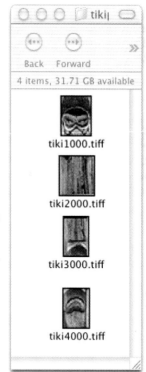

Figure 13-3: Merge multiple photos into one.

by a well-known Tiki carver) to create a clear image of the whole sculpture that I can then print out at 10" x 42". (I have the option to double the merged photo's size — just like the sculpture itself — without much loss of fine detail in the image.)

1. **Open the photos that you want to stitch together into one large, whole picture.**

   I create a folder for situations like this so that the photos are easily accessible when I'm navigating Photoshop.

2. **(Optional) Turn each picture to its side by opening each and choosing Image⇨Rotate Canvas⇨90° CCW. (See Figure 13-4.)**

   If you're merging a true landscape — that is, something horizontal — you won't have to do this step.

   Because computer monitors are more wide than tall, I rotate the images 90 degrees counterclockwise because it's easier to see them as one piece horizontally rather than vertically.

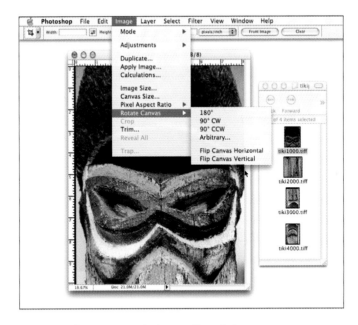

Figure 13-4: Rotate composite images if needed.

You could rotate the individual images within the work area of Photomerge. If you go that route, it would take you about the same amount of time, or maybe longer, than doing it in Photoshop first.

Figure 13-5 shows the icons of my images as they appear after I turn them on their sides. Now I'm ready to merge the photos that are in the folder on my Desktop.

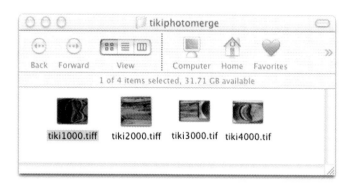

Figure 13-5: All my images are rotated.

3. **In Photoshop CS, choose File⇨Automate⇨Photomerge.**

4. **In the Photomerge dialog box that appears (see Figure 13-6), click the Browse button to navigate to the folder.**

   You can also navigate to files and open documents by selecting one from the Use drop-down menu.

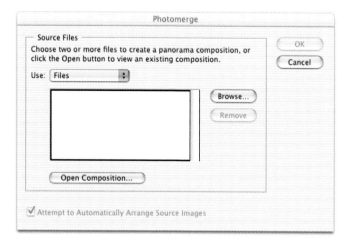

Figure 13-6: Browse for your files or folders here.

5. **Browse to find the folder you're merging.**

6. **Then click Open when the Open window appears onscreen.**

The program lists the images that you have in your project folder.

7. Mark the Attempt to Automatically Arrange Source Images check box so that Photoshop tries to connect your image using its automated process.

If you don't, Photomerge won't try to put your images together.

Because Photomerge couldn't put together my Tiki automatically, a dialog box came up to let me know that. I then arranged the images myself. In this case, I want the Tiki files that I rotate in Step 2.

You can add or remove files from the image you're merging by changing your folder selection to Files and browsing for the files you want. To remove an image, simply select the file that appears in the list and click the Remove button.

8. Click OK.

The program begins its merge. When the merge program finishes, it either displays the merged files as it sees fit or asks you to click and drag them from the top frame, where they are displayed, to the main part of the window.

9. If prompted, click and drag the merged files to fit them together like pieces of a seamless puzzle.

In the Tiki case, I got the prompt that said it couldn't fit my images together (probably because it sensed that it couldn't get them to mesh). I moved the images down to the main part of the window. They easily fit together because the ends are transparent, and you can see where the overlap is for each to fit them together. See Figure 13-7.

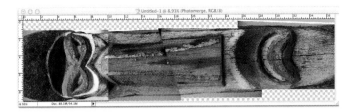

Figure 13-7: Time to flatten and rotate.

10. Flatten the image by choosing Layer⇨Flatten Image.

Photomerge makes a layer for each part of the picture. That means each picture is alone, within its own space, and the other images can be moved on top of it. (Hence, that's how you can "see through the images.") I discuss how layers work and can be manipulated in Chapter 14. *Note:* In Photomerge, you can't access your layers when the image is in the working space.

11. **(Optional) If you rotated your images in Step 2, rotate the merged image clockwise to stand it upright (vertically) by choosing Image⇨Rotate Canvas⇨90° CW.**

There! You have one whole picture of that large thing you couldn't fit into one frame (whatever that one large thing is). In my case, the Tiki is back together again, as tall as ever (see Figure 13-8).

Here are some other tips to bear in mind when merging:

- **Minimize tweaks.** Any time you transform your image, you move pixels around. That means that Photoshop has to *interpolate,* which can result in a loss of fine detail in the image. For more about interpolation and resampling, see Chapter 16.

  Transform your image very little. For example, transform it only to fill in a small piece of the frame that was left white or to even out an image if it's slightly cockeyed. If you overdo it, your image will lose too much resolution.

- **Make reparations.** To repair a merged photo, see Chapter 12 and do the same steps as repairing an old photo.

- **Tweak before you merge.** If your images vary a lot in hue and tone, you should tweak them before using Photomerge. If at some point in your Photomerge process, you see that the images are off in this manner, go back and work with your original images; then run Photomerge again after you tweak and resave the images in a folder.

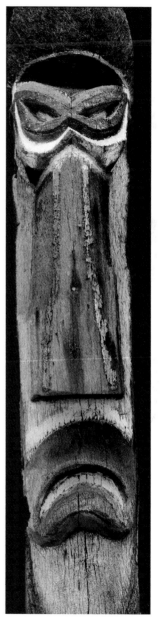

Figure 13-8: Post merging.

Pausing Photomerge

If the phone rings or you have to quickly scoot to pick up your child at school, don't click Photomerge's Cancel button if you have to leave your computer because you'll lose all the precious work you've done thus far. If you've got a dozen images to connect and tweak (they don't always snap together), it could take some time to piece them all together and to make sure each is in the right place.

To come back to a project in progress, click the Save Composition As button. This saves your work area as a *PGM* file, which is a file format that lets you click and drag all those pictures around in a work area. To return to your project, just click the Open Composition button (it toggles) and navigate to the PGM file that you saved. When you save this file, Photomerge saves all your images in layers. For more about layers, see Chapter 14.

Seamlessly Introducing Backgrounds in Photographs

Admit it — you've undoubtedly sometime taken a potentially great picture only to have the subject surrounded by clutter. Maybe you weren't careful enough about image composition, or you just couldn't help it that clutter runs through the background. Sure, you could try to take the picture again or maybe move the subject in front of a better background. When you can't change life, however — whether the disturbing culprit is a palm tree rising out from someone's head or an errant phone wire marring a crystal-blue sky behind a mid-century motel sign — change it in Photoshop. To do that, create a new background.

The Tiki that I use as an example in the preceding section is an object that doesn't fill each frame evenly. After I finish merging an object like a Tiki, I have to add a new cohesive background.

You can create simple backgrounds that match your picture by using the following technique:

1. **In Photoshop, open an image to which you want to add a background.**

   I change the background to a brick red.

2. **With the Eyedropper tool, click somewhere on the image.**

   This picks a color that is included within your photograph, which is insurance that you'll get a match to apply to your background. See Chapter 1 for more about matching colors.

3. **With the Paint Bucket tool, click the part of your picture's background that you want to change.**

This changes the part you clicked to whatever color you pick with the Eyedropper tool. In my case, the background has been changed to brick red, to match colors in the Tiki. (See Figure 13-9.)

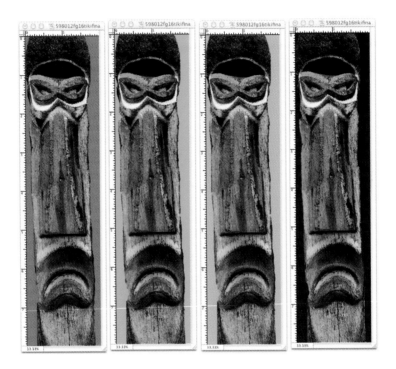

Figure 13-9: Use the Eyedropper and Paint Bucket tools to try different backgrounds.

At this point, maybe you're thinking about a couple of photographs to which you'd like to add a matching color background, but those photographs aren't white. Well, it's easy to make a background white.

To make a background white:

1. **Select the object(s) for which you want the background changed by using one (or more) of the selection tools (a marquee or lasso tool, or the Magic Wand for a solid-color subject).**

2. **Choose Select⇨Inverse.**

   Photoshop switches your selection from the objects that you select to everything but the objects you select (the background).

3. **After you check your selection and choose white for your background color from the Tools palette, press Delete.**

   Press the D key on your keyboard to set the foreground color to black and the background color to white.

You can get more natural-looking backgrounds by overlaying the Tiki onto another picture with a clutter-free background. Read more about this in Chapter 14.

Creating Art Photos through Symmetry

Another way to create unusual photography suitable to sell as art is to manipulate images in Photoshop by taking part of an image and duplicating it to create a symmetrical pattern. You can often find such opportunities to create symmetry from architectural sources, such as the fretwork intricacies of modern architecture, like the Eiffel Tower. Think of how a kaleidoscope takes crystals and creates several mirror images of them, or how you used to cut out valentines as a kid — half of a heart, from the folded side of a piece of paper, that opened into a whole heart.

To create your own symmetrical art, follow these steps:

1. **In Photoshop, open a picture of a shape or form that approaches a pattern of symmetry — say, a building or object.**

   To create something perfectly symmetrical in photography is a very difficult job — more fit for a surveyor — so don't worry if it's not perfect from one side to the other.

   For this example, I use the photo shown in Figure 13-10. You can use any photo for this art project. The purpose is to create sets of interesting lines — to play with them and slide them around with the Move tool — to make your own quasi-symmetrical masterpieces.

Figure 13-10: Start with a subject with interesting lines.

2. **Make a selection of one half of the subject and its surrounding background.**

   Because you're creating your own pattern using the existing symmetry, you need only part of the photo. See Figure 13-11. I eyed the bike and the reflection of the water to where I thought would be a nice place to make a break for cropping.

3. **Choose Edit⇨Copy.**

4. **Choose Edit⇨Paste.**

5. **Choose Edit⇨Transform⇨ Flip Horizontal.**

6. **Select the Move tool in the Toolbox (or press the V key on the keyboard) and reposition the upper layer.**

   Try to align the center edges.

7. **Use the Edit⇨Transform commands as necessary.**

Figure 13-11: Choose part of the photo to flip later.

   You might need to rotate or skew the upper layer a bit to get proper alignment at the point where the two halves meet.

8. **Flatten the image by choosing Layer⇨Flatten Image.**

   Flattening the layers of an image reduces the file size. For more about layers, see Chapter 14.

9. **Crop your new image as you see fit and then save it.**

   Cropping provides additional balance and cuts out the parts of the images that don't appear symmetrical.

   My final image is shown in Figure 13-12.

Figure 13-12: Horizontal and/or vertical rotation works well with symmetrical objects.

14

Using Layers to Create a Theme

In This Chapter

▷ Seeing how layers work

▷ Making a layered picture with a theme

*L*ayering images is one of the most powerful features of Photoshop. Remember working with an x-y axis in algebra? You can think of your image in terms of that plane. In more advanced math, you also have a *z axis*, which is a kind of space that moves up and down. You can think of other images that you lay over your original as being in that plane. A *layer* is just a picture file that Photoshop uses to make an image. Photoshop can merge many pictures together in a kind-of-third dimension called a *layer*.

For the purposes of this book, I leave heavy rendering of dozens of images to graphic designers. From a photographer's perspective (more specifically, *this* art photographer), if a photographic image is overdone with Photoshop, you move it into a different category of art — more toward graphics. For now, digital photography graphic designs have not sold widely as prints without the aid of mass production. In other words, designs do sell but mostly if they're part of a poster produced as part of an event, a gallery opening, movie premiere, or stage production. But, in the art world, you never know when this will catch on.

This chapter discusses how you can make interesting photo montages using Photoshop layers.

Using Layers in Photoshop

When working with layers in Photoshop, first show the appropriate palette. The Layers palette can be shown and hidden, like all of

Photoshop's palettes, through the Window menu (Window⇨Layers). See Figure 14-1.

You can layer any image one on top of the other by selecting a smaller image and dragging it onto a larger image. In the first example of layering a bit later in this chapter, I take a simple image — a cutout of an orange — and juxtapose it with an image of a natural window of stone.

 It's important to know the relative pixel dimensions of images you're combining. Use the Photoshop Image⇨Image Size command to check (and change) pixel dimensions so that you get the desired relative size of each element in your artwork.

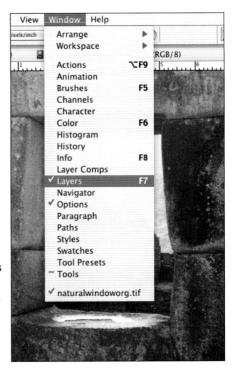

Figure 14-1: The Layers palette.

Feathering

Before I get into the fun of layering images, you need to understand the concept of feathering. This finishing technique is essential to help your superimposed images blend smoothly, preventing an upper layer from looking as if it's been pasted on top of your background (like a poster board project kids make in grade school).

To make the superimposed image blend in — and avoid a pasted-on hard outlined edge — feather a selection (choose Select⇨Feather) before copying.

Figure 14-2 shows you what happens when you select and feather and then click and drag a selection from one document to another (in this example, a plain white document).

The two basic ways to soften the edges of a selection with feathering are

✔ **Make a selection and then feather.** Use any of Photoshop's selection tools or commands to make a selection. Then use the menu command Select⇨Feather to feather the selection.

✔ **Set the feathering before making the selection.** Both the Marquee and Lasso selection tools offer a Feather field in the Options bar. Enter a value in the field before using the tool to make a selection.

Feathering Guide

2 pixels

2+10 pixels

2+10+50 pixels

2+10+50+100 pixels

Figure 14-2: Note the effects that different values of feathering have on an image.

Creating a simple two-layer project

Here's how you can move one image over another in Photoshop to get an awe-inspiring result for your viewers. I start with a simple two-image example:

1. **In Photoshop, open the two photos that you want to arrange together, one on top of the other.**

Here are the photos I use: an orange and part of an edifice of an Inca ruin that I call a *natural window,* as shown in Figure 14-3.

Figure 14-3: Setting a piece of fruit among ruins creates an artful still life.

2. **Make a selection of the area of one image that you want to copy to the other.**

   For a subject that's similar in color to its background but has a distinct edge (like the orange used in this example), the Lasso tool is a good choice. When there's a significant difference in color between the subject and the background, the Magic Wand tool or the Magnetic Lasso tool (both found in the Toolbox) might make selecting easier.

   You can set your feathering before using a selection tool, or you can feather afterward by using the Select➪Feather command. Generally, when you're selecting a subject with distinct edges to copy/paste into another image, a feathering value of 2 pixels is sufficient.

3. **Refine your selection.**

   As you can see to the left in Figure 14-4, you might need to fine-tune the edges of your selection. Hold down the Shift key and drag a selection tool to add to a selection; hold down the Option key (Mac) or the Alt key (Windows) and drag a selection tool to subtract pixels from a selection.

4. **Move your selected subject to the other image.**

   You have a couple of choices when you're duplicating the selected pixels into the second image:

   • *Copy and paste:* You can use the menu command Edit➪Copy, switch to the other image, and then use the command Edit➪Paste.

   • *Click and drag:* You can also simply select the Move tool in the Toolbox, click the selected pixels, and then drag the selection to the window of the other image.

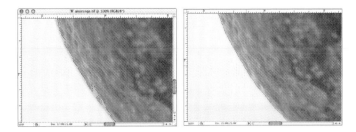

Figure 14-4: Select process makes or breaks a quality layering project.

5. **Position and transform as necessary.**

Use the Move tool to position the pasted pixels where you need them in the second image. You can also use Photoshop's Edit⇨Transform command to scale, rotate, skew, or otherwise fine-tune the appearance of the pasted pixels in the second image. Because Photoshop pastes onto a separate layer, you can use these commands without fear of making changes to the original background layer.

When using a Transform command, you'll see a *bounding box* surrounding the pixels on the layer. Drag the side or corner *anchor points* (the hollow boxes around the square, shown in Figure 14-5) to manipulate the pixels.

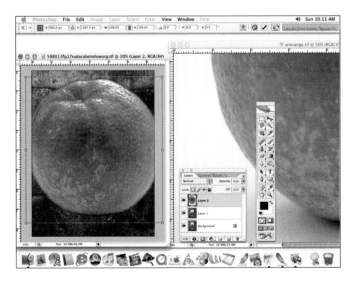

Figure 14-5: Drag anchor points to change the size and shape of the bounding box.

6. **Evaluate the composite for lighting and shadows.**

After you move and transform the pasted pixels, take a good look at the composited image and ask yourself these questions:

- Do the angles of lighting for the background and the subject match?

- Are there any places where a shadow should be falling on the new subject that no shadow is evident?

- Is the overall tonality of the composited image harmonious, or do you need to adjust the lightness/darkness of the new subject?

- Is there agreement in overall color between the new subject and the background?

As you can see in Figure 14-6, sometimes additional work with Photoshop's Image⇨Adjustment command is in order to completely unify the new subject with the original background. (See Chapter 12 for more information on using Photoshop's Curves, Shadow/Highlight, and other adjustment commands, as well as the Dodge and Burn tools for localized adjustments.)

Figure 14-6: Adjust color and tonality of the new subject to match the background.

Saving as an investment

Sometimes you invest a considerable amount of time in making a selection or need to interrupt your selection creation for any number of reasons. Rather than risk losing your work to date, choose Select⇨Save Selection. This command creates an *alpha channel* in Photoshop's Channels palette, which is actually your selection. Later, you can choose Select⇨Load Selection to convert that alpha channel back into a selection. If you find it necessary to later delete the alpha channel (because the selection has been refined and resaved with another name or the Channels palette is getting crowded), simply drag it to the Trash icon at the bottom of the Channels palette.

There's generally no need to flatten the layers in your image (unless you're desperate to save hard drive space or require a specific file format that doesn't support layers). Save your images as a Photoshop PSD file without using the Image⇨Flatten Layers command so that you have maximum flexibility to make changes or adjustments to the image.

Creating a More Complex Layer Project

Creating collages around a theme is popular in many art venues, from huge billboards in upscale shopping areas to advertising to small personal scrapbooks. A good theme leads to a good collage. When you keep to a specific theme — one that you've narrowed down to a simple focus — a viewer can easily understand your overarching message. For example, when creating a Roman collage theme, consider using appropriate elements such as round, arched, or fluted columns; marble/bronze trims and mosaic tile; decorative sculptures; and frescos from your photographs. The only limits to creating a theme are your imagination and source photos.

Here, I show you how to use Photoshop to put together a group of pictures — a collage — with multiple layers.

In a nutshell, you take a background, middle ground, and foreground and separate each with a solid color fill layer, which is then faded to become semitransparent. Each time you move a picture, Photoshop automatically creates a new layer for you.

Using Photoshop's Browse command (File⇨Browse), you can view your images while you navigate to them in different parts of your computer. In Photoshop CS2, *Bridge* (a separate program) automatically opens when you browse. You can open your collage images from Bridge; keep them open (and docked) so that you can toggle back and forth among them.

1. **Set up your background image.**

    a. *Open (double-click it from your browser window) a picture that you want to be the background of your document.*

    b. *Choose Image➪Image Size to set your image size.*

    I set mine to 8 x 10.

    c. *Check all three options at the bottom of the Image Size box.*

    I changed the width to 10, the height to 8, and the resolution to 300 pixels per inch (ppi), which is a resolution that's great for most inkjet printers because it balances image quality and file size.

    Experiment a little. Try different images until you get a background that you feel summarizes your theme. I chose an image of wooden marimbas, cropped so that they form a nice set of horizontal and vertical lines (kind of like railroad tracks) that also have perspective. The image is shown in Figure 14-7.

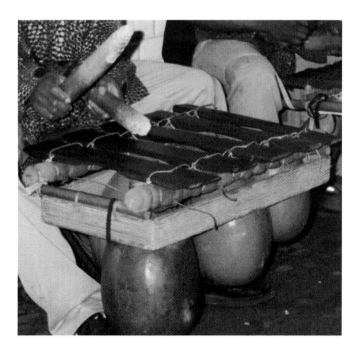

Figure 14-7: Background image for a music theme.

2. **(Optional) Use the Channel Mixer layer (Layer➪New Adjustment Layer➪ Channel Mixer) to convert your background to B&W — the first step to give it a sepia tone.**

I wanted a fairly bleached-out background (that is, lots of pure white tones) so that the middle ground and foreground images aren't over-shadowed by the background picture. Figure 14-8 shows the channel mixer values I used. I selected the Monochrome check box and tweak the slider bars to give lots of white tones. (For more about using the Channel Mixer layer, see Chapter 9.)

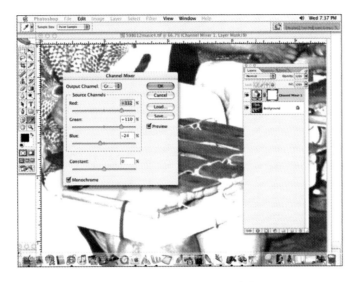

Figure 14-8: Convert your background layer to B&W.

3. **(Optional) Use a color balance layer (Layer⇨New Adjustment Layer⇨Color Balance) to make a sepia tone.**

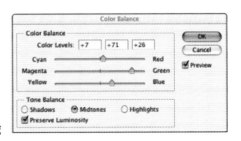

Figure 14-9: Color balance midtone values for a sepia tone.

You can choose any tone that you feel matches your images. Figure 14-9 shows the slider bars in the Color Balance dialog box. You can choose values for not only the midtones but also for highlights and shadows.

I chose a brown (sepia) tone to match the colors of natural wood instruments. To maintain a harsh contrast, I left the Preserve Luminosity check box unchecked. I needed this contrast because this layer will be covered with three fill layers later. I also chose to get my sepia tones by balancing only the midtones. I didn't use the Tone Balance options for the shadows or highlights. For more about creating an art photo by choosing from a variety of sepia tones, see Chapter 12.

4. **To choose a color overlay for the background, choose Layer⇨New Fill Layer⇨Solid Color and choose a faint color to soften the background.**

Click the color swatch to open the Color Picker. I chose a pale yellow (see Figure 14-10) from the Color Picker dialog box. To get the pale yellow, click in the vertical color spectrum bar of color choices to get in the vicinity of yellows, as shown in the Pick a Solid Color square work area.

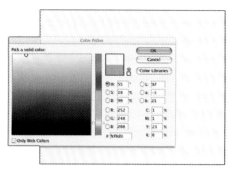

Figure 14-10: Make a new fill layer semitransparent to soften the background.

5. **Use the Opacity slider in the Layers palette to control how much you blend this color into the background picture.**

To soften your background, click Layer 1 in the Layers palette (Windows⇨Layer) and then reduce the opacity to 70%, as shown in Figure 14-11. Making a semitransparent overlay for your layers with pictures in them softens the subjects contained in the pictures.

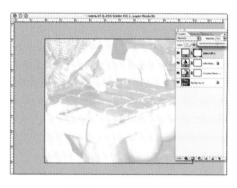

Figure 14-11: Reduce opacity to soften the background.

Reducing the opacity lets you blend two layers together so that you get, in essence, both pictures together. If you use a white fill layer, reducing the opacity gives a silky smooth look to the image you lay it over.

6. **Open another image and select an object to move to your collage.**

I selected my object to add (a street musician) with the Magnetic Lasso tool.

7. **Soften the edges of your selection with Select⇨Feather.**

For most subjects with defined edges, feathering one or two pixels is great. However, if you want very soft edges to more gradually blend your subject into the background, use a larger value.

8. **Copy and arrange your selection.**

Use the Copy and Paste commands (as described earlier in this chapter) or drag the selection with the Move tool onto the window of your collage background. If necessary, use the Edit⇨Transform command to scale, rotate, and otherwise manipulate the pasted pixels.

9. **(Optional) Using the Add a Layer Style button (the second one over on the bottom of the Layers palette drop-down menu), I put a color overlay to soften the image of the man just a little.**

I clicked the Add a Layer Style button at the bottom of the Layers palette and selected Color Overlay to bring up the Layer Style dialog box. I then chose a color via the Color Picker and used the slider bar there to adjust the opacity.

10. **Repeat Steps 4–8 for the additional images to move and make overlays for. You can tweak them along the way so that they fit as secondary and complementary — not primary — images in the collage.**

    For example, in Figure 14-12, I made a selection to apply a Brightness/Contrast adjustment to lighten the image (of children playing instruments). When copied into my collage, this image was less prominent and therefore didn't conflict with what became the primary image of the collage. I added just one more image after this one (the guy walking away with the horn).

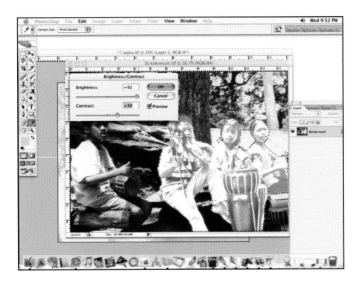

Figure 14-12: Secondary images get less detail than primary ones do.

11. **(Optional) Repeat Step 4 one more time, using white as a fill layer.**

    This unified my entire image with a softness — a subtle retreat from what a photograph taken with a normal lens would ordinarily give.

12. **Use a layer mask (Layer⇨Layer Mask⇨Reveal All) to clean up your image.**

    Click a layer in the Layers palette and then add the layer mask. Paint with the Brush tool, using black as the foreground color, to hide areas along the edges. Repeat for each additional layer that needs touching up, clicking the layer in the Layers palette and then adding a layer mask for that layer.

    For example, I noticed some black edges on the man playing the instrument. To soften them, I chose Layer 2 (where the man appears) and then chose Layer⇨Layer Mask⇨Reveal All. When I painted with black on the layer mask, my brush acted as an eraser, hiding that part of the layer. See Figure 14-13.

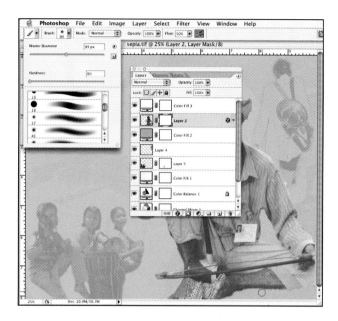

Figure 14-13: You can brush up your image using a layer mask.

13. Flatten the image (if desired), and you're done!

Remember that flattening the image blends all the layers into one layer, which reduces the file size but makes it nearly impossible to go back and make changes to your collage. Figure 14-14 shows my final result.

Figure 14-14: The final collage.

15

Using Photoshop for Special Effects

In This Chapter

▷ Using Photoshop filters to enhance your art photos

▷ Advanced Photoshop special effects

▷ Creating backgrounds in Photoshop

*P*hotoshop has literally hundreds of effects that you can use to manipulate an image. The choices available range from subtle to dramatic to (in my opinion) downright bizarre and surreal. How far you want to take your art photography from its original state is a matter of your taste and the outcome you desire.

For making saleable images that are superior prints, keep in mind the printing process as you move through your editing process. And with the special effects you can achieve with the special effect filters Photoshop offers, you can take a great photograph and tweak or twist it into something spectacular.

Experimenting with an image in Photoshop is a trial-and-error process; you won't really know the potential of the final result until you print the image (discussed in Chapter 17). However, you can twist and turn and tweak an image in Photoshop with a minimum amount of processing. In this chapter, I discuss using filters, creating a new background, and applying color enhancement.

Pick your finest images to tweak in Photoshop. Otherwise, you run the risk that your image won't have clear lines, shapes, and forms. Too, you're likely to get more image degradation when you run it through the various filters and options. Alternatively, if you have an image that you think is beyond salvage, you might just turn it into a gem with Photoshop's more powerful filters.

Photoshop Filter Effects

Filters in Photoshop work differently than those that you attach to your camera's lens (see Chapter 11). With so many choices, menu bars, values, colors, and patterns to choose from, you might wonder why you even need a camera at all! As a photographer, though, I'm sure you want to work with your own images, because in Photoshop, starting with your own exposures can let you create many effects from the same shot.

For example, Figure 15-1 shows before and after pictures of the Photoshop Watercolor filter applied to an architectural landscape in my attempt to bring the golden age of British watercolors back to life. Joseph Mallord William Turner, a British watercolorist, used the same hues as this tweaked landscape during his lifetime evolution from realism to abstraction. To see how to tweak an image like this, see the upcoming section, "Watercolor filter."

Most of Photoshop's filters are *destructive;* that is, they make permanent changes to the image. (Adjustment layers, on the other hand, are considered *nondestructive* because deleting the adjustment layer returns you to the original unchanged image.) Always make a copy of your image file before you

Figure 15-1: Use Photoshop's filters to transform your shots.

start making permanent changes to it. You can make the copy in the Mac Finder or Windows Explorer, or you can use Photoshop's Image➪Duplicate command.

Photoshop has too many filters for me to cite and show the effects of each here. The ones I concentrate on in this chapter are Gaussian Blur, Unsharp Mask, Plastic Wrap, Glowing Edges, Watercolor, Charcoal, Chalk & Charcoal, Graphic Pen, and Emboss. For more detail on these filters, see *Photoshop CS Timesaving Techniques For Dummies* (Phyllis Davis) and *Photoshop CS2 All-in-One Desk Reference For Dummies* (Barbara Obermeier), both published by Wiley.

When you apply some of the special effects of image processing programs, sometimes your image appears to have lost detail. Truth be told, some effects look no better than unwanted noise in your digital image. But then again, you might just craft an artistic view that is creative and compelling. Be very selective when using any filter in any image processing program because some filters work better than others. Some are meant to give your picture only a slight edge over the original.

Mies van der Rohe is a famous architectural designer who penned, "Less is more." This truism applies to when you process your images. Using one or two objects/subjects is best as well as using a uniform background. For more on creating flattering backgrounds, see the section, "Making a Background for Your Images."

Gaussian Blur filter

William Klein's famous photograph of a child, *Candy Store, Amsterdam Avenue, New York* (1954), was shot with effective blur. This blur effect left some critics referring to his work as photography that didn't meet standards of quality. Check out Klein's photo at

    www.masters-of-photography.com/K/klein/klein_candy_store_full.html

You can create a similar kind of blur via Photoshop's Gaussian Blur filter (Filter⇨Blur⇨Gaussian Blur). A good image to work with using this filter is one of a child. With this filter, you can take hard edges or contrast and mellow them both in the foreground and background. In Figure 15-2, sharp rocks transform to pillows to float upon, and humans turn into dreams.

Figure 15-2: Use the Gaussian Blur filter for a dreamlike setting.

To create the effect in Figure 15-2, see in Figure 15-3 the settings that I used. The Radius setting of 4.5 pixels is a good blur value whereby the image has enough contrast to be clear and enough blur to make it soft.

You can also use the Gaussian Blur filter to create intentional softening or blur in the background of your image. The Gaussian Blur filter is an absolute must if you want to produce a killer sky. Use this filter to take a mediocre sky and make it surreal.

Figure 15-3: Adjust Gaussian Blur settings here.

The Gaussian Blur filter can also produce a special other-planetlike special effect:

1. **Take an image in which you have a good bit of background sky and clouds.**

2. **Select the sky with the Magic Wand tool, using a tolerance setting (located in the top menu bar) of about 20 or 30.**

   To make continuous multiple selections, hold down the Shift key while selecting. For more about selection techniques, see Chapter 13.

   After your initial tap on your background with the Magic Wand tool, you can choose Select⇨Similar, which picks up most of the rest of the sky. This also works especially well with clouds. Pick one cloud with your selection tool and then choose Select⇨Similar to have all your clouds selected. Come to think of it, this technique also works with flowers and all kinds of objects that repeat themselves in tone and contrast.

3. **Choose Filter⇨Blur⇨Gaussian Blur.**

   The blur becomes more pronounced as you click and drag the slider (in the Gaussian Blur dialog box) to the right. My *before* and *after* images are shown in Figure 15-4.

Unsharp Mask filter

The Unsharp Mask filter (Filter⇨Sharpen⇨Unsharp Mask) adjusts the contrast at the edges of objects in your image. When you open an image and select this option, Photoshop calculates an amount, radius, and threshold. When you tweak to make your edges more crisp, you usually move the Amount and Radius sliders a little to the right and the Threshold slider a little to the left.

Figure 15-4: Make surreal backgrounds surreal with the Gaussian Blur filter.

Figure 15-5 shows how I took a shot of a box of dice and tweaked the image using Unsharp Mask to the max for a special effect that looks almost hand-drawn. The animated look of the picture using this drastic tweak can come in handy when you're building a layered cartoon image.

Figure 15-5: Tweak a shot with the Unsharp Mask filter.

For a special effect such as this, you can move the Amount and Radius sliders to their max values of 500% at 250 pixels at a Threshold of 0. The Unsharp Mask dialog box shows your image as you tweak the values.

Plastic Wrap filter

Sure, using Unsharp Mask is cool, but take it further. Building on the image in the preceding section, read on to see how you can continue to manipulate this same image in even more dramatic ways. Here I move on to the Plastic Wrap filter. Using this filter makes an image look as if you've wrapped your subjects tightly with, um, plastic wrap. Go figure. You can imagine what that looks like. But here, tweaking this image with the Plastic Wrap filter (an image that has been altered using maximum settings of the Unsharp Mask filter), you get a Surrealist effect. After using the maximum Unsharp Mask settings, you can use the settings shown for the Plastic Wrap filter in Figure 15-6.

Figure 15-6: Go surreal with the Plastic Wrap filter.

Glowing Edges filter

Applying the Glowing Edges filter (Stylize⊃Glowing Edges) makes an image's edges range from being subtly outlined with color to radiantly glowing, like neon at night. You tweak an edge's width, brightness, and smoothness (as shown in Figure 15-7) to get the effect you want.

Figure 15-7: Tweak the glow on edges here.

Watercolor filter

The Watercolor filter application is easy and requires only that you choose Filter⊃Artistic⊃Watercolor and then adjust the sliders so that the effect is to your liking. Check out the amazing transformation in the before and after floral image of Figure 15-8. (I used settings of Brush Detail: 10, Shadow Intensity: 1, and Texture: 2.)

Sometimes lightening your image by using the sliders in Shadow/Highlight (Image⊃Adjustments⊃Shadow/Highlight) and/or tweaking the Hue/Saturation option in Photoshop before using the Watercolor filter gives you a better result than using the filter alone.

Figure 15-8: Try different values to create a watercolor effect.

Sketch filters

If watercolors aren't your thing, take an image and convert it to a sketchlike image in Photoshop by using one of the sketch filters. I find this technique effective when starting with an image with lots of shadows, silhouettes from natural sunlight, and lines within architecture. Here are but a few of the Sketch filters that Photoshop offers.

Charcoal

Use the Charcoal filter (Filter➪Sketch➪Charcoal) to create streaked lines, just like you get when drawing with a charcoal pencil. Photoshop *posterizes* major edges with bold edges, turning darker shadows into highlights. Start with a heavily shadowed image, apply the Charcoal filter, and then lighten. See the results in Figure 15-9.

I chose the maximum Detail setting (as well as Charcoal Thickness: 5 and Light/Dark Balance: 37) because I had many dark tones in my original image that, when highlighted, still showed some detail through sketched lines in between the edges.

Figure 15-9: Use the Charcoal filter for a soft, hand-drawn effect.

Chalk & Charcoal

Use the Chalk & Charcoal filter (Filter⇨Sketch⇨Chalk & Charcoal) on images that have a good range of highlights, midtones, and shadows. This effect makes midtones mostly gray and chalky, and shadows turn to black charcoal lines. If your image consists only of a limited range of midtones, using the Chalk & Charcoal filter makes these colors flat and gray.

In the picture I chose, one with a darker foreground and lighter background, the lighter tones in back appeared hand-brushed with short diagonal strokes. As a result, in the foreground, the dark tones are medium to dark shades of gray, and the light that breaks through has a soft chalky appearance, as shown in Figure 15-10. Setting Charcoal Area and Chalk Area to 6 and Stroke Pressure to 1 produced this effect.

Figure 15-10: Create an effect of drawing with chalk and charcoal.

Graphic Pen

Use the Graphic Pen filter (Filter➪Sketch➪Graphic Pen) to give your image the feeling that your image was sketched in pen and ink. Figure 15-11 shows how an image can change from a clear photograph to one that was sketched fastidiously. You get more options in the directions of the strokes with this tool than with other sketch tools. In so doing, you can change the depth of detail depending on what direction the strokes go.

Figure 15-11: Go for the old movies "still" look in this transformation from photo to sketch.

I set the Stroke Direction to Horizontal, emphasizing the foreground and separating it from the fairly mundane background. I stuck to the middle ground (a setting of 10) on the Stroke Length and Light/Dark Balance (59).

Emboss filter

Use the Emboss filter (Filter➪Stylize➪Emboss) to stylize your image with a sculpted look, as shown in Figure 15-12. The Emboss filter is tricky in that at low values, it offers you a gray, claylike cover to your image — and at higher values, the claylike gray separates from your image's real color so that you've got double vision (not ordinary seeing double) in which you see your subject in color and a copy of your subject in a kind of claymation.

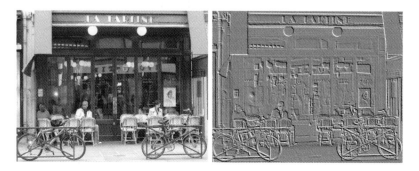

Figure 15-12: This filter makes an image look like pressed tin.

In this case I went for the conservative look of this filter with height values of 9 pixels — any more, and the shadows drift off onto entities by themselves. I tweaked the Angle to 49° because that gave me the most detail in the bikes and people. It also added a little dimension, which is the real deal with this filter. The Amount slider was set to 129% for this image.

Constructing a Composite à la Warhol Using Photoshop Filters

Time to turn up the flame a few notches. Take a very simple image — like an uncluttered basic portrait — and multiply it into a frenzy of color variations and repetition to emulate the work of Andy Warhol, an icon of pop art, who created startling and revolutionary block prints of repeating images. Here's how you can emulate his work via Photoshop from one simple image of your own.

1. **Open a color shoulders-up portrait (a head shot) and then use the Crop tool from the Tools palette to crop the image so it's a tight fit in the frame.**

   Start with a copy of your original so you still have your source image.

   I used Figure 15-13 to begin the process.

Figure 15-13: Start with a simple portrait to make a Warhol block print

2. **(Optional) Choose Image⇨Adjustments⇨Desaturate to take the color out of the image.**

   Desaturating an image is a simple way to change it to look as if it is black-and-white (B&W), clearing the way of all color so that the gray tones can be replaced with the bright, offbeat colors from the Gradient Map.

3. **Choose Image⇨Adjustments⇨ Gradient Map.**

   I clicked the sample gradient in the Gradient Map dialog box and chose the Rainbow gradient, as shown in Figure 15-14. I also

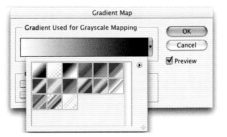

Figure 15-14: Click the drop-down menu to get gradients with colors.

selected the Reverse option because I liked the sharpness of the models features with this option.

Figure 15-15 shows what the Gradient Map tool does to your desaturated image.

4. **Save your base image.**

You can use this alone (um, stop here) or with other portraits produced in the same way to make a composite of like images (keep reading).

Figure 15-15: The base image after applying the Gradient Map tool.

To make it easier to find when you repeat the image in different color tones, save it in its own specially named folder on your desktop. And if you make a mistake, you can start over again with this image.

5. **Choose Image⇨Duplicate⇨*ImageName* as many times as you want the image repeated (where *ImageName* is the name of your original file).**

6. **Choose Image⇨Adjustments⇨Hue/Saturation.**

7. **Enter 20 for the hue for a picture that appears active on your screen (any picture).**

8. **Click OK and save to your project folder.**

9. **Repeat Steps 6, 7, and 8, adding 20 to the hue value each time.**

My composite contained nine images, so I did this eight times. (I renamed my original and tweaked that one last.) At the end of this, you have nine images open on your desktop. Each time you change the hue by 20, your image takes on a different gradient color. Continue to add 20 to the hue for each picture to reach the max hue (which is 180) after the ninth picture.

See Figure 15-16 to see the Hue/Saturation feature and the files duplicated.

10. **Choose File⇨Automate⇨Picture Package.**

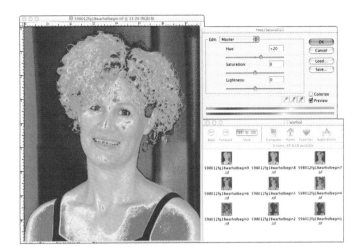

Figure 15-16: Up the hue for each image in the composite.

11. **Select the page size from the Layout drop-down list (Document section), choose the nine-picture option — (9)2.55x3.25 — as shown in Figure 15-17.**

12. **Click the first box (in the upper-right corner of the layout) and then navigate to your first picture.**

13. **Repeat Step 12 for the rest of the pictures, selecting a new picture for each box.**

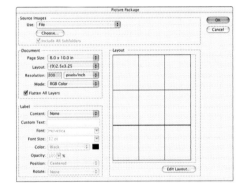

Figure 15-17: Choose nine pictures for your Warhol tribute.

14. **Click OK and wait a few seconds for Photoshop to make your block print.**

15. **After the block print is compiled, choose Layer⇨Flatten Layers to make all the prints in one layer.**

See Chapter 14 for more information about layers.

Figure 15-18 shows the final result.

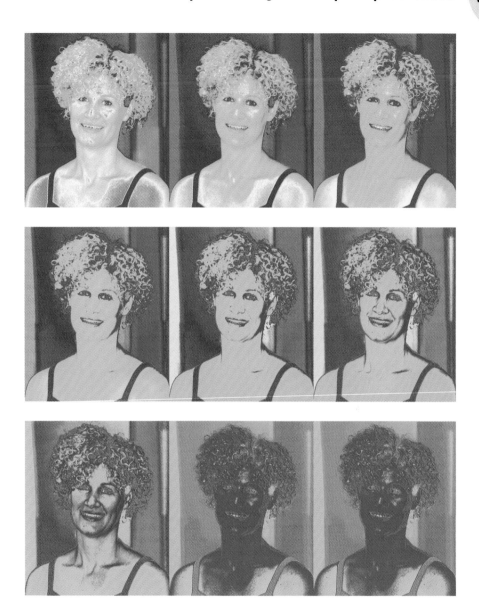

Figure 15-18: A Warhol tribute using Photoshop's Picture Package utility.

Making a Background for Your Images

Adding a different or dramatic background to an image can provide you with a whole new look and feel for an image. For example, using a fiery background could add spice to a shot of a supermodel or conjure up feelings of a native ritual when placed behind shots of South Seas' island Tikis. Let Photoshop do the work of cleaning up a less-than-optimal background and insert something artsy.

Here's how to make a fiery background:

1. **Open up a new Photoshop document.**

2. **Make the image 10 x 8 and the Resolution 300 pixels/inch.**

3. **Press the D key on your keyboard to set the default colors of black (foreground) and white (background).**

4. **Choose Filter⇨Render⇨Clouds to get a premade version of a Photoshop cloud image.**

5. **Choose Filter⇨Render⇨Lighting Effects.**

   Use this option to spread light among the clouds with a half-dozen slider bars, as shown in Figure 15-19.

At the top of the Lighting Effects dialog box is a drop-down menu that offers preset slider values for the sliders for the rest of the dialog box along with varying cloud type patterns. In addition, in the Preview window, you can click and drag shapes that Photoshop automatically inserts to redistribute the preselected light values.

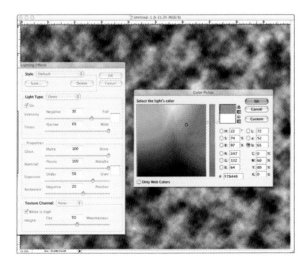

Figure 15-19: Use these sliders to make fiery clouds.

6. In the Lighting Effects dialog box, do the following:

a. *Choose Omni for the type of light (Light Type) to change the light distribution from the default ellipse to a circular pattern.*

b. *Click the white color swatch to the right of the Intensity slider to open the Color Picker.*

c. *From the Color Picker, choose a red-orange color for your fiery background.*

The cloud renders orange with black.

d. *Drag the Intensity slider to 50.*

Don't worry about the focus here.

e. *Under Properties, click the white color swatch next to the Material slider and navigate to red in the Color Picker dialog box that opens. (Click around until you get the shade you want.)*

f. *Drag the Gloss slider to 100, the Material slider to 100, and the Ambience slider to 20, as shown in Figure 15-20.*

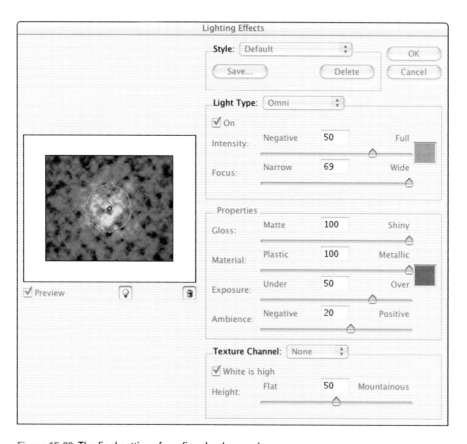

Figure 15-20: The final settings for a fiery background.

The final background image is shown in Figure 15-21. You could place an object — such as a Tiki — in the foreground. (To do so, use layers, as I discuss in Chapter 14.)

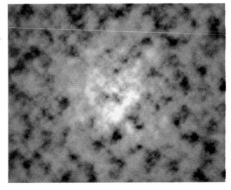

Figure 15-21: A fiery background is a perfect setting for images of a Hawaiian luau.

Part IV
The Final Output: Gallery-Worthy Prints

The 5th Wave   By Rich Tennant

"If I'm not gaining weight, then why does this digital image take up 3 MB more memory than a comparable one taken six months ago?"

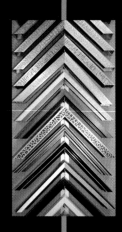

In this part . . .

Going on a photo shoot is fun, and playing with Photoshop is a blast, but when can I have a print to hold in my hands or put in a frame or sell? Here ya go in this part. Read Chapter 16 to master managing your electronic photo files (tedious, yes, but necessary). Chapter 17 gets you to that all-important Print button as well as the prep work that gets you to that point. Then comes presenting the final product to the world (and to clients) — matting and framing your photo, which I cover in Chapter 18.

16

Managing and Preparing Files

In This Chapter

▷ Discovering the purposes of different file formats

▷ Recognizing interpolation options Photoshop uses to enlarge your image

▷ Converting multiple high-resolution files for Internet uploading

▷ Constructing matrix images from multiple files

*P*aper files occupy space in a file cabinet, and digital files occupy space on a hard drive. Making sure the files don't burst out of their seams means keeping track of how big they are because file size is the very foundation upon which your computer will operate — lots of big files make a computer move like molasses. And keeping track of the space you're working in is largely dependent on your file sizes.

In this chapter, many of the common file types are defined in terms of their size with respect to keeping the image intact — that is, not losing detail in the image as you manipulate and process it along the way to printing.

Files become big in a variety of ways. It happens when you're not even thinking about it. Adding a layer, using a template, and moving documents from Word to Photoshop all require space in your computer and all make your files bigger.

After you get rolling in digital photography, you'll need more space to keep the large picture files. You can get a 160 gigabyte (GB) external hard drive from LaCie for about $100. It connects through your computer's FireWire port. *FireWire* is an extra-fast connection that will have your files moving from your computer to your external hard drive and back at lightning speed. See Chapter 3 for more about external hard drives.

For decent quality when printing to an inkjet printer, you want an image resolution of 300 pixels per inch (ppi) so that it retains quality. See Chapter 2 for more about what pixels are and how they make up your image.

Transferring an Image from Your Camera to Your Computer

Unless you print directly from a digital camera or the camera's media, digital images from your camera are stored on your computer.

Of course, an image can get into your computer from a variety of other sources, such as a scanner or the Internet. Downloading brings these image files onto your computer. iPhoto, by default on Macintosh computers, opens automatically when you connect the USB cable from your camera to your computer and turn on your camera. The program asks whether you want to download your images from the camera. Most other camera software that imports pictures from your camera, on both Windows and the Mac, does the same.

To work with each image in preparation for printing, you need an image editing program. Most digital cameras come with some sort of rudimentary software, but the program of choice is Photoshop (for professionals) or Photoshop Elements (for those with smaller budgets and/or less demanding requirements). Photoshop CS2 is the latest version and now includes Adobe Bridge, which can be used to browse and organize your image files.

From film/scanning

To bring into your computer a hard copy, film-based source image — whether a negative or a positive — you need to scan the image to create a digital copy. Although a dedicated film scanner is the tool of choice, purchasing a scanner that can scan both transparencies and *reflective materials* (such as photos and paper) lets you cover more bases for fewer dollars. See Chapter 3 for more about scanners.

If you're scanning print material and get lots of little dot overlays along with your scan, you can get rid of these in Photoshop by running your scanned material through the Gaussian Blur filter (Filter⇨Blur⇨Gaussian Blur). For more about Photoshop filters, see Chapter 15.

From a JPEG file

Almost all digital cameras can use JPEG files to record images, and some use only the JPEG file format. The camera holds these files on internal memory or on removable media that you slip inside them (see Chapter 3). You then download these stored images from your camera or removable media to your computer. Many cameras store your images in the Pictures folder of your computer, giving them various and sundry (and sometime long and boring) numbers.

Few professional photographers use the software that comes with their computer or camera to download and organize their images. You, too, can find better — and affordable — software, such as iView MediaPro (www. iview-multimedia.com) and Extensis Portfolio (www.extensis.com/en/ products/asset_management.jsp).

The JPEG file format uses compression to reduce file size, enabling you to store more photos on your camera's removable media than if you used the TIFF or Raw file formats. Although this is great when you're in the field, keep in mind that the process of saving in the JPEG format actual discards some of the image data. Repeatedly resaving as JPEG can severely degrade an image's appearance. Therefore, after opening a JPEG file in your image editing program and making changes, I suggest that you use the program's File⇨Save As command and create a TIFF file (which won't discard image data) rather than using the Save command to overwrite the JPEG. Don't worry, though, about opening/viewing/closing a JPEG — it's only the saving that can degrade the image.

From a Raw file

A *Raw* file consists of the unprocessed image data and information about that image data and the file, called *metadata*. (*Raw* means nothing less than what it says — no acronym here.) The metadata can include such information about the image as the shutter speed and f-stop, the white balance, the camera and lens used, and even (for some cameras) the actual spot at which the image was captured in the form of Global Positioning System (GPS) data. In addition, the metadata can include information about the image's file, such as the date/time the file was created, the file's size, and the filename.

When you make changes to a Raw file's appearance using Photoshop's Camera Raw plug-in (see Figure 16-1), the image itself is not changed. Instead, all the settings you select in Camera Raw are recorded to the metadata, where they can be accessed at any time. And because the adjustments are recorded to the metadata rather than actually made to the image itself, the original image is always available — unchanged and untouched. All you need to do is reopen the file in Camera Raw and apply different adjustments. Therein lies the beauty of working with Raw images — no matter how many versions you create and no matter how many changes you apply, the original, unprocessed image data always remains but a click away!

Photoshop CS2 has a really swift way of displaying the Raw file dialog box. It uses your camera's metadata to list (along the top part of the dialog box) the vital stats of your shot — camera type, Raw file type (each digital camera has a different Raw file type; CR2 is the type of file that Canon Rebel XT shoots in), ISO value, shutter speed, f-stop, and focal length. Notice the information at the top in Figure 16-1.

Figure 16-1: The Raw dialog box in Photoshop CS2.

Raw is an extremely valuable format for professionals; as soon as word gets out how nice this format is to tweak on your computer, everyone will join in on the fun. Several aspects of the image capture can wait until you download your photo onto your computer instead of getting bogged down to get the perfect shot in the field. Raw files are large; in the digital darkroom, the Raw conversion on multiple files can take some time. Because Raw files give more detail in terms of light and color, they are preferred among professionals to use during the editing process.

Using Raw files with Tiger and Panther

In Mac OS X Tiger and Panther (v 10.4 and 10.3, respectively), you don't need to download software for your digital camera. The Mac OS has its own utility called Image Capture (Applications⇨ Image Capture in Tiger). Connect your camera to the computer; when you click this utility's icon, a dialog box with your camera's model appears. From here, you have a choice to download some or all of your images (stored in your camera's memory). You can also access a drop-down menu (click Options) with various profiles, including those you've made to calibrate your monitor. (You'll want to use your calibration options when you go to open, edit, and print your images in Photoshop.) After you download the pictures, they're stored in the system's Pictures folder.

Shooting in Raw format is relatively easy (when your camera offers the capability). Within the menu (usually toggled to access while viewing your camera's LCD screen) of most dSLR cameras (for more about camera types, see Chapter 2) is an option to shoot in Raw format. Everything else stays pretty much the same as in other formats.

Some cameras do not allow you to shoot in Raw format when you're using an auto mode. (For more about auto mode, see Chapter 11.)

On most models, shooting in Raw format is only permitted in the *Creative Zone,* the zone where many of the settings are freed up to be set by you, the photographer.

When you edit a Raw photo, you can change the color balance and profile with the Raw data from the image just as if your camera was doing it during the shoot. If you convert the same photo to a JPEG file, much information is thrown away to make the file smaller *(compressed),* so you don't have as much color data to work with. A Raw photo comes to your computer as a 16-bit image so that the color and detail are strikingly clear. (16-bit color uses 16 bits — actual zeros and ones at the basic binary level — to record the color of each pixel. With 16 bits of data, you have an incredible number of possible different colors.) You need to convert the image to 8-bit color to save as a JPEG. You can convert to 8-bit color in the Camera Raw dialog box or by using the Photoshop Edit⇨Mode⇨8-Bits/Channel command. (In versions of Photoshop prior to Photoshop CS2, look for the command under the Image menu rather than the Edit menu.)

After you finish tweaking the white/color balance and levels in Photoshop or your camera's Raw processing software, you can save this file as a TIFF file and proceed with more tweaking in Photoshop or take it straight to press.

Are Raw Files a Raw Deal?

Each camera company makes its own Raw file format, perhaps because each wants users to use its company's downloading software and browser. Maybe it's a prestige thing. In order to deal with the variety of formats, Photoshop (www.adobe.com) has come up with a free converter (see Figure 16-2) to convert your image to its .dng format, referred to as a *digital negative* of your camera's Raw photo format.

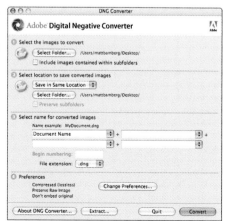

Figure 16-2: Convert Raw files here.

Fuji film's camera Raw files are labeled `.raf`. Canon has two kinds (`.crw` and `.cr2`), and Nikon and Olympus have their own, too (`.nef` and `.orf`, respectively). With so many file types (and so little time to learn about each), how does a digital photographer know what's going to be around next year or in a decade? Truth is, you won't.

Understanding the Relationship between File Type and File Size

Saving your files as TIFFs is the first step in keeping your image for a very long time. File➪Save As is the command that you use to convert a file to TIFF format in Photoshop (see Figure 16-3). There are many other files listed, but for the digital photographer who's interested in high-resolution, gallery-quality photographs, TIFF, JPEG, and Raw are the ones you'll be interested in using. TIFF offers some advantages: Its compressions algorithm (LZW), which is used to reduce the file size, doesn't degrade the image quality. Also, TIFF is compatible with most software with which you might use your images.

Figure 16-3: Saving file choices in drop-down Save As menu bar.

Defining and constructing a TIFF file in Photoshop

Most of the time, you'll convert to TIFF from either Raw files or JPEG files. To save hard drive space, you can make your TIFF file smaller (by about half) by compressing it. TIFF files don't compress as tightly as JPEGs do because the file is compressed in a *lossless* format. (In other words, when you open the file again, it's the same as the original.) Although TIFF format compressed files are still significantly larger than their JPEG brothers, some is better than none at all in terms of conserving hard drive space. See Chapter 2 for more information about JPEG file compression.

Five-megapixel cameras that shoot and store in JPEG (which most do) can give you a file anywhere from 1MB to 2.5MB, depending on the quality size you select in the camera's menu options. That same photo as an uncompressed TIFF requires about 14MB on your hard drive. With LZW compression (see Figure 16-4), the TIFF file shrinks to about 7MB, but that's still much larger than a JPEG — even at the highest quality setting.

Figure 16-4: Compress TIFF files for quick Internet transfer.

To ensure compatibility (and to make sure you'll be able to open your TIFF files years from now), use only LZW compression. Photoshop also offers JPEG and ZIP compression for TIFF files, but stick with LZW.

Creating a Web Gallery in Photoshop

If you want to put your photos quickly on the Internet, Photoshop has a quick way of converting not only each file but also setting up everything for you so that you can upload to any Web server. Web photos are usually small JPEG photos — say, from 4 to 60K. (There's a GIF format, too, which I don't cover here.)

Say you have a set of images of fruit that you want people to see on your Web site, and you want the images displayed so that users can easily navigate to them. Use Photoshop's Web Gallery option to convert your TIFF files to JPEG and display them on a Web page. The Web accepts only JPEG files and HTML code (an Internet computer language) to understand what to do with the files after they're uploaded to your Web server. (A *server* is a big computer that stores a multitude of Web sites.) To convert your high-resolution TIFF files to low-resolution JPEG files and the connected HTML code for uploading to the Internet (which will put them on display quite nicely, thank you), follow these steps:

1. **Locate the images you want to convert to JPEGs and put them into a folder.**

2. **Open Photoshop and choose File⇨Browser.**

3. **In Adobe Bridge, navigate to the folder that contains the images you want to convert.**

   Figure 16-5 shows the TIFF files that will be converted.

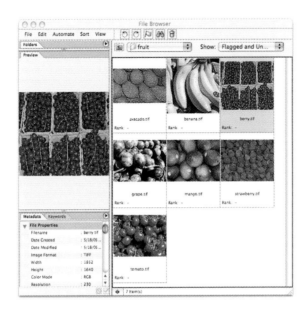

Figure 16-5: Convert TIFFs to JPEGs.

4. **Select all the photos in the folder by pressing ⌘+A (Mac) or Ctrl+A (Windows).**

5. **Choose Tools⇨Photoshop⇨Web Photo Gallery and select the settings, as shown in Figure 16-6, and then click OK.**

   When Photoshop processes your request, three folders appear on your Desktop — Images, Pages, and Thumbnails.

6. **Your new gallery opens in your default Web browser, ready for your review and approval.**

Web Photo Gallery offers a variety of different templates, with which you can produce galleries both simple and complex. To make your gallery available to friends and family via the Internet, contact your Internet service provider (ISP) or another operation about hosting your Web site. Your ISP can give you specific instructions for uploading your site to a Web server and assigning an address, known as a *Uniform Resource Locator* (URL), by which others can find and view your gallery.

Figure 16-6: Prepare a Web Gallery here.

Resolving Resolution Issues

If you want a clear print, you should aim to work with an image of at least 300 ppi at your desired print size. With a high-quality inkjet printer, you can use a somewhat lower resolution, but use 300 ppi as the target resolution.

When copying and pasting lots of stuff from file to file in Photoshop, have a standard resolution in mind to which you want to set each image. Photoshop automatically resizes an image if it's moved from one file to another at different resolutions.

Interpolation

When you change an image's pixel dimensions with the Image⇨Image Size command, you choose an *interpolation* method, which is an algorithm that Photoshop uses to re-create the image's appearance at its new size. To set an interpolation choice for Photoshop to use when transforming a selection within an image, choose Photoshop⇨Preferences⇨General (Mac) or Edit⇨ Preferences⇨General (Windows).

The interpolation options run as follows:

- **Nearest Neighbor:** I don't recommend this option for art photos because it produces rough edges, but it's great for some simple illustrations.

- **Bilinear:** This choice results in medium-quality interpolation, so it isn't a good option for art photography but can be excellent for blocky or irregularly shaped artwork.

- **Bicubic:** This option is fine for small changes to an image, such as minor resizing or transforming selections.

- **Bicubic Smoother:** This is a fine interpolation choice when enlarging images significantly.

- **Bicubic Sharper:** This option is great for reducing pixel dimensions because it keeps details sharp and well defined.

When considering enlarging an image for sale as art photography, start with an artful image — one that still looks good even if it loses resolution.

Resampling an image

Resampling an image, for all practical purposes, is enlarging or reducing the number of pixels with which the image is formed. The same image content is there (unlike with cropping), but a different number of pixels is used to represent the picture. Both increasing the number of pixels in the image (*upsampling*) and decreasing the number of pixels (*downsampling*, which you might do to create a Web version of a photo) can degrade the appearance of your image. When upsampling significantly, the image might look a little soft — out of focus. When downsampling, the fine detail in the image gets lost — eyes become blobs, grass becomes sheets of green, and diagonal and curved lines in the image can become jagged. Generally, as an art photographer, you're most likely to increase the pixel dimensions of a photo so that it can be printed at a larger size with good detail.

The left image in Figure 16-7 is a sign containing Egyptian hieroglyphics. I really liked the bird. This is a good subject for resampling because the blur that occurs when you resample softens the image — in this case, an image that took to softening well because it's etched in stone. I cropped the picture using the Crop tool from the Tools palette so that only the bird was in the image and then resampled it using the Bicubic Smoother (see the right image in Figure 16-7).

Resampling a person who is small in a picture by enlarging it ten times will likely not yield a good result, no matter how much you tweak it. Better to take another picture closer up (which, of course, could also have been done with the hieroglyph of the bird).

Figure 16-7: Resampling softens images.

You make an image grow, as I demonstrate with the preceding bird image, by using Photoshop's Bicubic Smoother interpolation method. Just follow these steps:

1. **Find an image that you think will take well to enlargement.**

2. **(Optional) If necessary, use the Crop tool to reduce the image to only the part that you want to enlarge.**

3. **Choose Image⇨Image Size.**

4. **In the Image Size dialog box that appears, mark the check boxes for Constrain Proportions and Resample, selecting Bicubic Smoother as the resampling method.**

   If the artwork contains layer styles, you also want to select the Scale Styles check box.

5. **In the Document Size area of the dialog box, enter your desired print dimensions and print resolution (usually 300 ppi).**

   You might use the upper part of the dialog box when preparing an image for a Web page, in which case you would need to work with specific pixel dimensions.

6. **When you're happy with the values, click OK and view your image.**

   Remember that you can always use the Edit⇨Step Backward command to reverse changes to your image.

Changing resolution without resampling

You might find a situation in which you need to change the resolution of an image while maintaining the original image's pixels. This is a trade-off: If you don't resample (change the number of pixels), you can change the resolution, but the print dimensions also change. For example, if you have an image 3000 pixels wide and the image resolution is 72 ppi, the print would be almost 42 inches wide. If you change the image's resolution to 300 ppi without changing the actual number of pixels in the image, the print size drops to 10 inches wide. Or, in a more practical sense, you can change the image's print dimensions without resampling, letting Photoshop determine the resolution.

Don't let your mind lock into *300 ppi* as a must-have resolution. It's generally better to *not* resample an image and print at a resolution of 250 ppi (or 360 ppi or 400 ppi or even perhaps 225 ppi) than it is to resample an image to 300 ppi for print. Avoid resampling if you can — that prevents the softening or loss of detail that can come with upsampling or downsampling.

To change an image's resolution without resampling, just do this:

1. **Open the image.**

2. **Choose Image⇨Image Size.**

3. **Deselect the Resample check box, enter your desired resolution, and then click OK.**

Printing Prep and Printing

In This Chapter

▶ Following a step-by-step printing process

▶ Matching your image in Photoshop with your printer output

▶ Processing your photo for superlative prints

*Y*ou have many options before you when printing your photos in the digital realm. You can print directly from iPhoto (on a Mac) or from the options within the software that came with your digital camera, which also likely contains some basic editing tools such as cropping and enhancing. However, most professionals and many amateurs use Photoshop to tweak their photos for the final output. Photoshop provides more alternatives to make sure your image keeps its detail, color, and contrast. (For more information about your photo's life as it's processed in Photoshop, viewed on your monitor, and transferred to a printer, see Chapter 3.)

In this chapter, I use a higher-end Epson Stylus Photo printer. Of course, models vary, but I think Epson makes excellent printers for art photos. (Many similar models are available, each printing at a variety of large sizes and able to print at sizes of 11" x 14" and larger.)

Discovering Proofs and Printing the Final Product

After your monitor is calibrated (as discussed in Chapter 3), you can make a *proof* — an estimate of what your print will look like when printed on the type of paper that you have in your printer — in Photoshop so that what you see onscreen is what you get in your print. The proof system works pretty well after you get the hang of it.

Here are the two ways you see an image in the proof-making process:

- **How the image is displayed on your monitor in Photoshop's *working space:*** This comprises Photoshop's tools and options and your image(s) displayed on your monitor.

- **From a soft proof:** In Photoshop, you can change the color and contrast of what you see in your working space to the color and contrast of how your image will look after printing. This copy of your image is a *soft proof.* The final result — a *hard proof* — is the output from your printer.

Your hard proof will never be exactly the same as your soft proof. There are just too many variables for that to happen, from how your monitor is calibrated to what interpretations Photoshop and your printer make from the colors it passes from one to the other.

You can tweak your soft proof (the copy that will be printed) two ways:

- **Look at it and tweak it using your own judgment.** This way, you can just make your original soft proof by going through the steps in "Preparing for Output" and then tweak it by eye for printing.

- **Create a duplicate copy** (one that you'll tweak to look like the original) before you set up the proof and apply the steps to your duplicate while you have your original onscreen until the soft proof and the original copy look alike.

Setting up a proof is a concept that has been taken from the hard copy print world to your LCD screen. Basically, a soft proof (which I refer to simply as a *proof* from here on out) is set up onscreen to see what your printer will print.

There are a multitude of choices in paper and printer models, each with specific profiles that you need to consider and set in Photoshop. In this example, I use an Epson printer and print on Epson enhanced matte paper. (The paper is what takes the ink and makes the color, so this is very important.) Profiles change when you change the paper you use. (More about that later in this section.) In the following steps, I show you how to set up your proof and save it as a profile you can later access. *Note:* I use Photoshop CS for this example, but I include notes regarding any changes in Photoshop CS2.

1. **With your image open in Photoshop CS, choose View⇨Proof Setup⇨ Custom (left, Figure 17-1).**

   The Proof Setup dialog box (right, Figure 17-1) opens, offering choices (Setup, Profile, Intent, Simulate) that I describe throughout this step list.

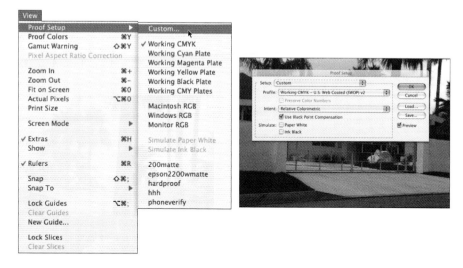

Figure 17-1: Begin to make a proof here.

2. **For Setup, choose Custom.**

   I choose Custom because I want a setup that matches my monitor and enhanced paper. Then I save this setting as phoneverify (see Figure 17-2) so that I can access it all the time. You have to pick a new paper if you change to glossy or other fancy papers.

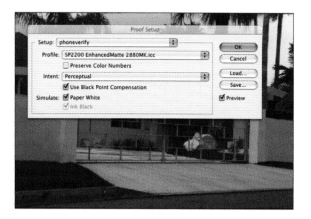

Figure 17-2: My selections for a proof.

3. **For Profile, choose the type of paper you're printing on.**

   Your printer driver software puts settings inside Photoshop from which you can choose for printing. It is from these settings that Photoshop recognizes the color of the medium (typically, paper) on which it's printing. This is important because the mixture of the paper's color and texture with the inks that are set into it is variable. A glossy paper takes ink differently than a matte paper, for instance.

   I choose EnhancedMatte 2880 (refer to Figure 17-2) because that's the paper I'm using, and I want a print at the highest resolution (the 2880 part). Epson has other choices in this drop-down list, so when I change paper, I can change this setting.

4. **For Intent, choose Perceptual and select the Use Black Point Compensation check box.**

   I choose Perceptual because it's the choice that's natural to the human eye. I could have gone with Relative Colorimetric. For vivid images like graphs or charts, I'd go with Saturation, which is standard and preserves the original colors more.

5. **For Simulate, select the Paper White and the Ink Black check boxes.**

   This tells Photoshop to match my image colors to the white of the matte paper.

6. **Save the profile by clicking Save and entering a name so that you can select it each time you later want to print, on any size enhanced matte paper.**

To soft-proof the image — that is, to see an onscreen representation of what the image will look like when printed — choose View➪Proof Colors. (Although some folks like to do all their work with Proof Color active, you might find that it's better for you to activate the command only when you want to double-check something in the image.)

Adobe has a system from which you can purchase technical help to solve any problem you have bringing your final Photoshop image to any type of printer. Help gurus can take you step by step through each Photoshop dialog box after you give them the type of paper and printer model that you have. The plan is worth its cost.

Preparing for Output

With proof in hand, printer turned on, and Photoshop opened to the image you want to print out, you're ready to produce your final paper output.

To get proper image quality for printing and selling, you either need to

- ✔ Scan your image from a negative or positive, sizing it or saving it when you download from your camera to your computer.

- ✔ Take a picture with a high-end (6 or more megapixels; MP) dSLR camera and download the picture to your computer and then open it in Photoshop. (Choose File➪Open and then navigate to the picture file in the Open dialog box.)

 Point-and-shoot cameras larger than 6MP can also be used for taking pictures to print at 13" x 19" inches and larger. That doesn't mean you can't print your images fairly clearly with a camera that takes pictures whose size is smaller than 6MP. It just means they won't be as clear as those that do.

Sometimes, you need to rotate your canvas if the image looks slightly cock-eyed. I usually eye it by a line that would be horizontal in a natural setting, like the horizon if you can see it in your image. Open the file in Photoshop and do a final rotation of your canvas. Choose Image➪Rotate Canvas➪Arbitrary. Small values from .5 to 2.0 are usually adequate for rotation clockwise (CW) or counter-clockwise (CCW) to correct handheld errors on a horizontal plane and to crop your image.

 Select Photoshop's Measure tool (under the Eyedropper tool in the Toolbox). Drag the tool along some line in the photo that should be horizontal or vertical. Now choose Image➪Rotate Canvas➪Arbitrary — the correct angle of rotation will already be entered, so you need only click OK!

After rotating your image, there are likely to be some areas of white along the edges. You can use the Clone Stamp tool to cover those areas or crop the image to eliminate them.

Making a Contact Sheet

Many of Photoshop's automate tools are great for making art pieces. For instance, you can create a group of portraits side by side in a new Photoshop document for an art collage.

One of the great things about Photoshop is its ability to work with virtually any image of any size. Use the TIFF format for the best results using any of Photoshop's file image manipulation packages in the Automate option (File➪Automate).

The following example will help you to understand how to set up multiple files so that they work together to create one image. Just take a series of images, of anything you want, and then put them together in Photoshop.

1. **Take a series of nine photos by setting your camera on an automatic timer mode.**

   Make sure that the background of each is at about the same focal length, as shown in Figure 17-3. Of course, you could make a contact sheet out of existing photos, in which case you would skip this step and go straight to Step 2.

Figure 17-3: Select pics from your browser for your contact sheet.

2. **Download the images into a folder on your computer in your camera's best-quality JPEG format.**

   You can convert the entire photo collage to TIFF format at the end.

3. **In Photoshop, choose File⇨Automate⇨Contact Sheet II and select your Source folder.**

4. **Choose your page size/resolution and select the number of rows and columns necessary to fit all the images in that folder onto one page.**

   Remember to choose the printable area of your page (such as 8" x 10") rather than the paper size (8.5" x 11") to allow room for the printer's margins. Because this image is destined to be printed as art, make sure to use 300 pixels per inch (ppi) as your resolution.

5. **Deselect the Use Filename as Caption option (for an art photo) and click OK.**

6. **Save your image as a TIFF file.**

You can, of course, apply some of your Photoshop magic to the resulting image. You might, for example, decide that the collage has more impact as a grayscale image (see Figure 17-4).

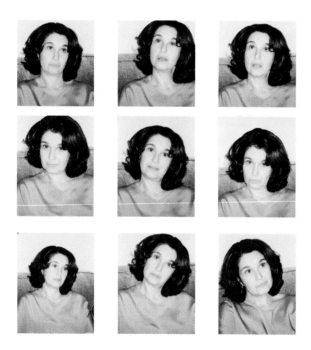

Figure 17-4: Contact sheets can be used for a variety of purposes.

Previewing Your Print

I continue processing my image for print within the Print with Preview dialog boxes. It's here that you set your printer to use Photoshop's colors and not Epson's or Canon's (or whatever printer model you have); you also specify the size of your paper and where on the paper you want your print.

1. **To access Print with Preview, choose File⇨Print with Preview.**

2. **When the Print dialog box comes up, click the Page Setup button to specify your paper size and print orientation (in the resulting Page Setup dialog box).**

I set my printer for (Epson) Stylus 2200 Photo US letter size. (All the Epson 2200 size possibilities are within this menu pop-up.) I also click the Orientation icon that indicates landscape mode. See Figure 17-5.

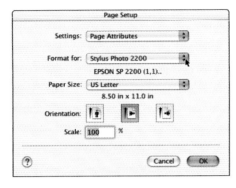

Figure 17-5: Specify paper size and direction.

After you make your choices, click OK to close the Page Setup dialog box.

3. **Back in the Print dialog box, set your printing options.**

In particular, in the Print Space profile (Printer Profile in CS2), make sure to select the printer's profile for the paper on which you're printing.

4. **Click Print and select your preset quality print choice.**

The printer's own Print dialog box opens, from which you make a selection from the Presets drop-down list.

I choose the mattequality preset. I saved this option because I print on this paper type again and again.

If your preset is already chosen, scroll through the drop-down menu and then reclick the preset to set it again. Otherwise, the image falls into default mode.

5. **Turn off the printer's own color management.**

The last thing that I do is to choose Color Management from the drop-down menu that falls after the Printer and Presets menus. Because I don't want the printer to decide my colors for me — I want Photoshop to decide — I select the No Color Adjustment radio button, as shown in Figure 17-6.

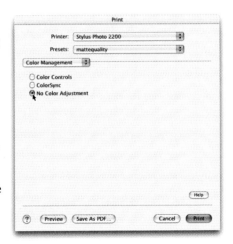

Figure 17-6: Choose from printing presets.

18

Framing and Matting

In This Chapter

▷ Buying or making mats

▷ Configuring mats for your photography

▷ Buying and assembling frames

▷ Framing on the cheap

*H*ow you frame your print has a great impact on its value. Your options are many in terms of finding a display for your digital photographs. If you're on a budget or just starting out, you can refurbish old frames or learn the craft of making or putting together the frames and mats yourself. If you're preparing high-end art for galleries and upscale stores, there are many places from which you can order frames and mats and other accessories online or through traditional retail.

Many galleries want only frame jobs that comprise professional mounting and acid-free papers. Read more about using acid-free papers and why they're important in the section, "Takin' It to the Mats."

Finding mats for your photographs goes hand-in-hand with finding frames for your photographs. When making framing choices, consider both the presentation of your work as well as how to protect it. You also have to consider the tastes and styles of your potential clients.

For the examples in this chapter, I show mats that are on the conservative end of the art spectrum because galleries and many stores want simple mats and frames for photography. You'll likely see many other options when you view mats for sale online or in catalogs, so keep your creativity and tastes in mind if you go with more fancy matting and framing.

At the end of the chapter are a few tips to help you put a picture inside ready-made frames. For the purposes of clarity in this book, the two types of frames that I refer to are

- **Ready-made frames:** These frames are put together for you, ready to accept your photo. They typically include the glass, the frame, and backboard (and sometimes the mat). All that's left is to put your picture inside. You can buy ready-mades in bulk.

- **Custom-made frames:** These frames are ones in which the entire frame is made for you with your picture in it. Although the convenience factor is high, this is an expensive method and I don't recommended using these for art photos that you sell.

Takin' It to the Mats

Mats, which are placed between the photo and the glass for both protective and aesthetic purposes, come in all colors, shapes, and sizes. Just about anything you want in terms of mat geometry is available. By *mat geometry,* I mean that you can find mats with openings other than the traditional squares and rectangles — oval, round, triangular. And complementing your photograph with a decent, reasonably priced mat is easier than ever. Stores today — both online and brick-and-mortar — can supply you with what you need to make your own or make them for you. Photography frames are easy to order, too, because of the specialized mats just for this purpose. I usually get my frames and mats together at the same place. To cut costs (especially when I try to sell a print for a higher profit), I shop around for the least-expensive mats that fit the frames I get from another supplier. Read more about where you can get mats and frames wholesale later in this chapter.

Before you start searching for mats, a little lesson in mat lingo will make things easier when you order. It's the language the mat guys use so they can build the right mat for your work. When you order your mats, whether you do so online or in a local frame shop, the framers will want to know how you want your image orientated, what size it is, as well as a few other pertinent pieces of information:

- **Orientation:** Let the framer know how you want your picture set up in the mat. Figure 18-1 shows you the ins and outs of landscape, portrait, and bottom-weighted orientation for mats and their openings.

- **Size:** State the shorter dimension first. For example, use 11 x 14 (inches) and not 14 x 11 (inches). That is, an 8 x 10 is always an 8 x 10 regardless of whether you display it landscape or portrait.

Always order your mat opening about an eighth to a quarter of an inch smaller than the image you'll place under it. For example, to order a mat for an 8" x 10" photo, order the opening cut to 7¾" x 9¾". If you don't, you could risk having the backing paper show up in the opening.

✔ **Double matting:** You don't need to state the dimensions of both mats. If your outer mat is 11" x 14", your inner mat will be one inch less, or 10" x 13". One inch on each side is the industry standard. For art photos, double matting is not common. Instead, many professionals choose a thicker mat.

✔ **Acid-free:** Sometimes called *conservation quality,* an acid-free mat isn't as susceptible to fading as ordinary mats and is important to prevent degradation of the photo paper.

✔ **Color:** Stick with basic white for a mat for your photo to satisfy the harmony it gives with the medium, especially if you're going to be evaluated by a professional for a gallery presentation. I think that white is the best color to use for a mat. If you have to play with color, go with pastels, like robin's egg blue. Of course, though, you might think that gray or black best complements your photograph.

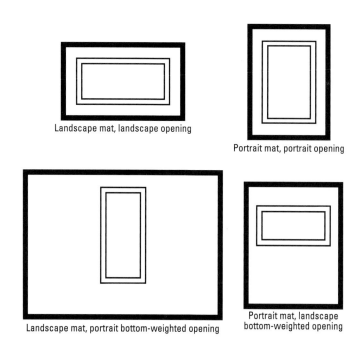

Landscape mat, landscape opening

Portrait mat, portrait opening

Landscape mat, portrait bottom-weighted opening

Portrait mat, landscape bottom-weighted opening

Figure 18-1: Mat configurations.

If your piece is designed to match *OPP* (a 1980s abbreviation meaning *other people's property* — most likely, their sofa), go to the local furniture store and ask the clerk what items people have been buying lately. Or, work with your client to match colors appropriately.

Comparing mat options

Whether you present your work to a high-brow gallery or sell your work in the neighborhood shabby chic palace, the advantages and disadvantages of mat buying for each kind of mat are described in Table 18-1. Prices in the table reflect the prices for acid-free mats.

Table 18-1	Mat Basics	
Type of Mat	*Advantages*	*Disadvantages*
Handmade from large mat boards	You can cut a custom mat for images in nonstandard sizes. (No need to resize the image in Photoshop.) Easily cut your mat's inside to match that of your printed photo. Costs fall rapidly after equipment purchase.	Good equipment takes up space, takes time to to master, and can be a bit expensive. (About $200.)
Precut mats from retail	No waiting (like an order) and no cutting. (Comes prepackaged in a variety of sizes and colors.) Mat price varies from $5 to $8, but many packages come with double mats.	Expensive. Sizes are limited, usually to 11" x 14" or 16" x 20".
Precut mats from wholesale	Professionals cut these, so any size is possible. Inexpensive (prices as low as $5 for an 18" x 22" mat with an 11" x 17" opening). Mats can be made/ordered with a frame as lower-priced package.	Usually takes a week to get made. Large orders are required.
Recycled	Very cheap; good for the environment.	Old mats can be discolored.

Cutting your own mats

You can certainly save money and have a lot of creative control when you cut you own mats. Purchase a mat cutter and mat boards and have at it. A variety of mat cutters are available. Check out `www.rockler.com` to find small mat cutters starting at $20 as well as a serious 40-inch cutter for $195. (At this site, on the left, under Departments, choose Tools⇨Picture Framing to see the cutters.) The high-end cutters include sliding guides and stops to make sure you don't overrun your cut. This Web site also includes a handbook for picture framing, "Home Book of Picture Framing" by Ken Oberrecht.

Buying mat board to cut is simple. You can easily order board online from places like http://jerrysartarama.com, which features acid-free mat boards that are reasonably priced. (Acid-free mat boards are made with materials that won't destroy your photos.) Boards (30" x 42") from this site run from $4 to $7 per piece. (A minimum order of 12 boards is required, and returns are not accepted.)

Small mat cutters, available at local art supply stores, allow you to make hand cuts with small guides (but you have to keep a steady hand). They're not easy to use, requiring great coordination to make the right kind of cut. An example is a Dexter Mat Cutter ($26.88) with a plastic knob that allows for cutting at any angle or depth.

When you cut a mat opening, you create a beveled edge — a very small 45° angle on the edge of the opening — while you cut, working within the thickness of the board, a place that's only a fraction of an inch thick. This can be a little tricky. Still, if you're adventurous and want to cut your own mats, it's not like you need the dexterity of a heart surgeon. It's only cardboard. Cutting your own mats lets you make any size you want and ends up being cheaper in the long run.

Keep these hints in mind when you do:

- **The more you do, the easier it gets.** Go ahead and take the first step. That's the hardest step — actually doing it.

- **Gather all your framing tools upfront.** You need a mat cutting kit, ruler, tape (double-faced), a burnishing tool, a razor blade, and linen tape.

  You can find mat kits at www.logangraphic.com.

Creating a mat in Photoshop

A mat doesn't have to be a physical piece of board; it can alternatively be something you craft within Photoshop as part of the image itself. Here's how:

1. **From an open image, choose Window⇨Layers to see your Layers palette.**

   For more about layers, see Chapter 14.

2. **Double-click the *Background* layer in the Layers palette and rename the layer.**

   This converts the background layer into a regular layer so that you can add a layer mask.

3. **To mask out part of the image so that you can frame it, use the Rectangular Marquee tool to select the part of the picture that you want framed, as shown in Figure 18-2.**

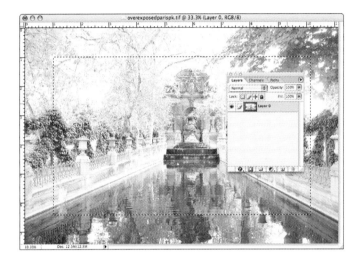

Figure 18-2: Choose the portion of the image you'll see in the digital frame.

4. **Click the Add Layer Mask button at the bottom of the Layers palette.**

See the result in Figure 18-3.

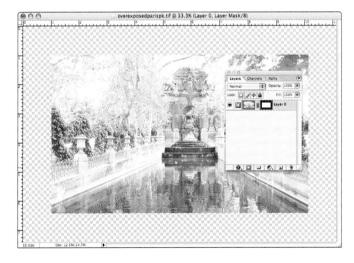

Figure 18-3: Select a layer mask.

The checkerboard area that you can see in the figure means that there's nothing there yet — no color, no picture, nothing. That's where the mat goes. Don't think that Photoshop tried to be "helpful" and created a checked mat for you.

5. **To add the equivalent of a mat, use the Stroke effect. Click the second icon — the Add a Layer Style button — at the bottom of the Layers palette, as shown in Figure 18-4.**

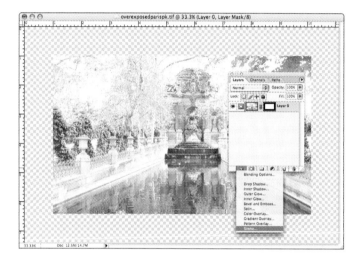

Figure 18-4: Choose the stroke effect.

6. **Choose your stroke settings — color, size, and position (Outside to create a mat effect). Drag the Layer Style dialog box to the side and watch what happens to the image as you move each slider.**

   Make sure the Preview check box is marked and move the sliders until you get what you like. You can see the settings I chose in Figure 18-5.

7. **Add a new layer by clicking the New Layer icon in the Layers palette (next to the trash can at the bottom) and move the new layer below your image layer in the Layers palette.**

   To change the order of the layers, click the new layer in the Layers palette and drag it downward until you see a heavy black line below the original layer; then release the mouse button.

8. **Select a color for the mat.**

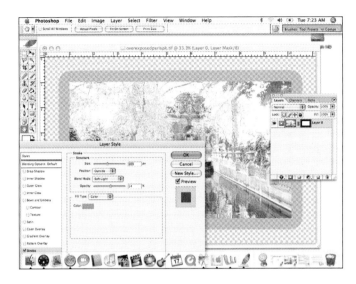

Figure 18-5: Tweak the matting effect that you want.

    a. Click the foreground color swatch in the toolbar.

    b. Select the Eyedropper tool.

    c. Find a place on the image where you like the color and click around until you see a color that you like in the foreground color swatch.

    d. Select the Paint Bucket tool.

    e. Click anywhere in your image to fill the lower layer with the selected color.

The "matted" image is shown in Figure 18-6.

Figure 18-6: Tweak and finish your mat in Photoshop.

Make your own poster

To gain your own sense of style, you can make a poster with text and image. You can decide on an era you want to re-create or a specific theme you want to create and choose a text that matches it. Images that are taken of shady spots (like under a tree over a lake in a park) and overexposed by +1.5 result in an exposure can look Impressionistic when printed. Add some borders and text that matches the image and you've got your own poster. Mass-produced posters are some of the most common saleable art in stores today.

Try using different Photoshop filters — Noise⇨Add Noise followed by Glass, Mosaic, or Gaussian Blur — on your mat layer for cool effects to make a poster out of your art. Read more about this in *Photoshop CS Timesaving Techniques For Dummies* (Phyllis Davis, Wiley).

The Great Frame-Up

Framing can be just as artful as the photography itself. If the frame isn't right for the photograph, you lose the total effect. And if you're trying to market your art, people won't buy it.

Your framing options are varied:

✓ **Frame kits:** You can order framing kits that include everything — glass/Plexiglass, hangers, pads (so the frame doesn't knock against the wall), mats, backing boards — but that need to be assembled. See the later section, "Buying online; finding Internet deals," for shopping sites that carry these kits.

Speaking of hangers . . . there are a few kinds:

- *Wires that stretch from one side to the other on the frame:* These are time consuming to put on.

- *One-piece metal hangers:* These are my favorite because all you have to do is hammer them onto the frame.

- *Metal hangers with screws:* Ugh. You need to have microscopic vision and robot hands to set and screw those beasts into the frame.

✔ **Order by parts:** You can order everything in parts from the four sides of aluminum frames to the hardware to put them together, each at its own price. Many artists order metal frames from Light Impressions this way. Their frames are professional quality but need to be assembled. Check out `www.lightimpressionsdirect.com` for their aluminum frame kits.

When choosing a frame, always consider your photograph. For example, you probably wouldn't want to put a heavy carved wooden frame around a photograph that's light and feminine (say, of your friend, the supermodel, splashing in the pool). Here are some examples of frame types and appropriate art to place within them:

✔ **Thick carved wooden frames:** These are great for cowboy/western or rustic photos. Sometimes a slimmed-down version of these frames can be a pleasant surrounding for nature photos.

✔ **Traditional black photography frames:** Sepia and black-and-white (B&W) photos look clean and professional in these types of frames.

✔ **Silver metal frames:** Something very modern looks good inside a metallic frame — say, glistening skyscrapers or city lights reflected on a body of water.

✔ **Bamboo-style frames:** Especially popular nowadays, a frame like this fits well with a print that's tropical or Polynesian themed. Try a bamboo-textured mat to add to the theme. (Color families are important here; use accents in reds and browns. See Chapter 1 for more about color families.)

✔ **Bright white frames with bright white mats:** This is what I use for my midcentury images. Many people in Southern California have modern homes with white walls. Framing signs in pure white blends with the walls so viewers can imagine they're looking at a real sign.

Here are other frame considerations:

✔ **Size:** Frame dimensions are usually given from the inside of the frame, so *11" x 14"* is the size of the opening of the frame and of the mat you'll put inside it. Obviously, if the *molding* (the actual frame material) is wide, the outside frame dimensions can be bigger.

✔ **Style:** Think of style as you would a bureau of drawers or other piece of furniture. Styles range from simple 18th-century Americana to embellished Spanish Colonial to (of course) simple contemporary, which is usually the most popular for photography. Figure 18-7 shows two types of frames that work with different photographic subject matter.

✔ **Material:** Frames come in a variety of materials, from synthetic material, such as polystyrene, to natural woods and metals. Any are suitable for photography.

Figure 18-7: Use different frames for different types of photos.

✔ **Color:** Basic black, the best choice of colors for your frame, is what galleries choose when displaying photographs. This has been the trend, but it's changing as photographers are getting more creative. Basic white, a color befitting a contemporary style, is more popular now, and I use it often (see Figure 18-8).

In fact, I frame in all white because my most popular subject — mid-20th-century signage — looks good that way.

✔ **Cut:** Choosing a frame can be daunting because of the thousands of moldings to choose from. Molding, the material from which framemakers make the frame, comes in a variety of widths, thicknesses, and cuts.

Figure 18-8: Basic white frames can be the perfect final touch for an art photo.

The cuts can be flat or angled or curved, sometimes using multiple inundations in the cut, all according to the style of the frame.

Here's what you should have on hand before you order and buy:

- **The size of your image:** I prefer making 8" x 10" images because I can sell them at a reasonable price. Making and printing them is less expensive both because of the ink required for the printer and the reasonably priced paper you can get at that size.

- **Know the size of your frame opening:** The size of your mat is the same size as your frame opening. With a good area of white space (yes, I recommend white mats only for photography), the viewer is directed toward the image.

Buying retail

You can find dozens of framing shops all over the world. However, you pay for convenience and expertise: Most retail custom framers charge three to four times more than what you'd pay buying a ready-made frame and putting the picture in yourself.

Most retail stores change the types of frames they offer by season. If you want a consistent product, buying at a retail outlet can be frustrating because what they have one month, they won't have the next.

Buying online; finding Internet deals

Quality is important in a frame, and when you shop online, you obviously can't tell how substantial the frame in terms of its weight or size. However, my experience has been that after you get used to buying on the Internet, frames and mats you end up with are as good as what you buy retail — and sometimes even better.

I went shopping for a 14" x 18" frame at a couple of outlets on the Internet. I realize that the quality of some frames is better than others, and thus, more expensive. For you bargain-hunters, here are the details and prices I found at the time of writing:

- **SendAFrame,** http://sendaframe.com: A bony wood, beveled, classic 11" x 14" frame with glass display is $22; arctic white, acid-free mat is about $10. Shipping costs vary by number of items shipped ($6 for the first and $2 for each additional; arrives in 3 to 5 business days [shipping is higher for faster delivery]; minimum order for most frames is two pieces. Some frame models come in packages of a dozen (like the ebony, black, wooden basic by Perennials; a pack of 12 is $81).

- **pictureframes.com**, `www.pictureframes.com`: The Black Tie Affair 14" x 18" frame is $39. Very-white rag (acid-free) 14" x 18" mat is about $12. Shipping costs vary by the price of the order, starting at $7 for orders less than $25 to $35 for orders around $300, all for next-business-day delivery. A 40 percent mix-and-match discount is available.

- **Picture Frames R Us**, `http://picture-frames-r-us.com`: A black gallery 14" x 17" (yes, really, 14" x 17") frame with mat is about $40. Shipping is a flat rate per order of $8, arriving in 5 to 10 business days. Minimum orders vary with stock ordered.

- **Picture This...Framed**, `http://Picturethisframed.com`: A flat black 14" x 18" wall frame, with single conservation-grade mat (acid free), clear acrylic glazing (glass substitute), and rigid board backing is about $64. Shipping charges range from $7 to $20; arrives in 3 to 5 business days. No minimum order is required.

Buying for the bargain

Although you can save a ton of money by buying your framing materials online, you can also find a local wholesaler or dig through thrift stores. In this section, I discuss how to buy wholesale and offer a few other cash-saving ideas for getting great frames and mats.

Your time is valuable

Streamlining your framing process saves you time and money. Although it can be more cost efficient to order mats from one place and frames from another, you're less likely to make errors in ordering if you order everything from the same place. *Bonus:* If that merchant makes a mistake, you can send the materials back and have them redone.

And speaking of getting it right the first time, getting your print right the first time also saves time and money; there's nothing worse than having a frame put together and finding that the image was printed wrong. Printing mistakes are easy to make and can also be expensive because each print uses quite a bit of ink — not

to mention the paper. Always check each dimension twice: both your mat size openings and the height and width of your frame's inner opening and overall size. Keep a record of these measurements in an Excel chart or Word table along with the number of each print, especially if you are printing *limited editions* (when you print a specified number of prints for the same image).

Finally, know the style of the mat you want before you choose your frame. Most framemakers offer mats with a variety of shapes for an opening. Although round openings and other such flares are nice, especially for older photos, you'll typically choose a traditional square opening.

Wholesale deals

You want to contact wholesale framers if you're buying large quantities of frames — say, 30–40 or more. These are the folks to cozy up to when you want to find the people who make the frames, cut the mats, cut the glass/Plexiglas, and assemble the parts so that all you have to do is open up the frame and put in the photo.

Buying frames and mats wholesale usually means you need to buy in bulk. However, *bulk* in the frame world doesn't mean that you have to spend thousands of dollars. Most places, both online and traditional stores, accept orders starting at $100–$200 dollars. If you plan to sell in a high-end store or work with a gallery, you need the same frame or type of frame for your images — and a lot of them — so buying in bulk makes sense.

As for buying mats in bulk, you can buy them for about $2 per piece, cut to a variety of sizes and for a variety of odd-sized prints.

If you're in the United States and order abroad — even from Canada — those businesses will likely ask you for your Social Security number. The Security Assistance Act of 2002 requires full electronic filing of all export information, which means that you must provide your Social Security number when you are shipped items from another country. And you always have the choice: If you don't want to give out your number, find a domestic supplier. For more information, go to `customs.ustreas.gov`.

Table 18-2 lists places where you can get ready-made frames wholesale. These shops offer a consistent supply so that you can go back and buy the same frame.

Many retail outlets and chain art stores such as Aaron Brothers Art Marts offer a wide selection of frames at good prices. Be on the lookout for sales via the Internet and in the newspapers. Get on mailing lists to receive coupons. These places are a blessing if you run out of stock when people want pictures fast: Vendors like this offer a wide selection of photography frames and pre-cut mats at good prices.

Table 18-2	Frame/Mat Wholesalers	
Company	*Phone Number*	*Online Contact*
Ready Made Frames 3359 North Lincoln Ave. Chicago, IL 60657	773-296-6696	
Frames LTD 975 E. 58th Ave. Denver, CO 80216	800-274-0706	

Company	Phone Number	Online Contact
Red Swan 2730 NE 14th Street Ocala, FL 34470	877-351-0776	
Framesmith DC 1350 "Q" St. NW Washington, DC 20009	202-518-2500	
PK Enterprise 25876 The Old Road #329 Stevenson Ranch, CA 91381		http://epictureframes.com
Frames and Images 440 North Cedar Bluff Rd. Knoxville, TN 37923	865-539-1997	
FrameMasters 8305 Merrifield Ave. Fairfax, VA 22031	703-573-5734	
Art Warehouse Inc. 12015 Nebel St. Rockville, MD 20852	301-770-5505	
Framemakers & Art Gallery 1649 Forum Place Suite #8 West Palm Beach, FL 33401	561-686-8299	
Mat Source 516 Commercial Street Glendale, CA 91203	800-216-6280	
Frames-Direct.com	800-733-2898	sales@frames-direct.com\
U-Frame Unit 22d Wincombe Business Park Shaftesbury, Dorset SP7 9QJ	0845 226 7249	www.pictureframes.co.uk/ start.asp
International Frame 3204 Polk St. Houston, TX 77003	713-224-6808	ipfw@mail.com
New York Frame 1800 Broadway St. Buffalo, NY 14212	800-878-1425	www.newyorkframe.com
Holliday Picture Framing 200 Bedford Street Hollidaysburg, PA 16648	800-442-3000	www.hollidaypicture frames.com/wholesale.php

(continued)

Table 18-2 *(continued)*

Company	Phone Number	Online Contact
Parthenon Framing Enterprises 140-4 Keyland Court Bohemia, NY 11716	800-667-0919	www.parthenonframing.net
Worldview Pictures 373 Dawson Drive Camarillo, CA 93012	800-543-9919	
New England Wholesale Frame and Molding Co. 22-R Main Street Reading, MA 01867	781-942-1188	www.newenglandframe.com
Howell Moldings L.C. 201 Overland Park Place New Century, KS 66031	800-748-8472	

Other great deals

You can find great deals on frames and framing supplies if you're willing to look around a bit. This list offers just a few more ideas on where to find great frames at great prices:

✔ **Discount designers:** Many contemporary designers use mass production to make affordable high-brow decorations for the home. This trend is a throwback to the 1950s when famous designers mass produced good-quality furnishings and made them cheap enough so more people could afford them. Here are just two examples:

   • *Umbra* (www.umbra.com), a home design company, offers frames that are great for photography and for your smaller pictures. An 8" x 10" inch frame by Tom Vincent has layered glass inserts that make the multiple photos this frame holds look as if they're floating. Umbra also has 11" x 14" Media frames ($22) available in six variations, made of aluminum with white, bevel-cut mats to hold your photo sets.

   • *Ikea* (www.ikea.com), a Swedish company, has huge outlet stores in major cities around the world that offer a great selection of frames. Most of their frames, however, do not come with mats, so look over the "Takin' It to the Mats" section, earlier in this chapter, and then order your mats using metric measurements. Any framer will understand these dimensions. For more about metric measurements, see the nearby sidebar, "It's English in the U.S. but metric everywhere else."

✏ **Thrift stores:** There they are, dozens of cast-offs stacked in a lonely corner, stray frames looking for new life in someone's home.

Refurbishing used frames from a thrift store is the most inexpensive alternative to traditional framing. Your options are limitless; millions of old but perfectly good frames are given to charities for sales at thrift stores every year. And the good news is that not many people sift through them, looking for a standard frame that you'd use for photography. Put in a good mat, and you have a saleable art piece. And if you're lucky, a useable mat will come with your frame.

You might have to sand and paint a thrift store frame because of bumps and nicks. Overall, though, ones I find in thrift stores are very refurbishable. When painting a frame, sand it lightly first (wood or metal) and then apply a flat or semigloss paint.

✏ **Nonprofit organizations:** Many nonprofit organizations, faith-based work programs, and other charities are in the framing business. A good example on the Internet is `www.kandu.org`, which works with the Michigan Rehabilitation Services and Community Mental Health to train workers. From their picture frame manufacturing plant that employs these workers in Holland, Michigan, you can order mats and frames by the box (from a selection of 150 molding choices). Orders can be placed by phoning 800-747-0728.

✏ **Garage sales/flea markets:** The possibility of finding great frames at a garage sale or flea market can be as limitless as at a thrift store. You have to scour these venues to find a gem or two — and you also probably have to refurbish what you find — but the prices can't be beat.

Earn extra income by selling art retail

Here's what I do. I order from a wholesaler who is a framer whom I found out about from an artist who sells at our local street fair. Every month, I pick up 30–40 frames to refill my stock. The wholesaler (City Art) charges me a fixed price each time for a 16" x 16" white frame and matching mat with an 8" x 10" opening. I also make smaller 11" x 14" prints for the Neon Museum to sell in Los Angeles, the home design store Room Service in Los Angeles, and Palm Springs Consignment, a local midcentury modern store, to sell in Palm Springs.

When I get the frames home, I go to work printing and numbering my images. I pull the existing staples from the frame, take out the mat, and then use white art tape to put my image behind the mat that came with the frame. Then I make my deliveries once a month to the three places that sell my art. (For the steps involved in framing your photos, see the later section, "Putting Together the Frame.")

It's English in the U.S. but metric everywhere else

Many places around the world use the metric system to measure art, including frames. Ikea offers great frames but uses this system to measure them. If shopping non-U.S. places for your frames, convert your images to metric measurements in Photoshop, which offers metric measurements in its Image Size dialog box (access by clicking the drop-down menu bar next to the height and width input options). If you're shopping where metric measurements are used, try converting your image to 20cm x 30cm and printing it out before you go shopping. That way, you'll be able to find a frame that fits. Ikea offers bulk frames of good quality at wholesale prices.

Putting Together the Frame

At some point, you'll put your ready-made frame together: that is, put your picture inside. Here are some steps to help you through the process:

1. **Gather the appropriate materials.**

   Figure 18-9 shows the parts:

   - *Photograph:* Your masterpiece!
   - *Frame/mat:* Chosen and cut for this particular photo.

Figure 18-9: Take the frame apart so you can sign the mat and tape the picture to it.

- *White artist's tape/scissors:* To affix the photo to the mat.

- *Glass cleaner/cloth:* To clean the frame before assembly.

- *Pencil/eraser:* To sign and clean up your mat.

- *Staple gun:* To put the frame backing on the frame when you're done.

2. **Disassemble the frame.**

   The backing typically comes stapled to the frame. You need to remove the backing (and also the mat, if you ordered one from the same company) so you can put the picture inside.

3. **Sign and number your mat.**

   Create a unique artful signature of your very own. Your signature should go on the bottom right of your mat; put the number of the print on the bottom left. If you have a name for your print, put it there also. The name for my print is *Tucson angled* because it's my second version of this picture. It will be numbered 1/50 because I make limited editions of 50.

   Signing your name in pencil on the mat is perfectly appropriate for photography artwork. If you use pencil and make a mistake when writing on your mat, use a magic Rub eraser (available at art stores) to get pencil marks and other smudges off your mat.

4. **Put just one piece of white artist tape, sticky side up, on your print along the top, as shown in Figure 18-10.**

   Attaching your mat to your picture requires only one piece of white art tape at the top of your picture. Using only one piece of tape allows the paper to grow and shrink in different weather conditions without rippling in the frame. ***Hint:*** You could also use acid-free photo corners along with the tape to help hold the photo in place.

Figure 18-10: Attach your tape sticky side up so you can put the mat on top.

Another method is to mount the picture. While some folks think that this hurts the true artistic quality of the print, it makes it impossible for your picture to wrinkle. Most frame shops have mounting machines as do FedEx Kinko's.

5. **Clean the inside of the frame with glass cleaner and let it dry.**

6. **Place the mat (with the photo taped to it) inside the frame.**

7. **Clear away any dust or other foreign material inside the frame and then staple the backing to the frame.**

8. **Attach a hanger if necessary.**

For more on hanger options, see the earlier section, "The Great Frame-Up."

My final product is shown in Figure 18-11.

Figure 18-11: The final product: A 16" x 20" landscape print.

Part V
The Part of Tens

The 5th Wave — By Rich Tennant

"Well, well! Guess who just lost 9 pixels?"

In this part . . .

This section contains only two chapters, but they're jam-packed with to-the-point info: the ten guidelines of digital art photography (Chapter 19) and ten very useful digital art tricks (Chapter 20).

Ten Photo Digital Art Rules

*A*rt is a lot of things to a lot of people. Create what you will, and what sells will follow . . . perhaps with a few tweaks in Photoshop, perhaps with a grainy image of your grandmother's backyard, or perhaps just being at the right place at the right time.

With Photoshop CS2 by your side, using its tools, like the cool new perspective options or Raw file capabilities, your images are perfectly ripe to become priceless images when you easily correct errors (like under- or overexposing pictures) with the click and drag of a slider.

These ten rules are easy to remember and can make your art more appealing as well as saleable.

Create with Classic Lines and Colors

The word *appealing* means different things to different people, especially in art. However, following your instincts with light, color, shape, and form (as I discuss in Chapter 1) and maybe a rule or two (say the Rule of Thirds) can help you produce a picture — like Figure 19-1 — that's attractive in many décors.

Figure 19-1: Light, color, and contrast produce desirable wall art.

Start with a Good Camera

The newest point-and-shoot cameras — both digital and film — produce some great results, like the photo shown in Figure 19-2. However, the spiffier (and pricier) digital SLRs (dSLRs) and film SLRs have more options, including toys that provide you with quicker response time when you press the shutter as well as additional manual settings that let you adjust your f-stops and shutter speeds in different light and contrast environments. Higher-end point-and-shoots (5 megapixel [MP] and higher) as well as dSLRs/film SLRs can produce effects that can deepen your colors and/or make your image look like an art piece. Both are suitable for you to create an outstanding photo, especially if you have fine weather and can balance your f-stop and shutter speed (as discussed in Chapter 6) to get the best of the scene and/or action.

Figure 19-2: Most middle-level and high-end cameras can shoot good photos.

Exploit the Right Light for Your Photo

From natural light's spectacular dawn and dusk window, where subtle light provides soft shadows, all photos are light dependent. Although you can certainly shoot indoors and use flash fill to augment existing light or provide the light you need, photos often look their best when shot under natural lighting conditions. The softness that natural light provides is often far superior than what emanates from artificial sources. Train your eye to seek out existing light, as in this photo of a plate of fresh bakery bagels (see Figure 19-3).

Figure 19-3: One light source and no flash makes these bagels fresh forever.

Keep It Small and Spectacular

Whether tiny wildflowers in a field, random and spontaneous, or a hybrid annual, fertilized and coddled, flowers shot at the macro level are transformed into other-worldly creations that captivate and explode with color. To get this close to your subject (as I did in Figure 19-4), use a macro lens or the macro lens setting (which most midrange and high-end digital cameras have). For more about lenses and cameras, see Chapter 2.

Figure 19-4: Shoot up close for great perspective.

Balance Items Onscreen and on Paper

Whether you're shooting or cropping your photo, balancing images is half the fun and a good part of the creativity in your art photography. Creating a sense of balance when taking a picture of a sculptural form is easy: It's already been done for you by the sculptor. What's important for you, the photographer, is to add foreground (or not add it); enhance color that puts your imprint on the remade art.

When taking pictures of signage, for example, I look for balance — lots of it, but not necessarily in the object of a whole because many parts of objects spark interest among viewers. Feel free to shoot from a weird angle or include objects that are of the same color or form, like a trio of pink clowns, a long row of silver bullet trains, or the gap between subway cars shot from the viewpoint of a child (stoop or lie down for this one), as shown in Figure 19-5.

Figure 19-5: Craft your photos with balance.

Organize Your Photos into Sets by Themes

Think in themes, from repetition to solitude to fun. Categorize your photos by subject to get started. Consider sports, transportation, or flying as themes. Transportation can have subcategories within it — motorized versus nonmotorized vehicles, for instance — to get even more focused. Figure 19-6 shows a horse-drawn carriage that emulates those of bygone eras, yet the picture was taken recently in the hippest section of San Diego, the Gas Lamp district.

Figure 19-6: One image can fit into a number of themes.

The photo fits into a number of themes, too, from photos of horses to transportation to moving things. Photo sets can help you resell an image many times and also provide you with an opportunity to sell more than one photo at once because they come as a set. (For more on photo sets, see this book's companion Web site, www.dummies. com/go/digitalartphotos.)

Know the Art Techniques of Thine Masters

You can emulate any masters, but instead of duplicating their work, create a new version, perhaps from a new perspective or a change of hues. Figure 19-7 shows a photo of the same church that van Gogh painted, which I tweaked using color balance and Photoshop's Twirl and Clouds filters. For more on using filters in Photoshop, see Chapter 15.

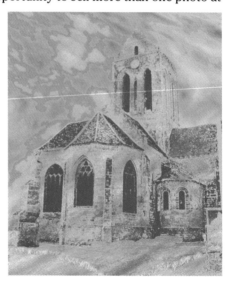

Figure 19-7: Emulate the masters' works using Photoshop.

Create a Story or Message

Capture as much detail and essence of your subject as possible in your photos to tell a story (as in Figure 19-8) or impart a message. For example, you're better off photographing a chef in a kitchen than in a silver mine (unless he's mining for truffles, I suppose). You don't have to step back and photograph to tell your story; you can also photograph close-up to get the details. For more about using photo sets to tell a story, see this book's companion Web site.

Figure 19-8: Create a story with photos.

Capture the Unexpected or Unreal

Artists often express themselves through the surreal. Salvador Dali painted forms that went beyond humanity in form and color to explain his fears and hopes. Figure 19-9 is a perfect example, featuring a man walking through a wall. (How often do you see that?)

Figure 19-9: Always keep an eye open for the unusual.

Sculptural elements ordinarily don't provide much contrast to make an appealing photograph. Using Photoshop's options when the photo is still in Raw format, you can tweak for contrast without losing detail and adding noise. There are multiple sliders (for exposure and contrast) that appear when your image comes up in a special Raw format window that you click and drag to change the look of your picture with almost the same results that you would get making the same changes out in the field. Add feeling to a photo like this by enhancing the details of the man's face as well as tweaking the foreground/background to see the rock and cement in which the man is embedded.

Always Have Your Camera with You

TV commercials used to call it *a Kodak moment* — those perfect snippets of life that demanded to be captured on film. When you always have a camera with you, you've got a sporting chance of catching all those vignettes of life that define us all. The ease and portability of digital cameras (as long as you have batteries) can help you sigh in relief that you were glad you had your camera. There's nothing like the concentration of a child when she or he is first learning how to ride a bicycle, or when, at only three years old, a boy decides to take to a skateboard, as shown in Figure 19-10.

Figure 19-10: Most things don't last forever, so always carry your camera!

Ten Digital Art Tricks

A fantasy is a dream that comes true. Digital art tricks can be those dreams, and they can come alive, beginning with thoughtful shots augmented with your creative use of Photoshop (or other image processors), from processing your Raw format photos to changing the hue and saturation of your image.

Real art begins with your imagination. In this chapter, I list a few tricks to help you to master image processing technology to get the best creative product possible.

Overexpose and Underexpose

As I discuss in Chapter 5, you can do a lot to make your image stunning while you shoot outdoors. When the sun shines on your subject, change your exposure compensation so that it reads in the minus column (underexposure) to deepen your colors. When you're shooting in deep shade, try upping your exposure compensation to the plus column (overexposure). You'll get an artsy effect that's almost impressionistic.

Photoshop CS2 comes to your aid also, letting you do anything you want with your exposure by just sliding the exposure slider when your image is in Raw format (if your camera shoots in that file type) just as if you were shooting. That's right! You can open and tweak your image in Raw format and get a chance to fool with your camera controls just as if you were on the shoot. (Yeah, that's right — no pixilation or image deterioration that you get when you tweak an image when it's in TIFF format. Read more about Raw file format in Chapter 16.) In Figure 20-1, altering the exposure changes the focus of the image as well as its appearance.

Figure 20-1: Raw files let you change your exposure just as you would while shooting.

Emulate the Masters

Some artists are easy to imitate via Photoshop techniques. For example, check out the Andy Warhol-like composite in Chapter 15. Run a search on other masters' names in a search engine to find other classic works and styles that you can re-create and tweak with your own style.

Figure 20-2 shows a staged piece (I hung a black sheet behind the subject and dressed him in dark clothing) — a Rembrandt replica, if you will. I searched for *Rembrandt* to come up with ideas that capture the view or mood with which I wanted to

Figure 20-2: Emulate the masters with composition and filters.

match my subject. In this case, the subject matched one of Rembrandt's almost to the tee. I then tweaked the original using a series of Photoshop's filters and options, much in the same way Rembrandt did on his canvas — applying layer after layer of paint to tweak the color and texture to achieve a surreal darkness. It works the same way in Photoshop — that is, you'll probably apply a series of different filters and/or options until you're satisfied. See Chapter 15 for more about Photoshop filters.

Shoot on a Cloudy Day

Light shining on objects makes color and shadows. Conversely, clouds and overcast conditions remove color and shadows. The gray tones resulting from a lack of shadows are filled with emotion. A broken wooden park bench among autumn leaves (see Figure 20-3), inches deep on the ground, offers symbolism that keeps the viewer in thought (that life, perhaps, isn't forever). Take advantage of this low-light opportunity to exploit the soft tone and variants of gray to compose an art photograph.

When clouds (and rain) abound, use black-and-white (B&W) film or switch your digital camera into B&W mode. Read all about B&W photography, including ways to tweak your gray shades with sliders in Photoshop's Channel Mixer layer. (Choose Layer⇨ New Adjustment Layer⇨Channel Mixer; then select the monochrome option.) Read more about that in Chapter 9.

Figure 20-3: B&W images bring focus to symbolic subject matter.

For images shot in color that you took in bad weather, try converting them to B&W. You just might be surprised by the results.

Create a Matching Background

Creating a natural-looking background for a picture is one of the first things you'll want to do as a digital photographer. Placing an object from one photo onto a faux background can clean up pictures that have too much going on in the background. Also, creating a background that has more contrast with the subject/object can make your subject or object stand out because you select your own background color, matching, muting, or enhancing it to get just the effect you want. One way to get a matching background is to use the Eyedropper tool to pick up another color from within the image.

Figure 20-4 shows a feathered image that I set into a new background. It's a handy option you'll probably want to use. Here are the steps:

1. **Select the image's background by using one of the Lasso tools to select your object and then choose Select⇨Inverse.**

2. **Set the feathering value by choosing Select⇨Feather and then typing in a value in the Feather Selection dialog box.**

   One or two pixels is generally sufficient.

3. **Add a new solid color fill layer by choosing Layer⇨New Fill Layer⇨Solid Color and then clicking OK in the New Layer dialog box.**

4. **With the Eyedropper tool, pick a color and click around on your subject/object until you get the background color match that you like.**

Figure 20-4: The background color of this lamp is a color contained within it.

You can duplicate any colorful image for a color study simply by choosing Image⇨Duplicate. You can make color study sets by changing one or two colors in the image to a different hue and/or saturation. You can change any color by tweaking the shades combined within them by adding a Hue Saturation Adjustment layer in Photoshop (Layer⇨Adjustment Layer⇨Hue/Saturation). For more about this option, see Chapter 12. Pair 'em up, and you've got an artsy set ready to go. (Bonus Chapter 1 on the book's companion Web site — www.dummies.com/go/digitalartphotos — has more information about photo sets.)

Playing with the selection tools can be a bit tricky (just about all the cool Photoshop techniques require that you first select something), but here's a hint that'll help: Press Option (Mac)/Ctrl (Windows) while you drag to take away from a selection area and press Shift while you drag to add to a selection.

Meld Layers to Create Motion

After you download or scan an image from film into Photoshop, you can multiply items within your image by selecting them, copying them, and pasting them into new layers over and over again, making a hundred layers if you want. By repeating copying and pasting, you can get parts of your image to move like an old-fashioned flip-book. The Go crosswalk man inside the stop light comes to life in Figure 20-5.

Figure 20-5: Layering objects can make them move.

Build Your Archive of Backgrounds

Having a variety of backgrounds can help you clean up your images if they need it. Sometimes you can't avoid clutter or distractions in the background of an image with a really good subject. In many of my pictures of signs, that's exactly the case. When this happens, I take the image and feather it into one of my blue sky backgrounds, as shown in Figure 20-6.

Figure 20-6: Clutter-free backgrounds have aesthetic appeal.

Take a picture of a blue sky, focusing on something small, like a plane. After you download that image, remove the plane using the Stamp tool. *Voilá!* A beautiful, unblemished sky to use as a background should a cluttered image need it.

No Photoshop tool can create a totally natural-looking sky (or clouds). People are smart: It's like a sixth sense. Create a fake sky, and they'll know. A real sky has dozens of shades of blue that vary according to where the sun is with respect to the shot. I've tried time and time again to reproduce this by painting my backgrounds blue using the Paint Bucket tool and selecting a sky blue color from the Color Picker. Although some shots of these one-tone, sometimes blazing-blue backgrounds have been effective, most have not.

Sometimes an image that you file as a potential background file is so beautiful that the image in and of itself will sell, like Figure 20-7.

Figure 20-7: Print simple images as is.

Don't Overdo Effect(s)

Pixilation happens when not enough data is in your file — so when you expand the image, it grabs from the nearest pixel and replicates it to fill the space. What you get with pixilation is *noise*.

When you perform an action in Photoshop — say, with a filter — the program shuffles data dropping and adding pixels to get the effect you want. When you perform the action once, you won't notice much difference in your image, and you also get the effect you want. Do the action over and over again, though, and Photoshop reshuffles pixels so much that your image begins to look noisy.

Figure 20-8: Too much sharpening can show the paper fiber of a scanned print.

Too much of Photoshop CS2's Smart Sharpen filter will also let you view the paper fiber from a scanned digital print. A furry rodent scanned from a glossy print and then run through the Smart Sharpen filter can produce the result shown in Figure 20-8.

Use the Edit➪Fade Command

If you end up with noise after giving your image all the tweaks you think it needs, you can use Edit➪Fade to reduce your changes, bit by bit (see Figure 20-9). Use the slider to take you back to where you started or within any percentage of the change that you requested in an action. Changing the blending mode can also have an incredible effect on a filter or adjustment.

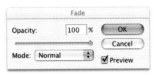

Figure 20-9: Use the Fade option to reduce opacity.

 If you want to undo the last thing you've done, use the Edit➪Undo command. If you decide you want it back (that's anything you do from selections to using tools and filters), choose Edit➪Redo after you undo what you did.

Keep Your Image in High Res on All Platforms

If you start out with an image that's 8" x 10" and 300 pixels per inch (ppi), you want to finish at the same size and resolution (res) — if that's the size you plan on printing. I scanned the photo in Figure 20-10 at 300 ppi from a negative. (The scanner was set to that resolution before the scanning process began. For more on scanning, see Chapter 3.) I then imported the image into Photoshop at the same resolution via the scanner software, saving it in Photoshop at 300 ppi resolution. Each time the image is printed, I use 2880 dots per inch (dpi), which is a value that ensures I get the most bang for my buck from what Photoshop doles out at 300 ppi.

Figure 20-10: A high-res image should stay that way from start to finish.

Index

A

Action/Motion mode, 100–101, 220
Adams, Ansel, 77, 110
A-DEP (depth of field) mode, 177
AGPs (Accelerated Graphics Ports), 65
alpha channels, 277
animal portraits, 138, 150–152
antistatic wrist straps, 64
aperture, 99
aperture priority (Av) mode, 161–162, 208
APS (Active Pixel Sensors), 38
Arbus, Diane, 77
architecture photos. *See also* B&W photos
  database site, 177
  at dusk, 17
  general rule, 14
  patterns, 21
Armstrong, Neil, 76
ASA speeds. *See* ISO speeds
atmosphere. *See* weather/atmosphere
    conditions
Auto (A) exposure mode, 219
Auto Color command, 238–239, 252
Auto Contrast command, 238
Auto Levels command, 238, 240
auto modes/settings. *See* digital cameras;
    special effects
Av (aperture priority) mode, 161–162, 208
AWB (Auto White Balance) mode, 166

B

B&W (black-and-white) photos
  adding sepia tones, 253, 279
  architecture
    camera settings, 176–177
    comparing B&W to color, 178
    line distortion effect, 178, 179
    ornamentation on, 181
    time of day, 179, 180, 181
    vanishing points, 179, 180
    vignetting effect, 178–179
  on cloudy days, 353
  getting into museums, 175
  getting model release forms, 185
  gray shades
    adding depth, 194
    adjusting contrast, 194
    adjusting levels, 196
    defined, 190–191
    highlights/midtones/shadows, 195–196
    in nature, 193
    tonal contrasts, 192, 193
  history of, 176
  landscapes, 192–193
  lightening areas, 241–242
  methods of getting
    B&W film in SLR cameras, 186, 190
    B&W mode on digital cameras, 186, 190
    comparing, 186–187
    converting color to B&W, 186,
      187–189, 292
    getting best quality, 189–190
    overview, 185–186
    warning, 187
  overview, 173–174
  photojournalism, 183–185
  portraits, 181–183
  printing, 196–197
  silver-gelatin prints, 195
  why shoot, 174–175
B&W mode, 186, 190
back lights, 134–136
backdrops, 140
background and foreground
  in B&W landscapes, 192
  in composition, 26–28
  in outdoor shots, 102–104
backgrounds
  building archives of, 355–356
  creating in Photoshop
    background layers, 278–280
    blue skies, 355–356
    matching backgrounds, 266–267,
      354–355
    with special effects, 286–287, 296–297
    white backgrounds, 267

balance. *See also* composition elements
Color Balance tool, 245–246, 252–254, 279
in composition, 14–15, 346
imbalanced color, 129–130
white balance, 163–166, 221
batteries, 45–46
Bellocq, E.J., 77
blur. *See also* night shots
depth of field and, 26, 99
fixing, 26, 128
intentional blur
using Av mode, 161–162
using Blur tool, 244
using Gaussian Blur filter, 285–286
in indoor shots without flash, 126–128
in night shots, 200–201, 203, 205
panning in Tv mode, 152
soft focus effect, 226
zooming while shooting, 225–226
ISO speeds and, 160–161
preventing with tripods, 181
bracketing exposures, 106–107, 209
Bridge, Adobe, 277, 302
Burn tool, 242
burst setting, 148–149

C

Candy Store, Amsterdam Avenue, New York
photo (Klein), 285
card readers, 47, 62
cards, graphics, 62, 65
cards, memory, 46–49, 50
CCD (charge-coupled device) sensors, 38
CD (Compact Disc) storage media, 57
Chalk & Charcoal filter, 290
Channel Mixer layer, 188–189, 278–279, 353
Charcoal filter, 289
chimping, 148
circles in composition, 19–20
Clone Stamp tool, 246–247, 250–252, 255
close-up (lens) filters, 231
Close-up or macro mode, 101–102, 219
close-ups. *See* portraits
clouds, 119, 193, 353, 356
collage projects, 277–282
color
CMYK mode, 67
how cameras interpret light and, 160–162

how light affects, 23–24, 154–155
imbalanced color, 129–130
intensity spectrum, 60
moods of, 156
out of gamut, 67
perception of, 23
primary/secondary/tertiary colors, 154
RGB modes, 67, 221
sepia tones, 253, 279
shades and tints, 154
weather/atmosphere and, 28, 172, 353
Color Balance tool, 245–246, 252–254, 279
color conversion (lens) filters, 231
color families, 24
color management, 61
color photos. *See also* Photoshop,
restoring old photos
color-blindness and, 158–159
comparing to B&W photos, 178
complementary/contrasting colors,
157–159
converting to B&W, 186, 187–189, 292
facing the sun, 110–111
indoor lighting and, 129–130
maximizing color
auto settings and, 160
EV compensation settings, 168–170
example, 167
f-stops, 161, 167–168
ISO/ASA speeds, 160–161, 162
in outdoor shots, 107–109
shutter speeds, 161
using the sun, 167–168
when shooting in shade, 171–172
white balance settings, 163–166
overview, 153–154
positioning camera, 156–157
Color Picker dialog box, 280
color saturation, 170, 243, 257–258
color temperature, 163–166
color wheel, 24, 154
compact CD storage method, 48
CompactFlash memory cards, 48
composition elements. *See also* digital art
photography
background/foreground, 26–28
balance, 14–15
color, 23–24
defined, 12–13
depth of field, 26

focus of interest, 13
in-camera cropping, 29–30
light/shadows, 16–18
lines/shapes/forms, 18–21
overview, 11
perspective, 28–29
positive/negative space, 24–26
Rule of Thirds, 15–16
simplicity, 13–14
subject placement, 21–23
computers. *See also* digital images
calibrating monitors, 61–62
choosing platforms, 60, 63
graphics capability improvements
Accelerated Graphics Ports, 65
adding RAM, 57, 63–64, 65
cleaning up hard drives, 58–59
external hard drives, 56–57, 62, 301
FireWire or USB 2.0 cable, 57, 64
graphics cards, 62, 65
graphics tablets, 62
LCD flat-panel monitors, 59–60
memory card readers, 62
multibutton mice (Macs), 62
workstations, 64
image file size and, 55–56
monitoring status of, 57–58
storage space, 56–59
contrast
adjusting
with Auto Contrast, 238
with Brightness/Contrast, 281
color tones, 238–239
overview, 194
in B&W shots, 192, 193
overview, 18
contrasting colors, 157–159
copyrights, 89, 92, 239
cropping images, 29–30, 248, 260–261
Curves command, 256, 257

D

da Vinci, Leonardo, 81, 140
Dadaism, 78
Dali, Salvador, 348
darkening image areas, 242, 256
depth of field
Ansel Adams and, 110
defined, 26, 99
in outdoor shots, 105–106

Desaturate command, 292
diffusion (lens) filters, 232
digital art photography. *See also*
composition elements
creating art that sells
B&W photos, 174, 188
choosing subject matter, 85–88, 91
copyright warnings, 89, 92
defining audience, 11, 84–85
finding niche markets, 87, 91
offering quality, 90–91
overview, 10–12, 75–76
posters, 329
preserving detail, 260
pushing the envelope, 88–90
repurposing old photos, 92–93, 188, 237
researching what sells, 87–88
selling retail, 337
defined, 7–8
defining yourself as photographer
finding the unusual, 83–84
overview, 11, 76
perspective, 80–83
right-brain/left-brain, 78–80
shooting what you like, 77
studying the masters, 77–78
overview, 343
rules
always carrying camera, 349
balancing images, 346
capturing the unusual, 348
using classic lines/colors, 343–344
emulating the masters, 347
using good cameras, 345
using natural light, 345
organizing in themed sets, 347
shooting up close, 346
telling stories, 348
tricks
building archive of backgrounds, 355–356
creating matching backgrounds, 354–355
emulating the masters, 352–353
fading/undoing/redoing edits, 357
keeping images in high-res, 357
melding layers to create motion, 355
not overdoing effects, 356
overexposing/underexposing, 351
overview, 351
shooting on cloudy days, 353

digital cameras. *See also* dSLR cameras;
  lenses
  A-DEP (depth of field) mode, 177
  auto exposure settings
    Action/Motion, 100–101, 220
    Auto (A), 219
    Close-up or macro, 101, 219
    Landscape, 101, 219
    Night, 101, 220
    overview, 97, 98, 100, 102, 218–219
    Portrait, 100, 108, 219
  AWB (Auto White Balance) mode, 166
  B&W (black-and-white) mode, 186, 190
  batteries, 45–46
  burst setting, 148–149
  color modes, 221
  defined, 38
  versus film cameras, 10, 33–35, 73
  flash, 44–45
  how they work, 38
  LCD displays, 33
  lens filters, 163, 230–233
  lenses, 40–43
  light meters, 38, 128, 209
  manual exposure settings
    Av (aperture) mode, 161–162, 208
    bracketing, 106–107
    f-stops, 99
    ISO speeds, 98, 122–123, 221
    M (Manual) mode, 208, 218
    overview, 43, 97–98, 102
    shutter speeds, 100
    Tv (shutter) mode, 152, 208
    white balance, 106, 221
  memory/storage media, 46–49
  monopods, 46
  overview, 36
  pixels/megapixels, 39–40, 51–52
  prices, 39, 40
  sensors, 9, 38, 40, 122
  tripods, 46, 47
  types of, 36–37
  viewfinders, 33–34
  websites, 39, 45
digital image editing. *See* Photoshop
digital images. *See also* JPEG files; Raw
  files; resolution; TIFF files
  creating Web galleries of, 307–309
  defined, 31–32
  downloading directly to printers, 50

editing software, 50
file sizes, 55–56, 301, 306–307
versus film images, 9–10, 32, 35, 73
saving as TIFF files, 53, 306–308
transferring to computers. *See also*
  computers; scanning photos
  from cameras, 49
  JPEG files, 302–303
  from memory cards, 50
  overview, 302
  RAW files, 303–306
  scanned film, 73, 302
digital sensors, 9, 38, 40, 122
disk drives. *See* hard drives
DNG (Digital Negative) Converter, 305
docking systems, 50
Dodge tool, 240–242
dpi (dots per inch), 73–74
dSLR (digital single lens reflex) cameras.
  See also digital cameras
  defined, 36, 37
  features, 38
  sensor size, 40
  viewfinders, 33–34
Duchamp, Marcel, 78
Dust & Scratches filter, 244
dust specks, removing, 255
DVD storage media, 57
dye sublimation printers, 69

E

Eggleston, William, 76
Emboss filter, 291–292
EV (Exposure Value) compensation
  defined, 168–169, 221
  enhancing color, 168–170, 221
  overview, 129, 218
exposure, defined, 100
exposure bracketing, 106–107, 209
exposure metering, 222
exposure settings. *See* digital cameras
exposures, double, 223–224
external hard drives, 56–57, 62, 301
Eyedropper tool, 256, 257

F

feathering image edges, 272–273

file formats. *See also* JPEG files; Raw files; TIFF files
  PGM, 266
  PSD, 277
fill flash, 112, 120, 171, 182
fill (studio) lights, 134–136
film format. *See also* ISO speeds; scanning photos
  B&W film, 186, 190
  versus digital format
    example, 148
    ISO and, 160
    overview, 9–10, 32–35, 73
  film sensitivity, 122
  film speeds, 160, 162
filters. *See also* Photoshop, filters
  for camera lenses, 163, 230–233
FireWire cable, 57, 64
fish eye lenses, 42–43
flare, 114, 115
flash
  defined, 44–45
  indoor shots, 131–132, 136, 182
  outdoor day shots, 112, 120, 171, 182
  outdoor night shots, 200, 204, 211–212
  portraits, 138–139, 182
flower close-ups, 346
focal lengths of lenses, 42
focus of interest in photos, 13
focus, out of. *See* blur, intentional blur
focus zone in-camera, 222
focusing systems in cameras, 38
foreground. *See* background and foreground
found art, 87, 91
Foveon digital sensors, 38
framing and matting photos
  frames
    buying online, 332–333
    buying retail, 332
    buying wholesale, 334–336, 338
    color, 331
    custom-made frames, 322
    cut, 331
    finding deals, 336–337
    frame kits, 329–330
    hangers for, 329
    ready-made frames, 322
    size, 330, 332
    style, 330, 331
    types, 330
    warning, 332
  image size and, 332
  mats
    acid-free, 323, 325
    buying wholesale, 334–336
    color, 323–324
    comparing types, 324
    creating in Photoshop, 325–329
    cutting own, 324–325
    double matting, 323
    finding discounts, 336–337
    orientation, 322, 323
    overview, 322
    size, 322–323
    warning, 323
  metric system and, 338
  overview, 12, 321
  steps in, 338–340
  streamlining, 333
f-stops, 99, 161, 167–168

G

gamma value, 60
Gaussian Blur filter, 285–286
glare, 114–117
Glowing Edges filter, 288
Googie images, 87
Gradient Map tool, 292–293
grain. *See* noise
Graphic Pen filter, 291
graphics cards, 62, 65
graphics tablets, 62

H

hard drives. *See also* computers
  cleaning up, 58–59
  external hard drives, 56–57, 62, 301
  internal hard drives, 56
Haring, Keith, 156
head shots. *See* portraits
Healing Brush tools, 251–252, 255
highlights, 195–196, 256, 258
Hockney, David, 76
hot shoes, 45
Hue/Saturation dialog box, 257–258

I

Image Size command, 260–261, 338
images. *See* digital images
Impression, Sunrise (Claude Monet painting), 22
Indiana, Robert, 184
indoor shots
  augmenting indoor light
    with flash, 131–132, 136
    with outdoor light, 132–133
    overview, 130–131
    using studio lights, 133–136
    using whiteboards, 133, 134
  without flash
    using available light, 125–126
    versus with flash, 131–132
    imbalanced color, 129–130
    intentional blur, 126–128
    overview, 124–125
    taming bright light, 128–129
  ISO speed settings, 122–123
  manual versus auto settings, 124
  overview, 121–122
  using tripods, 124
  white balance setting, 106, 124
infrared (lens) filters, 232
inkjet printers, 68
interpolation options, 309–310
ISO speeds
  defined, 98, 160–161
  ISO/ASA speeds, 160
  maximizing color, 162
  night shots, 200, 204–205, 206, 210–211
  special effects, 221

J

JPEG files. *See also* digital images
  adjusting contrast, 194
  overview, 302
  pros and cons, 52–53, 303
  saving as TIFF files, 303
  warning, 303

K

Kelvin (K) color temperature chart, 165
key lights, 134–136
Klein, William, 285

L

landscape photos
  Ansel Adams and, 110
  in black and white, 192–193
  at dusk, 17
  general rule, 14
  at night, 215
Landscape setting, 101, 219
Lange, Dorothea, 81
laser printers, 68
layers. *See* Photoshop layers
Leibovitz, Annie, 76
Lens Distortion filter, 179
lenses. *See also* digital cameras
  focal lengths, 42
  lens filters, 163, 230–233
  line distortion effect, 179
  overview of, 40, 40–41
  types
    fish eye, 42–43
    macro/micro, 84
    shift, 179
    short, 177
    telephoto, 41
    wide angle, 41, 42
    zoom, 40
  vignetting effect, 179
Leroy, Louis, 22
Levels tools, 196, 238, 240
Levitt, Helen, 77
light. *See also* color
  ambient light
    color temperature of, 163–166
    defined, 44, 108, 163
    in night shots, 204
  electric lights outdoors, 119–120
  how it affects color, 23–24, 154–155
  natural light, 345
light and shadows. *See also* composition elements; shadows
  architecture/landscapes and, 17
  color and, 23–24
  contrast and, 18
  overview, 16
  time of day and, 16–17
light meters
  defined, 38, 128, 209
  spot metering, 171
  tricking, 222–223
lightening image areas, 240–242, 256
Lighting Effects tool, 296–297

line distortion effect, 178, 179
lines/shapes in composition, 18–21

M

M (Manual) mode, 208, 218
Mac monitors, 62
Mac OS X Tiger and Panther, Raw files
    in, 304
manual settings. *See* digital cameras
Mapplethorpe, Robert, 76
mats. *See* framing and matting photos
Mbps (megabytes per second), 57
McCarty, Charlie, 183
megapixels, 39–40, 51
memory card readers, 47, 62
memory cards, 46–49, 50
Memory Stick cards, 48
metadata, 53, 303
meters. *See* light meters
midtones, 195–196, 256, 258
model release forms, 185, 239
Mona Lisa (da Vinci), 140
Monet, Claude, 22
monitors
    calibrating, 61–62
    CRT monitors, 59
    LCD monitors, 59–60
    Mac monitors, 62
    platforms and, 60
    resolution, 59
monopods, 46
Motion/Action setting, 100–101, 220
MultiMediaCard (MMC) memory cards, 49

N

negative/positive space in composition,
    24–26
neon sign shots, 205, 210
neutral density (lens) filters, 231
Night mode, 101, 220
night shots. *See also* outdoor shots in
    daylight
    architecture, 181
    with flash, 200, 204, 211–212
    without flash or blur
        bracketing shots, 209
        using exposure modes, 208

with intentional noise, 210–211
        ISO/ASA speeds, 204–205, 206, 210–211
        using metering, 209
        steps in, 206–207
        in well-lit areas, 205–206
    with intentional blur, 200–201, 203, 205
    landscapes, 215
    low light compensations
        ambient light, 204
        flash, 200, 204
        higher ISO/ASA speeds, 200
        longer shutter speeds, 199, 200–203
        wider apertures, 199
    moon shots, 212–214
    motion shots, 200–201, 203
    neon signs, 205, 210
    overview, 199
    progression shots, 203
    reflections, 216
    shadows, 216
    subjects lit from beneath, 212
    tripods, 201–202, 211, 214, 215
    weather, 216
noise
    cleaning up, 211, 244, 255
    defined, 9, 122
    digital noise, 122, 211
    fading, 357
    intentional noise, 210–211
    ISO speed and, 160, 161, 162–163
    luminance noise, 122, 211
    from pixilation, 356

O

outdoor shots in daylight. *See also* night
    shots
    adding flash fill, 112, 120
    using auto exposure settings
        Close-up, 101
        Landscape, 101
        Motion, 100–101
        Night, 101
        overview, 97, 98, 100, 102
        Portrait, 100, 108
    with back to the sun, 107–109
    at dawn or dusk, 113, 114
    depth of field, 105–106
    facing the sun, 109–111

outdoor shots in daylight *(continued)*
  flare, 114, 115
  foreground/background, 102–104
  getting maximum color, 107–109
  glare, 114–117
  including electric lights, 119–120
  using manual exposure settings
    bracketing, 106–107
    f-stops, 99
    ISO speeds, 98
    overview, 97–98, 102
    shutter speeds, 100
    white balance, 106
  at noon, 113
  overview, 97–98
  shadows, 111–113
  water, ice, and snow, 115–117
  weather conditions, 117–119, 193, 353
overexposure
  defined, 161
  fixing, 238
  intentional, 227–228, 351
  preventing, 108
  Raw files and, 351–352

P

panoramic photos, 224–225, 261–266
people. *See* portraits of people
perspective in composition, 28–29
perspective of photographers, 80–83
pet portraits, 151–152
PGM file format, 266
photo sets, 3, 347, 354
photojournalism, 183–185
photos. *See* digital images; film format
Photoshop. *See also* backgrounds; printing
    in Photoshop
  Bridge program, 277
  Browse command, 277
  Camera Raw plug-in, 186, 187, 303–304,
    305, 351–352
  creating photo mats, 325–329
  creating symmetrical art, 268–270
  cropping images, 260–261
  DNG Converter, 305
  enlarging images, 310–311
  fading edits, 357

filters
  Chalk & Charcoal, 290
  Charcoal, 289
  Dust & Scratches, 244
  Emboss, 291–292
  Gaussian Blur, 285–286
  Glowing Edges, 288
  Graphic Pen, 291
  Lens Distortion, 179
  overview, 242, 284–285
  Plastic Wrap, 288
  Reduce Noise, 211
  Sketch filters, 289–291
  Smart Sharpen, 128, 243, 356
  Unsharp Mask, 243, 286–288
  warning, 284
  Watercolor, 284, 288–289
fixing
  blur, 128
  line distortion, 179
  vignetting, 179
Image Adjustments commands
  Auto Color, 238–239, 252
  Auto Contrast, 238
  Auto Levels, 238, 240
  Color Balance, 245–246, 252–254
  Curves, 256, 257
  Desaturate, 292
  Gradient Map, 292–293
  overview, 237
  Shadow/Highlight, 256
Image Size command, 260–261, 338
interpolation options, 309–310
Levels histograms, 196
Lighting Effects tool, 296–297
overview, 50, 259–260
Photomerge panoramas, 259, 261–266
Picture Package tool, 293–295
redoing edits, 357
Rotate Canvas commands, 262, 265, 317
Save As dialog box, 306–307
selection tools, 249, 267
selections
  adding to/taking from, 355
  continuous multiple, 286
  saving, 277
  similar object groups, 286
Toolbox tools
  Blur, 244
  Burn, 242

Clone Stamp, 246–247, 250–252, 255
Dodge, 240–242
Eyedropper, 256, 257, 266–267, 354
Healing Brush, 251–252
overview, 240
Paint Bucket, 266–267
Sponge, 243
Spot Healing Brush, 251–252, 255
undoing edits, 357
Web Photo Gallery, 307–309
Photoshop, restoring old photos
adjusting contrast, 238
color
adding sepia to B&W, 253
adjusting levels, 238, 240
adjusting saturation, 243, 257–258
balancing, 245–246, 252
correcting tones/contrast, 238–239
enhancing, 254, 256–258
copyrights/release forms, 239
cropping before fixing, 248
darkening areas, 242, 256
fixing photo damage, 249–252
fixing under/overexposure, 238
lightening areas, 240–242, 256
minimizing grain/noise, 244
overview, 237, 247
removing scratches/specks, 244, 255
removing shadows, 246–247
scanning photos to restore, 248–249, 251
sharpening details, 243
smoothing object edges, 244
undoing edits, 240, 311, 357
Photoshop layers
adjustment layers, 189, 284
alpha channels and, 277
background layers, 278–280
Channel Mixer layer, 188–189,
278–279, 353
complex collage projects, 277–282
defined, 271
feathering image edges, 272–273
flattening, 189, 277, 282
layer masks, 281–282
Layers palette, 271–272
melding to create motion, 355
Opacity slider, 280
saving selections, 277
simple two-layer projects, 273–277

Photoshop special effects. *See also* special
effects
3-D sculpting, 291–292
Andy Warhol pop art, 292–295
artist sketches, 289–291
backgrounds, 286–287, 296–297
blurring/softening, 285–286
converting color to B&W, 186,
187–189, 292
crisp-edged flat cartoon, 286–288
glowing image edges, 288
not overdoing, 356
overview, 283
plastic wrap, 288
posterizing effect, 289
warning, 284
watercolors, 284, 288–289
PictBridge standard, 50
pixels
defined, 39, 51
megapixels, 39–40, 51
ppi (pixels per inch), 73–74
resolution and, 51–52
pixilation, 356
Plastic Wrap filter, 288
platforms, 60, 63–64
polarizing (lens) filters, 230
Portrait mode, 100, 108, 219
portraits of animals
in black and white, 151
with flash at night, 212
intentional blur, 151–152
overview, 138
pets, 151–152
wildlife, 150–151
portraits of flowers, 346
portraits of people
in black and white, 181–183
candid portraits, 147–149, 183
close-ups in the sun, 108
extreme close-ups, 27
getting model release forms, 185
inanimate "people", 149
minimizing flash, 138–139, 182
overview, 137–138
red-eye reduction, 138
traditional posed portraits
using backdrops, 140
body parts, 143–146
groups, 146
non-smiling subjects, 141–143

portraits of people *(continued)*
  traditional posed portraits *(continued)*
    overview, 138, 139
    personalizing, 143
    smiling subjects, 140–141
  using zoom lenses, 139
positive images, 92
positive/negative space in composition, 24–26
ppi (pixels per inch), 73–74
print output, 61
print paper, 67, 70–72, 314, 316
print quality, 67, 317
print resolution, 73–74
print sizes, 72
printers
  choosing, 66–67
  color modes, 67
  downloading images to, 50
  overview, 258
  types
    color laser, 68
    dye sublimation, 69
    inkjet, 68
    pros and cons, 69–70
    snapshot, 69
printing in Photoshop
  black-and-white photos, 196–197
  contact sheets, 317–319
  getting best quality, 317
  on-screen proof setup, 313–316
  overview, 12, 66, 313
  preparing for output, 316–317
  setting options, 319–320
  technical help for, 316
  warnings, 314, 320
prosumer digital cameras, 36, 37, 38

R

RAM (Random Access Memory), 57, 63–64, 65
Raw files. *See also* digital images
  B&W option, 187
  converting to DNG format, 305
  defined, 53–54
  editing
    using Camera Raw, 303–304, 305
    color balance/profile, 305
    color saturation, 170

contrast and depth, 194
  exposure, 351–352
file extensions, 53, 305–306
fixing vignetting, 179
in Mac OS X, 304
metadata, 53, 303
pros and cons, 53–54
software to read/convert, 54
warning, 305
red-eye reduction, 138
Reduce Noise filter, 211
reflections, 216, 225
Rembrandt, 352–353
rendered images, 59
resolution
  image resolution
    changing without resampling, 312
    interpolation options, 309–311
    keeping in high-res, 52, 357
    megapixels and, 39
    overview, 73–74, 309
    pixels and, 51
    resampling, 310–311
  in LCD versus CRT monitors, 59
  native resolution, 59
  print resolution, 67, 73–74
  scanner resolution, 74, 248, 251
  sensor resolution, 38
RGB color mode, 67
Rotate Canvas commands, 262, 265, 317
Rule of Thirds, 15–16

S

Save As dialog box, 306–307
saving images
  JPEGs as TIFF files, 303
  selections in layers, 277
  as TIFF files, 53, 306–308
  unfinished work in Photomerge, 266
scanning photos. *See also* digital images;
    film format
  advantages of, 36, 73
  choosing scanners, 73–74, 249, 302
  configuring scanners, 74
  resolution, 74, 248, 251
scratches/specks, removing, 211, 244, 255
Secure Digital (SD) memory cards, 49
sensors, 9, 38, 40, 122
sepia tones, 221, 253, 279
servers, 307

Shadow/Highlight command, 256
shadows. *See also* light and shadows
  enhancing, 256, 258
  flash fill and, 112, 120
  in grayscale, 195–196
  maximizing color, 171–172
  in night shots, 216
  in outdoor shots, 111–113
  playing with, 15
  removing, 246–247
shapes/lines in composition, 18–21
sharpening details, 128, 243, 286–288, 356
shutter speeds
  defined, 100, 161
  night shots, 199, 200–203
  Tv (shutter priority) mode, 152, 208,
    228–230
silver-gelatin prints, 195
Sketch filters, 289–291
sky backgrounds, 286–287, 355–356
skylight (lens) filters, 163, 230
Smart Sharpen filter, 128, 243, 356
SmartMedia (SM) memory cards, 48–49
snapshot printers, 69
soft-diffused (lens) filters, 232
special effects. *See also* blur, intentional
    blur; Photoshop special effects
  using auto modes/settings
    Action, 220
    Auto (A), 219
    B&W/color/faux sepia, 221
    Close-up or macro, 219
    exposure compensation, 221
    exposure metering, 222
    focus zone, 222
    ISO, 221
    Landscape, 219
    Night, 220
    overview, 218–219
    Portrait, 219
    white balance, 221
  double exposures, 223–224
  flowing water like velvet, 228–229
  intentional blur, 226
  intentional noise, 210–211
  intentional under/overexposure,
    227–228, 351
  using lens filters, 232–233
  overview, 217
  panoramic shots, 224–225
  reflections, 225

tricking light meters, 222–223
  zooming while shooting, 225–226
Sponge tool, 243
Spot Healing Brush tool, 251–252, 255
star (lens) filters, 232–233
still lifes, 77
stock photos, 88
stop-action shots, 98, 100–101, 220
storage media, removable, 46–49
storage space on computers, 56–59
studio lighting, 133–136
subject matter, 11, 85–88, 91
subject placement, 21–23
symmetrical art, 268–270
symmetrical balance, 14

T

telephoto lenses, 41
texture, 21
TIFF files. *See also* digital images
  adjusting contrast, 194
  advantages, 306
  compressing, 306–307
  converting to JPEGs, 307–308
  defined, 53
  saving images as, 53, 306–308
  warning, 307
time of day. *See also* night shots; outdoor
    shots in daylight
  B&W architecture photos, 179, 180, 181
  light/shadows and, 16–17
toner, 68
triangles in composition, 19, 20, 146
tripods
  defined, 46, 47
  improvising, 215
  indoor shots, 124
  outdoor night shots, 201–202, 211, 214
Turner, Joseph Mallord William, 284
Tv (shutter priority) mode, 152, 208,
    228–230

U

underexposure
  defined, 161
  fixing, 238
  intentional, 227, 351
  Raw files and, 351–352

undoing edits, 240, 311, 357
Unsharp Mask filter, 243, 286–288
USB cable, 57, 64
UV/skylight (lens) filters, 163, 230

V

van der Rohe, Mies, 285
van Gogh, Vincent, 81, 346
vanishing points, 20, 179, 180
viewfinders, 33–34
vignetting effect, 178–179
Vincent, Tom, 336

W

Warhol, Andy, 292, 295, 352
water, ice, and snow shots, 115–117
water flowing like velvet effect, 228–229
Watercolor filter, 284, 288–289
weather/atmosphere conditions
    clouds, 119, 193, 353
    color and, 28, 172, 353
    fog or mist, 117–118
    haze or steam, 193
    night shots, 216
    overview, 117
    rain, 118
    smog, 172
Web Photo Gallery feature, 307–309
Web sites
    Adobe, 54, 61
    Apple, 59
    book's bonus chapters, 3, 149
    information sites
        color management, 61
        digital art, 175
        inkjet printers, 68
        PictBridge, 50
        print papers, 197
        U.S. Customs, 334
    model release forms, 185
    moon phase calendar, 214
    photographs
        architecture, 177
        digital art forms, 175
        Garry Winogrand, 197
        master photographers, 77

NOAA, 117
    William Klein, 285
shopping sites
    backdrops, 140
    batteries, 45
    digital cameras, 39
    Epson printers, 70
    external hard drives, 56
    frame kits, 330
    frame/mat discounts, 336–337
    frame/mat wholesalers, 335–336
    graphics cards, 65
    image-organizing software, 303
    ink cartridges, 68
    LCD flat-panel monitors, 59
    mat boards and kits, 325
    mat cutters, 324
    Raw format-reading software, 54
Sony, 59
sportshooter.com, 148
white backgrounds, 267
white balance settings
    defined, 106, 124
    maximizing color, 163–166
    special effects, 221
white out, 208
whiteboards, 133, 134
wide angle lenses, 41, 42
wildlife portraits, 150–151
Winogrand, Garry, 197
workstations, 64

X

xD-Picture memory cards, 49

Z

zoom lenses, 40, 139
zooming while shooting, 225–226